POTTERY AND PRACTICE

Pottery and Practice

*The Expression of Identity at
Pottery Mound and Hummingbird Pueblo*

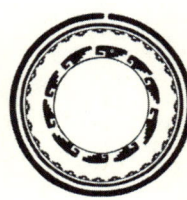

Suzanne L. Eckert

UNIVERSITY OF NEW MEXICO PRESS | ALBUQUERQUE

© 2008 by the University of New Mexico Press
All rights reserved. Published 2008
Printed in the United States of America
14 13 12 11 10 09 08   1 2 3 4 5 6 7

LIBRARY OF CONGRESS CATALOGING-IN-PUBLICATION DATA
Eckert, Suzanne L., 1970–
   Pottery and practice : the expression of identity at
   Pottery Mound and Hummingbird Pueblo / Suzanne L. Eckert.
       p. cm.
   Includes bibliographical references and index.
   ISBN 978-0-8263-3834-1 (CLOTH : ALK. PAPER)
1. Pottery Mound (N.M.)
2. Chaves-Hummingbird Pueblo Site (N.M.)
3. Pueblo pottery—New Mexico—Rio Puerco Valley
   (Rio Arriba County-Socorro County)
4. Pueblo Indians—Ethnic identity.
5. Pueblo Indians—Religion.
6. Excavations (Archaeology)—New Mexico—Rio Puerco Valley
   (Rio Arriba County-Socorro County)
7. Rio Puerco Valley (Rio Arriba County-Socorro County, N.M.)—Antiquities.
I. Title.
      E99.P9E24 2008
      978.9'52004974—dc22
                            2007042575

Book and jacket design and type composition by Kathleen Sparkes
This book is typeset using Minion Pro OTF 11/13.5, 33P;
Display type is Cronos Pro OTF family.

To Popi

I miss you

and

To Marcus and Lucien

I can't wait

Contents

List of Figures   ix

List of Tables   x

Acknowledgments   xiii

CHAPTER ONE
Pottery and Practice
    An Introduction   1

CHAPTER TWO
Understanding the Creation, Maintenance, and
Transformation of Social Boundaries through Practice Theory   9

CHAPTER THREE
Pottery Mound and Hummingbird Pueblo
    Archaeological and Temporal Context   15

CHAPTER FOUR
Communities of Practice in the Lower Rio Puerco Area   31

CHAPTER FIVE
Identifying Potential Homelands for Immigrants Living
in the Lower Rio Puerco Area during the Fourteenth Century   43

CHAPTER SIX
Communities of Identity in the Lower Rio Puerco Area   57

CHAPTER SEVEN
Social Integration and Ideology
    A New Ritual System along the Lower Rio Puerco   81

CHAPTER EIGHT
Pottery and Practice in Fourteenth-Century
Villages along the Lower Rio Puerco   97

APPENDIX A
Pueblo III and Pueblo IV Pottery Types
Produced in the Lower Rio Puerco Region   107

APPENDIX B
Seriation of Ceramic Types from the Lower Rio Puerco District   123

APPENDIX C
Description of Petrographic Temper Types   145

APPENDIX D
Code Sheet and Summary Tables for Faunal Analysis   153

References   175

Index   197

List of Figures

1.1 The American Southwest showing the location of the study area in relation to major prehispanic pueblo regions   4

3.1 Map of the Lower Rio Puerco area   16

3.2 Hummingbird Pueblo   22

3.3 Pottery Mound late component   24

3.4 Pottery Mound early component   25

3.5 One-meter contour map of Pottery Mound   26

4.1 Sherd, igneous rock, and quartz-mica schist temper characteristic of pottery produced in the northern portion of the study area   34

4.2 Three examples of Hidden Mountain igneous rock temper characteristic of pottery produced in the southern portion of the study area   34

4.3 Scoria rock sample from Hidden Mountain   34

5.1 Micaceous clay temper characteristic of utility pottery produced in the central Rio Grande district   46

5.2 Weathered pumice temper, one of numerous igneous tempers characteristic of pottery produced in the northern Rio Grande district   46

5.3 Timeline showing date ranges of major types in Pueblo glaze wares   49

5.4 Photos of exterior designs common to fourteenth-century glaze-decorated pottery produced in the Acoma area, the study area, and the Rio Grande region   51

6.1 Partial vessels recovered from Hummingbird Pueblo   63

6.2 Agua Fria Glaze-on-red vessels recovered from Pottery Mound   64

6.3 San Clemente Glaze-on-polychrome bowls recovered from Pottery Mound   65

6.4 Pottery Mound Polychrome vessels recovered from Pottery Mound   66

6.5 Miscellaneous decorated bowls recovered from Pottery Mound   67

A.1 Rio Grande Glaze Painted rim forms   113

B.1 Correspondence analysis results showing relative contribution of ceramic types on excavation levels from the Lower Rio Puerco area   126

B.2 Correspondence analysis results plotted by *k*-means three-cluster solution   128

B.3 Rim forms on pottery recovered from Hummingbird Pueblo and Pottery Mound in the Lower Rio Puerco area   139

List of Tables

3.1 Summary of chronological data for Hummingbird Pueblo and Pottery Mound based on ceramic seriation and associated absolute dates   27

3.2 Excavation levels (Site/Unit/Level/Locus) by phase   28

4.1 Column percentages of locally produced decorated and utility wares by site and phase   33

4.2 Column percentages of attributes that reflect different aspects of technological style on locally produced wares for each site by phase   36

5.1 Column percentages of nonlocally produced decorated and utility wares by site and phase   45

6.1 Design attributes recorded for whole and partial vessels from Hummingbird Pueblo and Pottery Mound   69

6.2 Slip color combinations for common local pottery types, Phases 2 and 3 percentages combined   70

6.3 Icons recorded for whole and partial vessels from Hummingbird Pueblo and Pottery Mound   71

6.4 Icons recorded on sherds from Hummingbird Pueblo and Pottery Mound   72

6.5 Percentage of locally produced Pueblo IV pottery types recovered from Phases 2 and 3 at Hummingbird Pueblo and Pottery Mound   73

6.6 Row percentages of decorated types by technological attributes for major decorated types by phase   76

7.1 Number of occurrences of icons by ceramic type as recorded on sherds   86

7.2 Summary of bird taxa from Phase 1 Hummingbird Pueblo   88

7.3 Summary of bird taxa from Phase 2 Hummingbird Pueblo   89

7.4 Summary of bird taxa from Phase 3 Pottery Mound   90

7.5 Recovered artifact types and cubic meters of excavation by phase   91

7.6 Room-to-kiva and room-to-plaza ratios for Pottery Mound, Hummingbird Pueblo, and contemporaneous sites in the Rio Grande and Western Pueblo regions   94

A.1 Counts and percentages of ceramics by excavation levels: Matte Painted Wares and Western Glaze Ware   117

A.2 Counts and percentages of ceramics by excavation levels: Rio Grande and Lower Rio Puerco Glaze Wares   119

A.3 Counts and percentages of ceramics by excavation levels: Utility Wares   121

B.1 List of ceramic types used in seriation   125

B.2 Factor loadings, eigenvalues, and percent variance for first five factors from CA of ceramic type assemblage   127

B.3 Mean and standard deviation for k-means three-cluster solution as well as mean ceramic date (MCD) for each cluster   129

B.4 Excavation levels (Site/Unit/Level/Locus) presented by k-means three-cluster solution   130

B.5 Selected excavation units used to examine the relationship between k-means cluster assignment, stratigraphic placement, and sherd density   131

D.1 Summary of major taxa from Phase 1 Hummingbird Pueblo   170

D.2 Summary of major taxa from Phase 2 Hummingbird Pueblo   171

D.3 Summary of major taxa from Phase 3 Hummingbird Pueblo   172

D.4 Summary of major taxa from Phase 2 Pottery Mound   173

D.5 Summary of major taxa from Phase 3 Pottery Mound   174

Acknowledgments

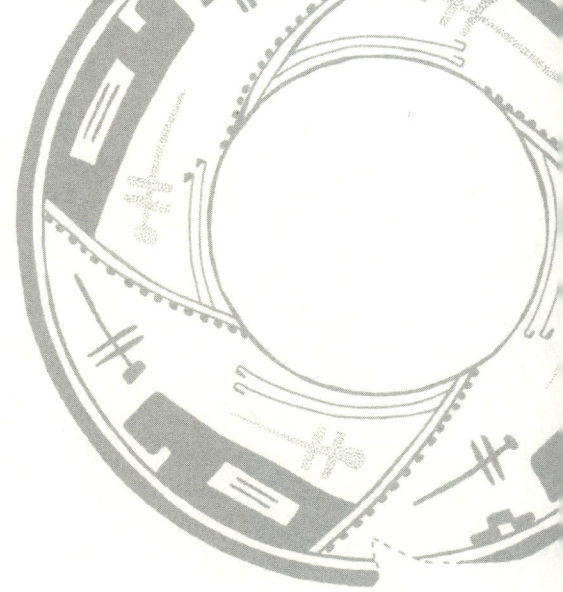

There have been many folks who have helped in this endeavor, some in small ways, some in large. I hope I have thanked you all along the way, and if not, I hope I remember to include you now.

This manuscript began as my PhD dissertation through the Department of Anthropology at Arizona State University in Tempe. As such, I am greatly indebted to my dissertation committee: Keith Kintigh, Katherine Spielmann, Judith Habicht-Mauche, Geoffrey Clark, and Michael Adler. They have provided insightful comments throughout the entire process, insisting upon clarity of argument. Keith and Judith, through different means, have taught me whole new ways to think about what I do and why it is necessary. I need also to thank Linda Cordell for her direction and advice; Linda has provoked me to consider the general anthropological significance of archaeology and the place of my research within that context.

Each group of people has a unique collective identity and personality, and I thank such various groups for taking me in and helping me in countless ways, both large and small, to finish this research: the staff of the Maxwell Museum of Anthropology, especially Bruce Huckell, Mike Lewis, and Sonya Urban; the staff at the Laboratory of Anthropology in Santa Fe, especially Tony Thibodeau, Jeremy Kulisheck, and Dody Fugate; the staff at the Laboratory of Tree-Ring Research, especially Jeff Dean; the unusually mismatched group of students at Hummingbird Pueblo during the summer of 1998, especially Maxine McBrinn; and the archaeology faculty in the Department of Anthropology at Texas A&M, especially Bruce Dickson.

This research would have been impossible without the financial and technical support of various individuals and institutions. The research was funded in part by the National Science Foundation (Award #0109885), an Arizona State University Graduate Research Grant, and the Department of Anthropology at ASU Graduate Research Award. Judith Habicht-Mauche provided supplies and unlimited access to the Ceramic Laboratory, Department of Anthropology, University of California, Santa Cruz. I am especially grateful to Paul Boni of the Department of Geology, University of Colorado, Boulder, for making the majority of petrographic thin sections for this study and doing an excellent job. And a special thanks to

Bruce Tanner of the Department of Earth Sciences, University of California, Santa Cruz, who was kind enough to make a few last-minute petrographic slides.

This research also benefited greatly from support from various private and native groups. A whole bunch of thank-yous go to Richard Chaves and his family, who not only permitted me to work on their ranch, but also went above and beyond the call of duty on numerous occasions to make sure my students and I were safe and comfortable. Dr. and Mrs. Hibben, as well as Kit Sargeant, made all of their resources from Pottery Mound and Hummingbird Pueblo available to me. I am also grateful to Isleta and Laguna pueblos for allowing me access to Pottery Mound and Hummingbird Pueblo.

There are numerous individuals who have offered moments of sanity and escape from the daily grind, as well as those who have participated in intense discussions resulting in epiphanies and excitement concerning the work we do. Thank-yous to Andrew, Brian, Cynthia, Deb, Greg, Jill, Jim, Tiffany, and my graduate students. A special thanks to Tiffany for her excellent faunal analysis and to Andrew for reading an early draft. Thanks also to Deb for suffering through so much with me; I could not ask for a better friend.

Thank you, thank you, thank you to my husband, Keith Maggert. Without your support, I would not be where I am. And last, but not least, thanks to all the dogs I have loved along the way.

CHAPTER ONE

Pottery and Practice

An Introduction

This research is motivated by a desire to better understand the signaling of multiple social boundaries by individuals in the archaeological record and specifically examines decorated pottery from central New Mexico to argue that fourteenth-century potters used their wares to emphasize contradictory social boundaries, often on the same vessel. Using practice theory to frame my interpretations, I examine technological and decorative characteristics on glaze-decorated vessels to argue that potters used their pottery to emphasize social boundaries between ethnic groups with different migration histories. At the same time, they used this same pottery to help integrate disparate ethnic groups by signaling village-wide participation in a shared ritual system. This complicated, and seemingly contradictory, patterning in the ceramic assemblage reflects the complexity of fourteenth-century potters' identity and the decisions that individual potters made in regard to their own social boundaries.

Although this book focuses on fourteenth-century Pueblo potters, the identification of social groups and social boundaries is a fundamental aspect of archaeological research. Whether analyzing gender differentiation in the American Southwest (chapters in Crown 2000), social districts in Mesoamerica (Altschul 1987), or the development of political differentiation in Peru (Hastorf 1990), archaeologists search for evidence of past social groups. A consideration of social boundaries is inherent in studies of ethnicity, culture groups, migration, gender roles, social hierarchies, economics, and urbanization. However, the phenomenon of social boundaries raises three problems for archaeologists in terms of both theory and practice: (1) defining what is meant by "social boundary," (2) identifying boundaries through material culture, and (3) understanding the articulation of multiple social boundaries, which creates complex patterns that are difficult for archaeologists to study.

Defining "Social Boundary"

The distinction between "social group" and "social boundary" is subtle and yet important for archaeological research. A social group is a number of individuals who are classified together within a society based upon some socially meaningful characteristic that is shared by all members of the group. Among any society, there will exist multiple social groups; at any given time, an individual within any society may belong to more than one social group. Social groups can exist within and between households, villages, and communities; they might be based on biological kinship, fictive kinship, economic activities, ritual sodalities, class, ethnicity, gender, or political power (Hitchcock and Bartram 1998; MacEachern 1998). Social groups within a society may also be ranked: age may take precedence over gender, or vice versa, when determining etiquette in a given social situation. Finally, social groups are fluid: they can be disassembled or redefined as one generation replaces another, as groups move or change relative sizes, as resource availability changes, or as new groups are introduced into a given situation.

Social boundaries are the conceptual and behavioral practices of individuals that divide them into social groups based on culturally defined factors; in other words, social boundaries are the culturally defined practices of individuals that allow them to claim or deny membership within a given social group. Social boundaries can be reflected in language, dress, body adornments, household crafts, ritual practice, architecture, or many other aspects of culture. Of course, one's ability to signal membership within a social group will be regulated by societal norms: it would be difficult for a male to signal membership in a traditionally female social group if other members of society did not recognize his membership, and it would be meaningless to signal membership in a social group with signs that were only meaningful to the individual. What is of interest in this discussion is how an individual within a society may choose to signal multiple social boundaries that potentially contradict, crosscut, or complement one another; further, an individual may change his or her social boundaries with context or over time.

I distinguish between two types of social groups, and their corresponding social boundaries, in this study focused on fourteenth-century Pueblo potters in central New Mexico: communities of practice and communities of identity. Communities of practice are social networks in which Pueblo potters learn their craft from other women in the community (Stark 2006). These communities are defined by a shared history of practice and not by spatial constraints. Due to migration, marriage, and other forms of social movement, multiple communities of practice can exist within a given village, while a single community of practice can crosscut multiple villages. Patterns in local pottery styles, both technological and decorative, result from potters making different decisions throughout the production process but using a similar set of tools and techniques available to all potters within an area. Some of these decisions are conscious and may reflect intentions to ally themselves with specific social or economic groups. But some of these decisions are unconscious and reflect the general context of socialization and cultural reproduction; in other words, they result from a community of practice.

Communities of identity are social networks in which potters share a group identity. This identity could be based in a shared language, migration history, religion, kinship, or some other social process. Communities of identity may be nested: as individuals move between social contexts and interact with kin, other village members, or long-distance exchange partners, they may move in and out of different communities of identity, emphasizing membership in the community of identity that most benefits them within a particular social context. As communities of identity are based upon social perception, they may or may not correspond to communities of practice. Depending on the nature and organization of craft production, multiple communities of practice can exist within a single community of identity, or vice versa.

Identifying Social Boundaries Using Material Culture

An important theoretical framework that enables archaeologists to conceptualize the fluidity of social boundaries, and their relationship to material culture, comes from practice theory. This theory was developed by Pierre Bourdieu (1977, 1984) as a means of understanding the construction and maintenance of power relations in societies (Fowler 1997; Robbins 1991). Bourdieu was not interested in "fixing" behavior in society (Robbins 1991), but rather was interested in understanding the dynamics behind the decisions that people actually make on a day-to-day basis. Practice theory focuses on the activities of individuals as they undertake their daily routines. This focus on daily routine is well suited to archaeological research, as daily routine creates much of the patterning that we see in material culture (Stark 2006).

Bourdieu argued that material culture is strategically used in the reproduction of social practice (Barrett 2001) but that social practice structures the understanding of the context in which that material culture is used. As such, material culture is both the "medium and the outcome" of practice (Giddens 1984:174). The material culture that archaeologists work with thus becomes the residue of active debates, dialogues, and negotiations between different social actors (Stark 2006:20–23). An important concept from Bourdieu's work that is used to study material culture is *habitus*. Habitus reflects culturally specific ways of doing things—cultural patterns and traditions that are generally unconscious forms of practice. Working with the concepts of practice theory, especially habitus, allows archaeologists to consider social boundaries as "something people do" (Hegmon 1998:272) rather than as a static social form.

The fourteenth-century Pueblo world in central New Mexico (figure 1.1) provides a productive arena for the study of dynamic social boundaries through the lens of practice theory. Between AD 1275 and 1400, a demographic transformation in the Pueblo world resulted in a new social landscape (Adams 1991; Adams and Duff 2004; Spielmann 1998a). As part of this transformation, two processes linked the creation and maintenance of new social boundaries in much of the Pueblo Southwest: aggregation of populations into large villages and migration of kin-based groups into already occupied regions resulting in immigrants

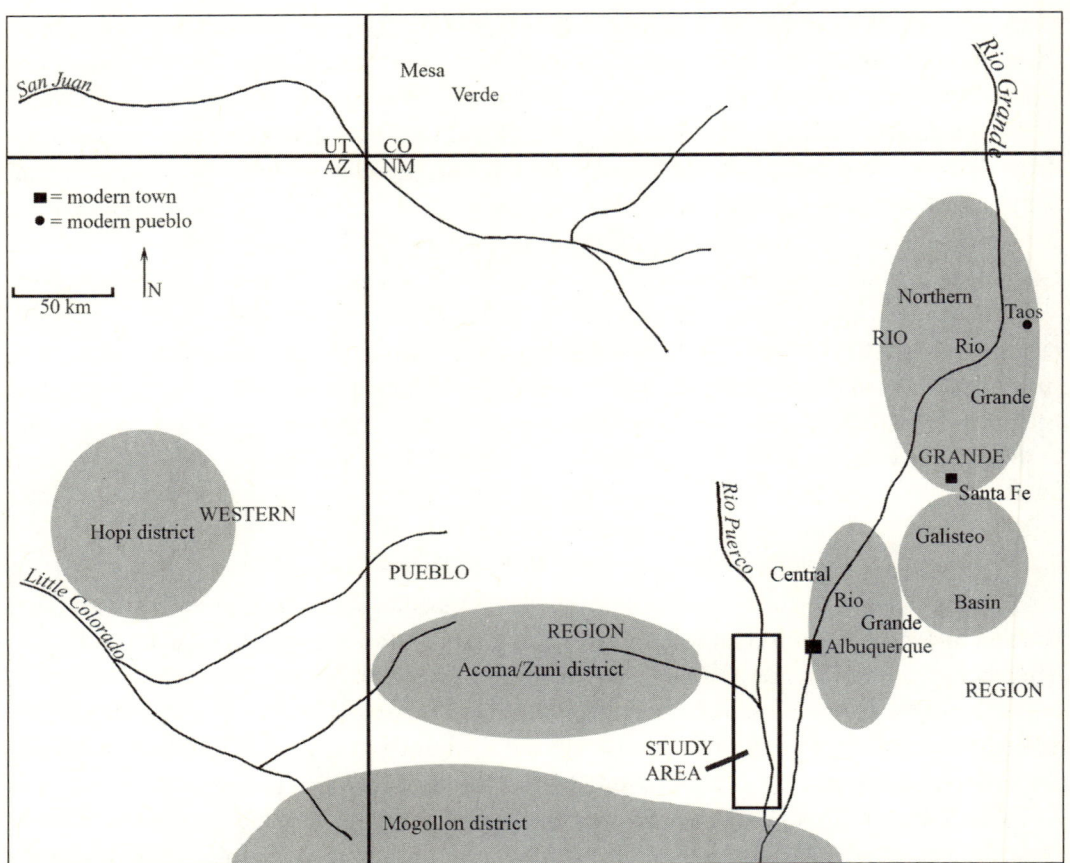

FIGURE 1.1. The American Southwest showing the location of the study area in relation to major prehispanic pueblo regions.

living in close proximity to established groups (Adams and Duff 2004). These processes must have led to fundamental shifts in notions of community, appropriate social interactions, and how ritual practice articulated with these other social dynamics. In this book, I examine archaeological data from the Lower Rio Puerco drainage in central New Mexico to reach a better understanding of these issues within newly established villages.

The Lower Rio Puerco district is an ideal area in which to examine immigration and social change. The culture history of the Lower Rio Puerco area is similar to that of the Western Pueblo region but with a lower population density. Starting in the late 1200s, the inhabitants of the area aggregated (Eidenbach 1982; Roney 1996). At the same time, a large-scale migration of various Pueblo peoples into the Rio Grande valley occurred (Beal 1987; Cameron 1995; Crown et al. 1996; Lekson 1995). Due to topography and geographic location, the Lower Rio Puerco district would have been an ideal corridor for groups moving from either the Mesa Verde or Western Pueblo regions into the Rio Grande valley. The study area is even mentioned as a migration pathway in the oral traditions of some modern Pueblo groups (Brandt, personal communication 1996; Cordell 1995; Hawley 1950). The fourteenth-century population of the Lower Rio Puerco area represented both indigenous and immigrant groups living together within two villages. This mixture of immigrants and natives required the negotiation of new social boundaries within each village, negotiations that are reflected in the pottery produced during this socially dynamic period.

The Articulation of Social Boundaries with Other Social Dynamics

In examining the creation and maintenance of social boundaries, I explore specifically the articulation of multiple social boundaries that were the result of two important social processes in fourteenth-century Lower Rio Puerco villages: migration and ritual practice. In this volume I consider how residents of two villages transformed their social boundaries in an attempt to reproduce their social order within a context of immigration and new ritual practice. To do this, I analyze decorative, technological, and formal attributes on pottery to isolate evidence of kin-based social groups, some of which were comprised of immigrants, within each village. Further, ceramic, architectural, and faunal data are used to argue that both local and immigrant residents of these villages adopted a new ritual system. A part of this system included the development of a new suite of ritual-based social boundaries that crosscut ethnic-based ones. These transformations in the social order were not planned but rather developed in an organic fashion as people attempted to cope with the tensions inherent between different ethnic groups who were living together.

Migration has important consequences for the development and transformation of social boundaries between indigenous and immigrant groups living together within a Pueblo village. Migration is one of the most important concepts of modern Pueblo thought because "it is necessary for the perpetuation of life" (Naranjo 1995:247). Narrative histories focusing on past migrations often provide one important facet of Pueblo ethnic identity (Edelman 1979; Nequatewa 1936; Parsons 1926; Strong 1979). "Ethnic groups are culturally ascribed identity groups, which are based on the expression of a real or assumed shared culture and common descent" (Jones 1997:84). Importantly for this volume, ethnicity is a self-conscious identification with a particular social group and is, at least partly, based on a specific locality of origin (Shennan 1989:14).

Ethnic identity is often associated with a certain set of morals, worldview, and way of doing things that goes unquestioned among those who share the same ethnicity (Barth 1969; Ofstadt 1981). But when ethnic groups confront one another, as is often the case after migration, identity comes to the forefront of social concern, especially if the two groups live in close proximity or compete for certain resources (Barth 1969; Hodder 1979a; Ofstadt 1981). Such social tensions between immigrant and local groups have become part of Pueblo oral tradition (Parsons 1939; Stanislawski 1979); further, these tensions may have led to the development of a new ritual system during the fourteenth century in the Pueblo Southwest.

According to Michelle Hegmon, Roy Rappaport (1979) has defined ritual as a "relatively invariant and formal sequence of actions that is established through tradition" (Hegmon

1989:6). Among historic Pueblo groups, ritual is an important arena where social boundaries can be negotiated. Pueblo ritual organizations create social networks and loyalties that help to crosscut, and potentially conflict with, kinship lines. For example, the Zuni divide themselves among kin-based clans; integration of clans is achieved through membership in various ceremonial organizations including curing societies and kiva groups (Ferguson 1989; Kroeber 1917; Parsons 1939). These various ritual organizations create non-kin-based relationships and obligations that need to be respected to preserve proper balance in both society and the cosmos.

Factionalism between historic Pueblo groups sometimes resulted in the splintering of a village, with part, or all, of its residents emigrating (Schroeder 1979; Titiev 1944:69–99). Ritual practice played a role in determining where some of these migrants moved. There are historical cases of villages fissioning "through the movement and recruitment of religious groups . . . to other villages" (Brandt 1994:17). Similar recruitment may have occurred in the prehispanic era. For example, ritual practitioners in the fourteenth-century Upper Little Colorado River area appear to have been actively recruited by residents of the Hopi and Zuni regions (Duff 2002). Andrew Duff (2002) speculates that these recruits were incorporated into their new village with a certain amount of social power associated with their unique ritual ceremonies, while the residents of Hopi or Zuni who had recruited them gained local prestige. Pueblo ritual practice, then, can act as a form of social currency, as a way for groups to negotiate their relative ranking within their own village or to buy their way into a new village.

Members of a Pueblo group who own highly ranked ritual knowledge have a stake in certain ideologies that continue to uphold the established hierarchy, while members with lower ranked ritual knowledge (or no ritual knowledge) have less interest in maintaining the status quo (Titiev 1944:201–3). Further, membership in different kin-based and ritual-based social groups can lead to conflicts of interest for individuals within the society. The inherent instability in such social tensions can lead to cultural transformation as power relations between different groups and the members of each group are negotiated (Titiev 1944). If these tensions cannot be overcome, then the resulting social conflict may lead to violence or the fissioning of a village's population (Levy 1992). This study is ultimately concerned with recognizing these tensions and negotiations in the prehispanic record.

Organization of This Volume

The relationship between ethnicity, migration, and ritual practice is multilayered. These social dynamics interact with one another to create a rich, complexly patterned material culture. Within any society, multiple social boundaries exist that may contradict, crosscut, or complement one another; further, social boundaries are fluid, changing with context and over time. The remainder of this book is concerned specifically with the social boundaries that existed between immigrant and local ethnic groups within two fourteenth-century villages in central New Mexico and how these social boundaries were crosscut by village-wide participation in the same ritual system.

Chapter 2 outlines practice theory, the theoretical framework through which I interpret my data patterns throughout this volume. There are two reasons why this theory is an ideal framework for archaeological research. First, practice theory enables archaeologists to conceptualize the fluidity inherent in social boundaries as the result of daily negotiations made by the actors who participate in numerous social groups. Second, practice theory provides the concept of habitus, which reflects the culturally specific practices that result in much of the material patterning studied by archaeologists. The basic principle of this theoretical framework is that the ordering of daily life reflects the broader organizational principles and social categories in which an individual lives. Further, through habitus, cultural perceptions and the resulting material products can transform and change when faced with new environmental and social situations.

Chapter 3 provides the archaeological and temporal context from which the data were collected. This study focuses on data collected from two villages located in the Lower Rio Puerco archaeological district of central New Mexico. Although the district was populated from the Archaic period (5500 BC–AD 500) through the Pueblo IV period (AD 1300–1450/1500), this volume focuses primarily on the fourteenth century. This century is marked by dramatic transformations in group identity, social organization, power structures, and ritual practice and so is ideal for examining the interplay between multiple social boundaries.

In chapters 4 and 5, evidence for the presence of immigrants in the Lower Rio Puerco region is examined and communities of practice in the area are defined based on ceramic data. Pottery production and technological data, as well as architectural data, are presented in support of the argument that immigrants moved into the study area during the late 1200s or early 1300s. These chapters argue that at least some of these immigrants were from the Western Pueblo area, as well as possibly from the Mogollon area and northern Mexico. Evidence is presented to support the argument that these immigrants, along with separate kin-based groups from the northern and southern portions of the study area, were living together in two large villages. I identify four communities of practice living within the study area and argue that they reflect four social groups with distinct migration histories.

Chapter 6 considers communities of identity in light of migrations into the study area during the fourteenth century. Decorative and technological evidence suggests that pottery was used to signal identity based on different migration histories. Migration histories play an important role in modern Pueblo ethnic identity. As such, migration has important consequences for the development and transformation of social boundaries, especially in contexts where immigrants and indigenous groups live together within a village. As the basic social unit in middle-range societies is normally kin based, and the basic unit of migration is likely to be kin based, one set of social boundaries in a postmigration environment in the prehispanic Southwest would most likely have occurred along kinship lines. When a kin-based group moved into a large village, they would be confronted with daily, face-to-face interaction with other family groups. Some of these families were immigrant groups, and so regular interaction must have occurred between people with different ethnic identities as well as different kin relations. Social negotiations would have been required between and within these groups living within a village as they struggled to make sense of their new social context.

Chapter 7 continues a consideration of communities of identity, but with a focus on ritual practice. Pueblo ritual practice provides an arena where social boundaries can be both negotiated and contested. The modern Pueblo ritual system is one in which members of a village are segregated by membership in various medicine societies, clown sodalities, moieties, hunting and war societies, and katsina groups. These ritual-based groups create social networks and loyalties that crosscut kin-based groups. Although participation in public ceremonies provides participants and witnesses the chance to reaffirm their belief in the ritual system, the potential for conflict lies immediately beneath the surface. The ranking of different ceremonies and ritual knowledge within a village, ritual secrecy and its role in village social hierarchies, and the ownership of ritual paraphernalia and ceremonies by specific kin-based groups all provide the seed for underlying social tensions within a village. The inherent instability in such social tensions can lead to cultural transformations as power relations are negotiated and contested.

Chapter 8 synthesizes the data and interpretations presented throughout the volume. This research contributes to the field an explanation of the seemingly contradictory patterns in material culture as reflecting the dynamic nature of daily decisions made by people attempting to negotiate their place in a new social landscape. The coalition of various groups into two large villages in the Lower Rio Puerco area during the fourteenth century would have required transformations in group identity, social organization, and power structures. Such transformations occur through daily attempts by both immigrants and indigenous groups to reproduce their social order in the changed context of aggregation and interaction. A socioreligious system would have developed as community leaders and members faced the daily decisions and obligations of living in a village with residents of diverse backgrounds. During the fourteenth century, many villages were established throughout the Pueblo world that created different combinations of ideology and ritual to cope with the social stress brought on by disparate groups living together. But for as many villages that were successful in this endeavor, there were at least as many villages that were not successful. This process fundamentally transformed the Pueblo social landscape, eventually leading to the diversity of villages we see today.

CHAPTER TWO

Understanding the Creation, Maintenance, and Transformation of Social Boundaries through Practice Theory

This volume works within the framework of practice theory to investigate the dynamic nature of multiple social boundaries and how such boundaries articulate with material culture. Practice theory interprets human behavior as being physical, social, and mental; individuals act as agents of practice by reproducing physical behaviors, social understanding, and mental "know-how" (Reckwitz 2002). Practice refers to these interrelated aspects of routine human behavior, including "forms of bodily activities, forms of mental activities, 'things' and their use, a background knowledge in the form of understanding, know how, states of emotion and motivational knowledge" (Reckwitz 2002:249). A practice—be it making a pottery vessel, cooking a meal, courting a lover, or raising a child—cannot exist in isolation. However, a practice can be reproduced through enactment of a variety of different, and often unique, actions (Ortner 1984; Reckwitz 2002); for example, a certain "practice" of cooking can be enacted by preparing numerous kinds of meals with various types of foods, while a "practice" of pottery making can be enacted by producing any number of vessel forms for a variety of purposes. This concept of practice is closely related to Marxist praxis and has its roots in Marxism; however, the former has come to reflect the idea that action has both a physical and social component, while the latter tends to reflect a purely social phenomenon (McGuire 1992).

Pierre Bourdieu, Practice Theory, and Habitus

Practice theory was developed by Pierre Bourdieu, a French philosopher and anthropologist, in the 1970s as a way of overcoming the dichotomy of structuralism and subjectivism when attempting to understand the construction and maintenance of social hierarchies (Bourdieu 1980; Fowler 1997; Ortner 1984; Robbins 1991). Through Bourdieu's emphasis on individual action rather than rules or social norms, his theory is related to agency theory. Both frameworks view culture change as the result of individuals' collective behaviors; however, practice theory does not focus as closely on individuals' intents and motivations, but rather on the outcome of individuals' actions (Stark 2006). Bourdieu was not concerned with outlining social "rules," but with understanding how people knew "what was possible and proper to the occasion, or of what pushed against the acceptable and transgressed convention" through the monitoring of reactions by others within a group (Barrett 2001:153). This level of practical knowledge would be continuously reproduced as it was validated through the very fact that "it worked" and not through some disembodied enforcement of societal rules.

Bourdieu (1977:33–38) provided the example of "official kin" and "practical kin" to help illustrate how practical knowledge helps anthropological understanding of social structure. Official kin are biological relatives, especially those who are outlined by ethnographers' genealogies. Practical kin are relatives, biological and fictitious, who are recognized within a society through oral tradition, ritual sodalities, friendship, illegitimate relationships, or such other cultural constructs. Official kin only exist on the theoretical level; that is, official kin represent the biological relationships between individuals as recorded by an ethnographer through observation or as described to an ethnographer by individuals who are presenting an official account of the group. Practical kin exist on a day-to-day basis and are the product of strategies (conscious or unconscious) that require cultivation and maintenance. Although there is overlap between official and practical kin, the point is that "kin relationships are something people *make*, and with which they *do* something" (1977:35, emphasis in original); they are the result of practices that produce, reproduce, and transform social behavior.

Bourdieu's focus on the activities of individuals as they undertake their daily routines makes practice theory an ideal framework for archaeologists. Bourdieu argued that material culture is strategically used in the reproduction of social behavior (Barrett 2001), but social behavior is what structures the understanding of the context in which that material culture is used. The patterning in material culture that we see in the archaeological record, then, is both the medium and the outcome of practice by individuals as they went about their daily routine (Giddens 1984). To explain the relationship between material culture and human behavior, Bourdieu developed the concept of habitus. Arguably the most important concept to come out of Bourdieu's work (Throop and Murphy 2002), habitus is a set of tendencies (and not rules) that develops as a practical solution to a particular demand within the framework of certain environmental and cultural conditions. As such, it can transform as the demand changes or as the environmental or cultural conditions change. Further, it may transform gradually, as long as there is a "close fit" between the practical solution and the cultural and environmental framework in which it functions (Dietler and Herbich 1998:247).

Critics of Bourdieu

The major critique of Bourdieu is that practice theory is most insightful as a theory of cultural reproduction and weakest as a theory of cultural transformation (Ortner 1996; Rowlands and Kristiansen 1998). Sherry Ortner (1996:17) has referred to this theoretical framework as a loop "in which 'structures' construct subjects and practices, but subjects and practices reproduce 'structures.'" She proposes a "subaltern practice theory" as a means to break out of this theoretical loop of reproduction. In this updated version of the theory, one would "look for the slippages in reproduction, the erosions of long-standing patterns, the moments of disorder and of outright 'resistance'" (1996:17). While Bourdieu never specifically addressed resistance, or counterpractice, as part of his theory, his later work does provide a discussion of how practice would allow for cultural change.

In considering cultural transformations, Bourdieu (1980) argued that social actors may be linked to one another through different social domains, such as kinship, class, and religion. Conflicts of interest may arise from participation in these separate domains; cultural transformation results from the negotiation of the contradictions, tensions, and power relations between these domains and the social actors who participate in them. For example, the Zuni and Hopi divide themselves into kin-based clans as well as into various ceremonial sodalities (Ferguson 1989; Kroeber 1917; Ladd 1979; Parsons 1939; Titiev 1944). These clans and ritual groups crosscut one another; membership in both a clan and in various ritual organizations requires obligations that need to be respected to preserve proper balance in Zuni society. As a result, a dispute between two individuals would potentially result in other Zunis being faced with conflicting loyalties and thus motivate them to help find a quick and peaceful solution. If no peaceful solution is to be found, each individual would have to choose sides in the conflict based upon their own desires and interpretations of their social obligations.

Further, when responding to contact with new groups, social actors will redefine and reinterpret daily practices in ways that both help to make sense of the new social context as well as to best meet their own interests (Sahlins 1981). In so doing, social actors may transform the very culture they are attempting to preserve. By trying to make the unfamiliar familiar, they change the familiar. For example, James Deetz (1996) notes that early African Americans, often working under strictures placed on them by slavery, used the materials of their immediate environment (the southern United States) to create housing, food, and pottery vessels that harkened back to their origins (western Africa). By using their habitus on the materials available to them in their new social and natural environments, they created a new material culture that was neither African nor English American but was a reflection of both.

Practice Theory, Archaeology, and the Study of Social Boundaries

Miriam Stark (2006:33–35) outlines three reasons why archaeologists working in North America have recently turned to practice theory to help them interpret the past. First, practice theory can work as a middle-range theory to help bridge the gap between apparently disparate theoretical approaches (Dobres and Robb 2000). For example, economic archaeologists tend to work within either an ecological or Marxist framework of human behavior

(Sheridan and Bailey 1981); practice theory could help bridge the gap between these theoretical approaches by viewing patterns in material culture as a result of people's daily negotiations when confronted with a variety of choices based within both class tensions and environmental parameters. Second, practice theory, especially the concept of habitus, parallels previous concepts in American archaeology. Specifically, the measuring of "what people do"—be it Irving Rouse's (1939) concept of mode, James Hill and Evan's (1972) approach to classification, or Hegmon's (1998) approach to social boundaries—has deep roots in the history of archaeological thought in North America (Stark 2006). Third, and finally, practice theory is attractive because it provides a methodological approach that lends itself to archaeological data (Stark 2006:34). Daily practice patterns material culture; the archaeologist must interpret these patterns.

In regard to the study of social boundaries, practice theory allows for the consideration of social boundaries as "something people do" (Hegmon 1998) rather than as a static social form. Bourdieu (1980) argued that habitus developed through people's tendencies to act in certain ways based upon their perceptions of the cultural and environmental choices available to them. Techniques, along with other patterned behaviors, are formed through habitus (Dietler and Herbich 1998). For archaeologists, artifacts often preserve the physical attributes that provide clues concerning the techniques that created them, allowing us to interpret the conditions in which these items were produced, used, and discarded. An excellent example of the application of these concepts when examining anthropological social boundaries comes from the work of Michael Dietler and Ingrid Herbich (1998) among the Luo of western Kenya.

Dietler and Herbich (1998) examined pottery production among the Luo and were able to define ceramic micro-styles (incorporating technical, formal, and decorative attributes) between different potter communities. These micro-styles were not created through an explicit set of rules; in fact, although potters could distinguish vessels made in their community from vessels made in other communities, they were hard-pressed to explain what attributes defined "their style." These micro-styles are the result of women learning the craft from their husbands' female relatives as part of the general resocialization process after marriage. Any expression of identity in the creation of the micro-style is largely understood in the social context of production and is not necessarily meant to signal identity between potter communities. No micro-style can be identified by a single attribute, but rather must be identified by a set of attributes. There is also a range of variation for any single attribute; potters follow a set of tendencies, habitus, which guides their perceptions of the acceptable range of variation in choices at different stages of production. Further, these micro-styles are not static; change may occur at any point in the production process as a result of any variety of demands. For example, some potters recently began to use crushed brick temper when old vessels for crushed sherd temper were unavailable. Natural sources of crushed rock are not considered within the acceptable range of variation, despite the fact that a neighboring potter community uses crushed rock temper.

Practice theory can also be used for the identification of the maintenance and transformation of social boundaries in the archaeological record. Kent Lightfoot and colleagues (1998) found that Kashaya (Native Californian) women and Aluttiq (Native Alaskan) men attempted to maintain their distinct social identities in interethnic households at Fort Ross, where both groups had been displaced to during the first half of the 1800s. Kashaya women were able to assert their identity in daily activities focused on food preparation, mundane tasks such as cleaning and refuse disposal, the organization of domestic space, and the use of material culture specific to their foraging tradition. Aluttiq men were able to assert their identity through the choice of situating houses near the ocean, the consumption of seafood, and the use of material culture specific to their maritime tradition. However, in the process of spouses reproducing their own cultures, cultural transformations also took place as they responded to one another and accommodated themselves to a new social context. New foods were consumed by both spouses; new foodways were developed that incorporated the cooking of marine, terrestrial, and domesticated animals together in Kashaya ovens; new raw materials were used to produce native artifact forms; and innovations took place in landscape modification techniques. Spouses do not appear to have deliberately created a new multicultural identity; rather, they were creating cultural innovations that allowed them to work and live within a new social setting and still behave within their perceptions of being a proper Kashaya or Aluttiq.

These two studies show that through daily routine—pottery production, cooking, refuse disposal—individuals repeatedly construct and reproduce their underlying structural principles, worldviews, and social identities. The basic principle of practice theory is that the ordering of daily life reflects the broader organizational principles and social categories of an individual. Further, both studies provide examples of how, through habitus, cultural perceptions and the resulting material products can transform and change when faced with new environmental and social situations. As such, these studies provide examples of how studying material culture can provide insights into the process by which social boundaries are negotiated.

The remainder of this volume explores how residents of two fourteenth-century Lower Rio Puerco villages transformed their social strategies in an attempt to reproduce their social order in the context of aggregation and immigration. Working within practice theory, I analyze decorative, technological, and formal attributes on both whole vessels and ceramic sherds to isolate evidence of changes in group identity and ritual practice in each village over time. These transformations in the social order were not planned, but rather developed in an organic fashion as people attempted to cope with the tensions inherent between different kin-based groups living together.

CHAPTER THREE

Pottery Mound and Hummingbird Pueblo

Archaeological and Temporal Context

Social boundaries in the archaeological record are examined through analysis of data collected from Pottery Mound and Hummingbird Pueblo, two thirteenth- and fourteenth-century villages located in the Lower Rio Puerco archaeological district (Eckert and Cordell 2004) in central New Mexico (figure 3.1). The Rio Puerco in central New Mexico is sometimes referred to as the Rio Puerco of the East to distinguish it from the Rio Puerco of the West, which runs southwest from western New Mexico into eastern Arizona.

Two aspects of the district's culture history require attention for this study. First, the district was populated from the Archaic period (5500 BC–AD 500) through the Pueblo IV period (AD 1300–1450/1500). Thus, the local population had a long history of residency before immigrants entered the area in the late 1200s and early 1300s. Second, two distinct ceramic traditions characterized the district during the Pueblo II (AD 900–1175/1200) and Pueblo III (AD 1175/1200–1300) periods. These two ceramic traditions can be thought of in terms of two separate communities of practice (Dietler and Herbich 1998; Stark 2006). The significance of these two aspects of the Lower Rio Puerco culture history is discussed in the next chapter. This chapter provides a brief description of the environmental, cultural, archaeological, and temporal setting for the two villages examined in this study.

Pottery Mound and Hummingbird Pueblo were occupied during one of the most dramatic periods in the Pueblo Southwest. The thirteenth and fourteenth centuries are

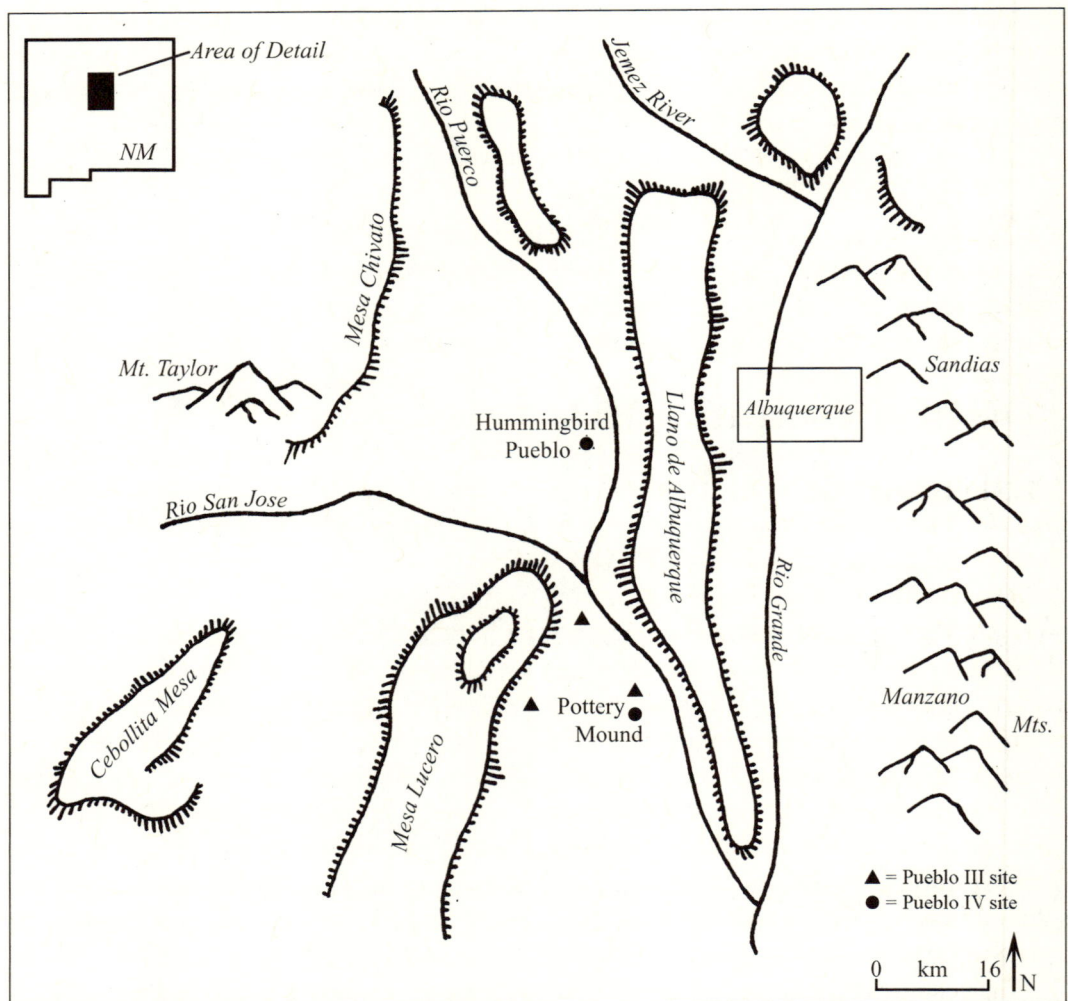

FIGURE 3.1. Map of the Lower Rio Puerco area showing location of sites pertinent to this study and surrounding geological features.

characterized by complete abandonment of some areas, population increase in other areas, and the nucleation of populations into large villages (Adams and Duff 2004; Adler 1996). This period of dramatic shifts in settlement paved the way for the development of social, cultural, and religious practices that continued through Spanish contact to the present (Spielmann 1998a). Dramatic population reorganizations during this period include the complete abandonment of the Mesa Verde area, abandonment of much of the Western Pueblo area, and the corresponding dramatic population increase in the Rio Grande region (Cameron 1995). Immigrants from the Mesa Verde, Western Pueblo, and Mogollon areas all appear to have moved into the Rio Grande region (Duff 1998), resulting in greater cultural diversity in this one region than previously experienced in the Pueblo world. These two centuries are marked by dramatic transformations in group identity, social organization, power structures, and ritual practice and so are ideal for examining the interplay between social boundaries and these other social processes.

Environmental and Geological Setting

The Lower Rio Puerco valley was not the most attractive of Southwest environments for Pueblo groups to live in; however, considering its long occupational history, the valley was not unattractive for settlement. Today, the valley is primarily desert grassland; however, some shrubs and sparse juniper woodlands occur on valley slopes, and a riparian environment characterizes the main water channel (Eidenbach and Gossett 1982:14–17). The area has an average elevation of 5,500 ft and is semiarid: modern yearly rainfall averages 21.5 cm, with two-thirds (68 percent) of that rain falling between May and October. Although the growing season (frost-free days) is adequate for corn agriculture, occurring between April and October and averaging 163 days (Gerow 1998), soil studies of the valley suggest that the potential for agriculture in the valley was extremely limited (Love et al. 1982).

Wild resources are, and presumably were, abundant. An intensive vegetation survey of the valley's main ecological zone identified 100 plant species: only 5 of these species were historically introduced; 63 native species were identified as potentially useful to humans; and 33 native species were identified as being edible (Tierney 1977). This survey was conducted in an area immediately northeast of the Lower Rio Puerco district and is similar to it geographically. It is reasonable to assume that prehistoric residents in the study area would have had access to a similar range of floral resources. The largest available faunal resources in the district during the prehispanic era were mule deer and antelope; however, rabbit and other small game were also available. Further, it has been suggested that ducks and other migratory waterfowl were seasonally collected for food (Emslie 1981).

The geology of the Lower Rio Puerco district is complex due to extensive fault activity, warping of the underlying basin, and ongoing erosion (Fitzsimmons 1959; Kelley 1977; Love et al. 1982). Overall, the landscape is one of alternating uplands and drainage bottoms dotted with isolated volcanic plugs. Major geologic formations include the Datil Formation, Ceja Formation, Abo Formation, and Santa Fe Formation. Various igneous, sedimentary, and metamorphic rocks are present in these formations. Culturally important geological features in the district are abundant. Extensive outcrops of sedimentary rocks along the western portion of the valley could have provided white-firing clays, while volcanic features throughout the district could have been a source of buff-, brown-, and red-firing clays (Warren 1982a). Potential temper materials for pottery available in the area include hornblende latite, hornblende syenite, vesicular basalt, rhyolite, olivine diabase, and quartz sand (Warren 1982a). Chert, light-colored petrified wood, quartzite, obsidian, and intermediate igneous rocks were all available for chipped stone manufacture from gravel layers throughout the district (Gossett 1982; Warren 1982b). Finally, basalt, sandstone, and limestone outcrops could all have provided material for grindstones as well as masonry construction.

Cultural History

With the exception of work at Pottery Mound and Hummingbird Pueblo, archaeological research in the Lower Rio Puerco area has been sporadic and limited in scope. Research in the region is mostly the result of surveys and limited excavations associated with construction and other land management projects. Most reports are limited in circulation and are part of the infamous gray literature of the field. Further, much of the land in the district is incorporated into various Indian reservations with the result that access to some data is currently restricted. The following summary has been gleaned mostly from Chada (1993), Eck (1981), Eidenbach (1982), Gerow (1998, 2001), Luhrs (1937), Roney (1996), Schaefer and Huntley (2000), Swift (1988), Washburn (1974), Wimberly and Eidenbach (1980), and ARMS site files.

PALEO-INDIAN THROUGH PUEBLO II PERIODS

Discovery of early period sites along the Lower Rio Puerco is hampered by the fact that many have been buried, often under 1 to 3 m of sediment (Eidenbach and Gossett 1982). Most early sites are found in the walls of arroyos after exposure through erosion. Even with this consideration, archaeological surveys in the district indicate that humans were in the area possibly as early as the Paleo-Indian period (10,000–5500 BC) (Judge 1973), but definitely during the Archaic period (5500 BC–AD 500). The Archaic period was one of adaptation to local conditions, including the intensive exploitation of a broad range of plant and animal species. This period marked the beginnings of a more sedentary way of life (Irwin-Williams 1967). Archaic period sites have been found throughout the study area, usually dated with projectile points. Based on survey data, Archaic occupations are often part of a larger, multicomponent site. In general, the Archaic component consists primarily of lithic scatters; occasionally there is a large ash stain identified as a hearth.

Basketmaker sites (AD 500–700) have been reported in the district and are usually dated by the presence of Lino Gray pottery, an undecorated ware distinctive for its conspicuously protruding sand temper. This period is marked by the introduction of two major technical innovations: pottery and the bow and arrow (Irwin-Williams 1973). Further, Linda Cordell (1979) has argued that basic aspects of Pueblo life—storage, maintenance of long-distance exchange networks, and construction of special ceremonial rooms—were established late in this period. Identified Basketmaker III sites are most often artifact scatters composed primarily of lithic debitage with a low frequency of Lino Gray sherds; however, sites with ground stone, pithouse architecture, surface hearths, and storage pits have all been reported.

The Pueblo I period (AD 700–900) in the Lower Rio Puerco area is marked by the appearance of small pithouse villages and increased variability in ceramic manufacture and decoration. Sites are usually dated by the presence of mineral-painted black-on-white pottery types, especially Red Mesa Black-on-white (B/w). Pueblo I sites probably reflect dispersed, semi-independent households located across the landscape due to the demands of low technology agriculture (Irwin-Williams 1973). These farmsteads may have been organized into larger social networks through participation in regional exchange and ceremonial systems. In the study area, Pueblo I sites are characterized by shallow pithouses, fire-cracked rock scatters, ceramic scatters, and possible adobe architecture.

Pottery types found on Pueblo II (AD 900–1175/1200) sites in the study area suggest that the district was on the boundary of two different ceramic traditions. This ceramic boundary may reflect potter communities within the district that participated in different social and economic networks (Roney 1995). The first decorated pottery tradition, found on sites in the *southern* portion of the Lower Rio Puerco district, is predominantly Socorro B/w, an unslipped, mineral-painted type with rock temper. Pueblo II sites in this portion of the study area are often no more than a ceramic and lithic scatter associated with fire-cracked rock. The few architectural sites have irregular site plans, with 2–20 masonry rooms. There is no indication that occupants of these Pueblo II sites were integrated into the contemporaneous Chacoan system. Instead, the Socorro B/w recovered from these sites suggests that residents of the area may have been integrated with communities to the south and southwest (Marshall and Walt 1984; Roney 1995).

The second decorated pottery tradition, found on the few sites recorded in the *northern* portion of the study area, tends to be locally produced variants of Cibola White Ware with white slip, mineral paint, and sherd temper. During this time period, Cibola White Ware is associated with the Chacoan interaction sphere. It is important to note that Pueblo II occupation in the Rio Puerco valley was centered along the *Middle* Rio Puerco drainage (just north of the study area). Further, the decorated pottery recovered from sites in the northern portion of the study area matches that of decorated pottery recovered from sites along the Middle Rio Puerco (Durand and Hurst 1991).

Among the Pueblo II sites in the Middle Rio Puerco area are two Chacoan outliers: Guadalupe Ruin and the Eleanor site. These outliers were likely established in, or by, an indigenous Rio Puerco population (Gerow 2001). As local residents (including those in the northern portion of the study area) became integrated into the Chacoan interaction sphere, social and economic factors may have led to a less dispersed settlement pattern focused on these outliers. This settlement focus on Chacoan outliers seems to have resulted in the near-abandonment of the southern portion of the Middle Rio Puerco valley and much of the *northern* portion of study area. Pueblo II movement of residents from the Lower Rio Puerco area into the Middle Rio Puerco area may account for the increase in population in the latter witnessed during this period (Gerow 2001).

SETTLEMENT AGGREGATION

This study is concerned with social developments during the Pueblo III (AD 1175/1200–1300) and Pueblo IV (AD 1300–1450/1500) periods. With the collapse of the Chacoan system, much of the Pueblo II population in the Middle Rio Puerco area appears to have moved south, back into the northern portion of the study area (Durand and Hurst 1991; Tainter and Tainter 1995). The technological and decorative similarities between Pueblo II pottery in the Middle Rio Puerco area and Pueblo III pottery in the Lower Rio Puerco area support this cultural continuity (Durand and Hurst 1991). As with the previous period, two ceramic traditions characterized the study area during the Pueblo III period. Pueblo III pottery in the northern portion of the study area continued to be slipped and tempered with crushed sherd; however, potters began to use a combination of carbon and mineral components in their paint (Durand and Hurst 1991; Roney

1995). In the southern portion of the study area, the unslipped, rock-tempered Socorro B/w continued to dominate pottery assemblages, along with an unnamed type (Warren 1982a) that could be considered a slipped variant of Socorro B/w.

The Pueblo III (AD 1175/1200–1300) occupation along the Lower Rio Puerco appears to correspond with broad demographic developments in the Zuni and Acoma areas of the Western Pueblo region. In general, these areas witnessed a gradual transition from small, dispersed roomblocks to communities consisting of either multiple, aggregated roomblocks or a single large, planned pueblo (Dittert, personal communication 2000; Kintigh 1996). Numerous small, dispersed Pueblo III sites have been recorded in the study area, mostly on the slopes of mesas or low hills (Chada 1993; Eidenbach 1982; Luhrs 1937; Roney 1996; Tainter and Tainter 1995); however, two aggregated roomblocks and two possibly planned pueblos dating to the Pueblo III period have also been identified in the study area.

The two aggregated Pueblo III (AD 1175/1200–1300) communities identified in the Lower Rio Puerco area are Cerros Mojinos (Bandelier 1892; Fenenga 1956; Fenenga and Cummings 1956) and the Hidden Mountain site (Marshall and Walt 1984). Adolph Bandelier (1892) originally recorded Cerros Mojinos as separate roomblocks. Two of the roomblocks were excavated as part of a pipeline clearance and a "dozen-odd similar sites" (Fenenga and Cummings 1956:243) were reported to be within a 1.5 mi radius of these excavations (Fenenga 1956). The Hidden Mountain site (LA 415) consists of a group of 122 rooms, 18 pit structures, and 27 rock cairns located along a volcanic ridge. Pottery from the site dates it to the late Pueblo III/early Pueblo IV period. Michael Marshall and Henry Walt (1984:188) have argued that this site "was primarily inhabited as a fortified sanctuary of domestic character by various corporate groups."

Two large, possibly planned, Pueblo III (AD 1175/1200–1300) roomblocks have also been recorded in the Lower Rio Puerco area. Recent excavations (Eckert 1999) uncovered a Pueblo III roomblock with unusually deep trash midden deposits buried beneath the Pueblo IV site of Hummingbird Pueblo. However, little is known about the size or layout of this Pueblo III site. Also, Frank Hibben recorded a relatively large Pueblo III roomblock, which has since washed into the Rio Puerco, near the Pueblo IV site of Pottery Mound (Hibben 1955; Voll 1961). Unfortunately, no maps of this site have been found in Hibben's notes.

NUCLEATION INTO VILLAGES

The Pueblo IV (AD 1300–1450/1500) occupation of the Lower Rio Puerco drainage parallels developments in the Zuni, Hopi, and Acoma areas of the Western Pueblo region as well as much of the Rio Grande region. In general, during the Pueblo IV period, populations throughout the Pueblo world nucleated into large, often planned, pueblos (Adams and Duff 2004). The Pueblo IV occupation in the study area consisted of two nucleated villages, Pottery Mound (LA 416) and Hummingbird Pueblo (LA 578). Pottery Mound is located in the southern portion of the study area, near the confluence of the Rio Puerco and Rio Grande. Ceramic types on this site date it to the Pueblo IV period, with no evidence of earlier or later occupations. Hummingbird Pueblo is located in the northern portion of the study area, approximately 22 mi due west of Albuquerque and 15 mi north of Pottery Mound. Ceramic types recovered from this site suggest that the main body of Hummingbird Pueblo dates to the Pueblo IV period, with a smaller Pueblo III component beneath. Both sites were occupied into the 1400s. These two sites are discussed in greater detail below.

Currently, the timing of abandonment of the Lower Rio Puerco region remains uncertain. Abandonment of Hummingbird Pueblo probably occurred sometime during the mid- to late 1400s; Pottery Mound may have been occupied into the 1500s. These abandonment dates are based upon a handful of ceramic rim forms recovered from the surface of these sites. Overall, after AD 1500, there is little evidence of occupation along the Lower Rio Puerco until the possible reuse of the area during the Pueblo Revolt (Eidenbach 1982).

The social effect of the Pueblo IV (AD 1300–1450/1500) population reorganization on the residents of the Lower Rio Puerco area is the focus of this research. Pottery from both Hummingbird Pueblo and Pottery Mound suggests technological and decorative influence from the Western Pueblo and Rio Grande regions. Especially significant is the introduction of glaze ware technology into the Lower Rio Puerco area, which quickly replaced the previous black-on-white traditions (Eckert 2006a). The shift from carbon- and mineral-painted, white-slipped pottery to glaze-painted, red-slipped pottery was a dramatic transition in terms of both decorative and technological style. Despite this dramatic change, the two tempering traditions witnessed in previous periods continued, with potters at Hummingbird Pueblo normally selecting sherd temper and potters at Pottery Mound normally selecting rock temper.

Hummingbird Pueblo

Hummingbird Pueblo consists of over 200 rooms, about half of which were constructed with masonry, the rest being adobe (figure 3.2). The majority of data from Hummingbird Pueblo used in this study come from trash middens and stratified trash-fill excavated under my direction during the summer of 1998. These excavations were part of a larger, multi-institutional project directed by Michael Adler of Southern Methodist University and Linda Cordell of the University Museum, University of Colorado, Boulder. My Hummingbird Pueblo data are augmented by data collected in subsequent years by Adler. Finally, near-complete vessels from Hummingbird Pueblo, collected by Frank Hibben intermittently from the 1950s through the 1980s, were analyzed and are discussed in later chapters. These vessels are curated at the Maxwell Museum.

The pueblo appears to have been built through accretion of roomblocks around three plazas. The masonry portion of the site is built atop a trash mound. The mound and roomblock combined cover an area approximately 55 × 55 m and almost 5 m of elevation. Two other roomblocks to the north and east of the masonry mound are built of adobe. Although multiple floors are apparent in some rooms, and remodeling occurred in at least the masonry portion of the site, no evidence for multiple stories has yet been found.

Hibben uncovered one kiva (West Kiva) in the masonry roomblock during his excavations in the 1980s; however, the exact location of this kiva is unknown. More recent excavations directed by Adler have uncovered one rectangular, trash-filled kiva (K01 in figure 3.2), also in the masonry roomblock. Neither of these kivas had murals. However, K01 contained a ventilator, deflector, and fire pit complex along the northwest wall.

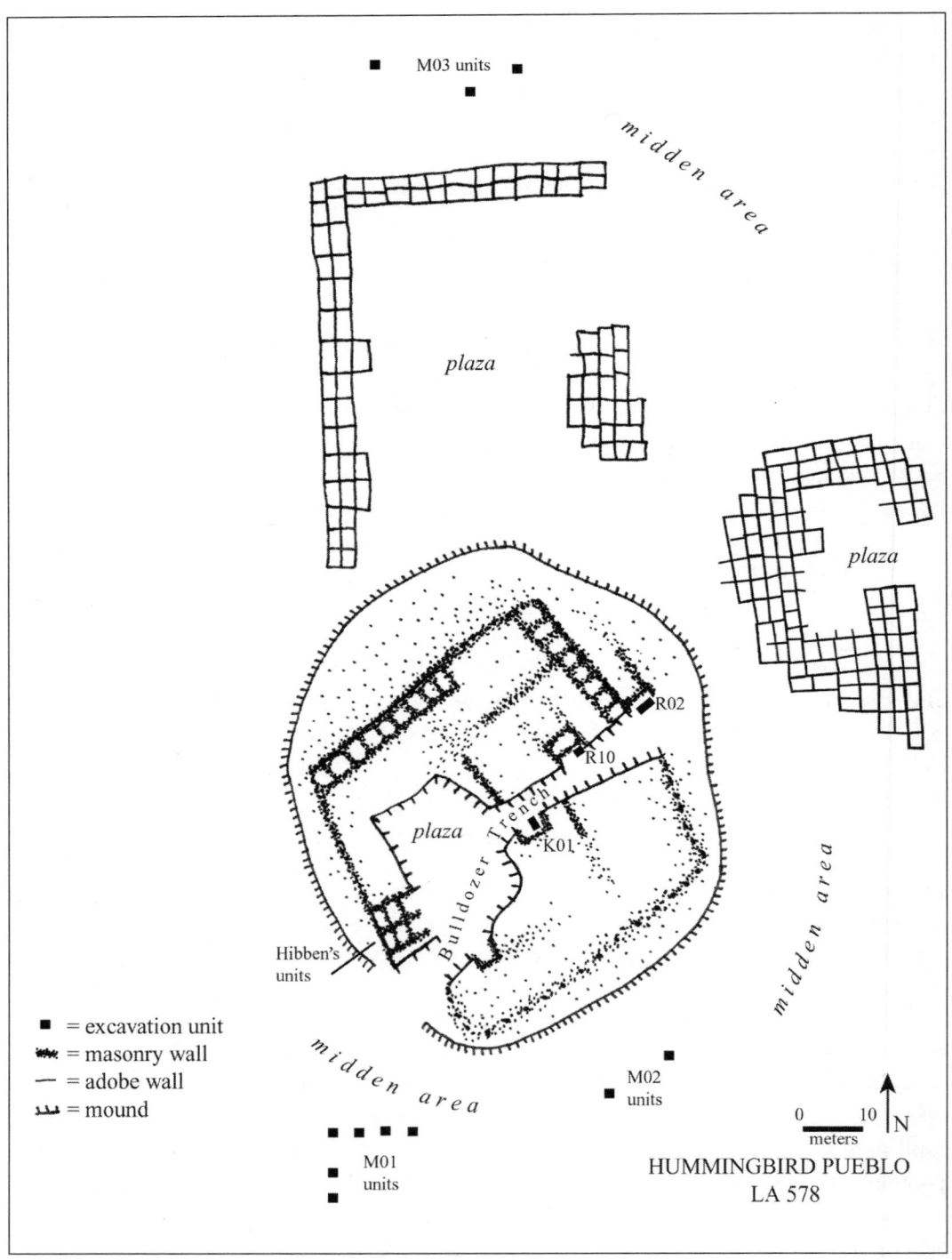

FIGURE 3.2. Hummingbird Pueblo. Map is author's interpretation of maps produced by Adler (2002, 2003) and author's 1998 field notes. NOTE: size of excavation units is exaggerated to show location.

During my 1998 midden excavations, a stone-robbed masonry roomblock associated with black-on-white pottery was discovered beneath one midden area (M01 in figure 3.2). The extent of this roomblock is uncertain, although it covers at least 50 sq m of area beneath the middens and may continue under the Pueblo IV portion of the site. Although no absolute dates are associated with this Pueblo III roomblock, the ceramic seriation discussed below suggests that it dates to the late 1200s.

Pottery Mound

Pottery Mound was constructed of adobe-walled rooms loosely surrounding four plazas (Hibben 1975). The majority of data from Pottery Mound used in this study come from Linda Cordell's 1989 excavations of 3.4 m of stratified trash. Artifacts and documentation of Cordell's 1989 excavations are available at the Maxwell Museum, University of New Mexico, Albuquerque. A collection of 150 petrographic thin sections from the Pottery Mound ceramic assemblage, part of the larger Elizabeth Garrett Thin Section Collection, is housed at the Laboratory of Anthropology in Santa Fe and was graciously made available for the analyses discussed in later chapters. Finally, complete and near-complete vessels from Pottery Mound, collected by Frank Hibben during the 1960s and 1970s, were used in this research. These vessels, along with maps and documentation from Hibben's work, are stored at the Maxwell Museum.

Although Hibben (1975) described the site as having been 3–4 stories high, later work found evidence of only a single story (Cordell, personal communication 2001). Based upon my recent examination of field maps housed at the Maxwell Museum, the site appears to have been constructed of multiple roomblocks (figure 3.3). There is also evidence of extensive remodeling. The main portion of Pottery Mound is notably mounded. Hibben (1975) believed this mound to be the first construction at the site with later roomblocks being built into and over most of it. While Hibben initially described this mound as a Mesoamerican-inspired pyramid (1966), he later notes its similarity to mounds at many sites in Arizona and to Casas Grandes in northern Mexico (1975).

I take no issue with the existence of the mound; however, I offer a different interpretation. After analysis of the four field maps and limited documentation available, I have come to believe that there may be an early component (albeit Pueblo IV) of roomblocks and kivas (figure 3.4). Some portions of this early component are evidenced by walls beneath the pueblo presented in Hibben's published maps (1966, 1975); other portions I gleaned from the remodeling of kivas (such as Kiva 8 into 9) and the trash-fill reported for some kivas and rooms. I argue that these early component roomblocks were eventually filled with trash; late component roomblocks were then built atop the resulting mound (figure 3.3).

Hibben reported the mound to be approximately 73 × 73 m and at least 4 m high. Although Hibben's maps report this mound as being almost perfectly square (as portrayed in figure 3.3), a later map of the site produced by Cordell has a mound with a much more ambiguous shape (figure 3.5). The high points on Cordell's map correspond to known roomblocks and backfill piles from previous excavations. However, Cordell's map was made years

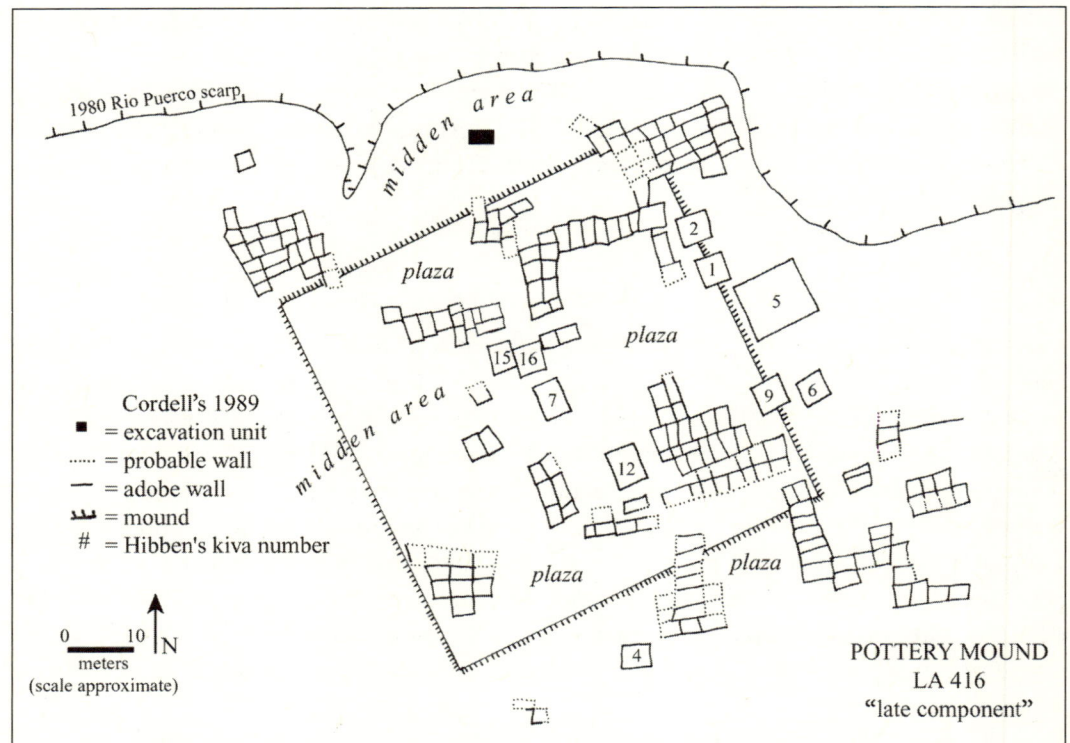

FIGURE 3.3. Pottery Mound late component. Map is author's interpretation of map produced by Hibben (1966, 1975) and field maps curated at the Maxwell Museum.
NOTE: scale is approximate and Kiva 9 is a remodeled version of Kiva 8 in figure 3.4.

after Hibben's excavations, which were not backfilled, so the site had been damaged by extensive erosion. I believe that the final result of remodeling and trash-fill at Pottery Mound was a mound—partially the remains of earlier roomblocks, and partially stratified trash—measuring, at its highest, 4 m. Although such trash accumulation has been observed at other sites, including over 3 m of stratified trash at Pueblo Blanco (Graves and Spielmann 2000), my interpretation of Pottery Mound's mound is speculative, and it may never have enough data to be confirmed.

One cannot discuss Pottery Mound without mentioning its 16 excavated kivas. Two large "moiety" kivas were identified at the site, one rectangular (Kiva 5) and the other round (Kiva 10), both with murals (Hibben 1966). If my interpretation of site construction is correct, these two kivas were not used contemporaneously. Instead, Kiva 10 was in use during the early component of the site, while Kiva 5 was in use during the late component. An additional 14 rectangular kivas, 12 of which had multiple layers of murals, were excavated (Hibben 1975). All kivas contain a ventilator, deflector, and fire pit complex, oriented either to the south or east. At least four kivas (Kiva 8, 9, 10, and 12) are noted as having had benches; a tunnel

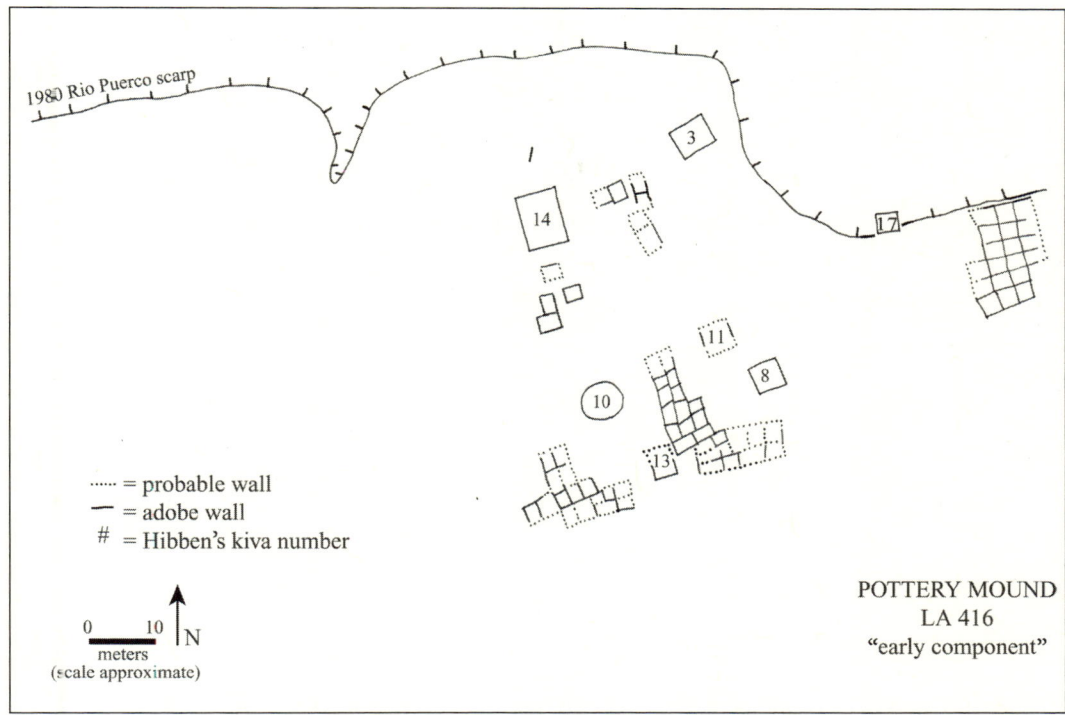

FIGURE 3.4. Pottery Mound early component. Map is author's interpretation of maps produced by Hibben (1966, 1975) and field maps curated at the Maxwell Museum.
NOTE: scale is approximate.

connected some kivas to one another (Kiva 1 and 2) or to other rooms. Kiva 9 is actually a remodeled version of Kiva 8; remodeling episodes in other kivas were also noted. At least two kivas (Kiva 11 and 14) had extensive burning, and many were trash filled. Finally, many of the floor slabs in the kivas were pierced with holes assumed to have served as loom anchors (Hibben 1975).

The most spectacular, and well-reported, aspects of Pottery Mound are the colorful, multilayered murals recovered from 14 of the kivas. Over 800 separate murals were recorded. Frank Hibben (1975) discusses the iconography of these murals in detail, while Patricia Vivian (1961), Helen Crotty (1995), and Polly Schaafsma (2000) all offer comparative analyses. Along with these published accounts, numerous unpublished manuscripts by various authors are available through the Maxwell Museum. To summarize the content of the murals here simply does not do them justice; they are painted in 20 different colors with great attention to detail. A wide range of subject matter is portrayed, including anthropomorphic figures, bears, mountain lions, dogs/coyotes, game animals, reptiles, dragonflies, horned serpents, snakes (Adams 1991:35), at least 12 identified species of birds (Emslie and Hargrave 1978), feathers, offerings, clouds, rainbows, rain, and lightning bolts. Anthropomorphic figures

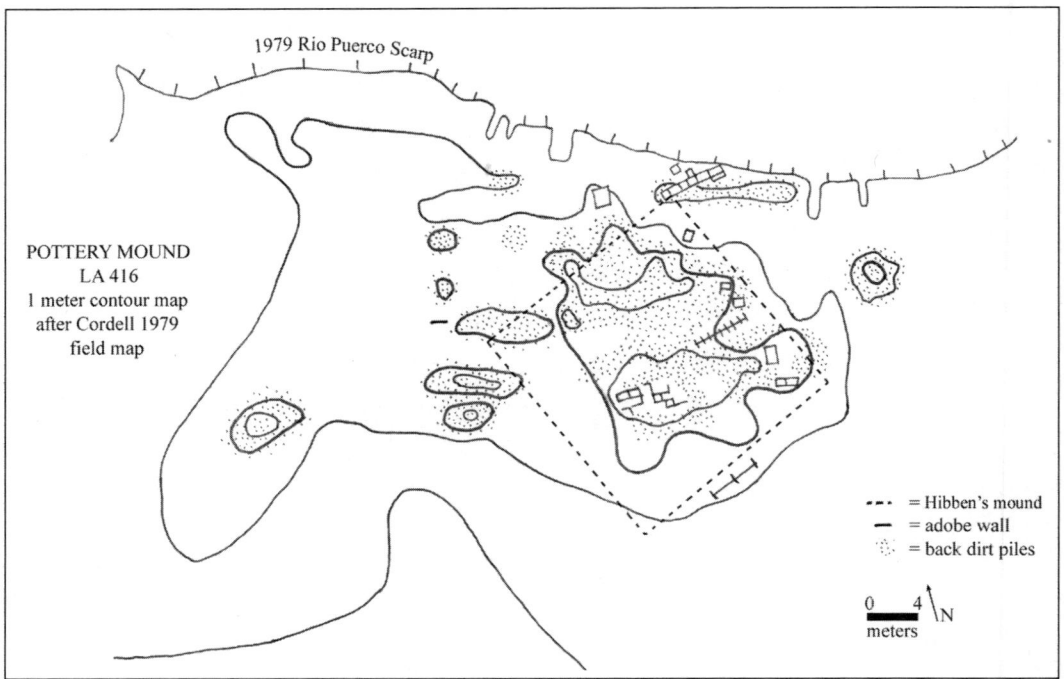

FIGURE 3.5. One-meter contour map of Pottery Mound based on field map from Cordell's 1979 field season (on file at the Maxwell Museum). Back-dirt piles are from Hibben's numerous previous seasons of excavation.

have been recorded wearing kilts, masks, headdresses, and necklaces; these figures have also been recorded carrying shields, weapons, wands, jars, and birds (Crotty 1995). Regardless of the splendid nature of these murals, they provide only anecdotal data for the present research as examination of any original photographs of the slides is currently not possible at the Maxwell Museum, and it is not clear how accurately murals are portrayed in Hibben's original work on the subject (1975).

Pottery Mound and Hummingbird Pueblo: A Timeline

A seriation of pottery types was used to create a timeline for Pottery Mound and Hummingbird Pueblo (pottery types are described in appendix A; statistics and ceramic counts for the seriation are described in appendix B). In archaeological research, seriation is most commonly the ordering of observations relative to time (Duff 1996). In the current seriation, the observations are counts of decorated and undecorated ceramic types from stratified trash deposits. Combining the seriation with mean ceramic dating and the available absolute dates, I created a timeline for excavation levels from Hummingbird Pueblo and Pottery Mound that consists of three consecutive phases ranging in time from approximately AD 1275 to

TABLE 3.1. Summary of chronological data for Hummingbird Pueblo and Pottery Mound based on ceramic seriation and associated absolute dates.

Phase	Mean Ceramic Date	Associated Absolute Dates
1 (AD 1275–1350)	AD 1286	none
2 (AD 1350–1400)	AD 1387	**Hummingbird Pueblo** 2 dendros, piñon, trash-fill, 1391r **Pottery Mound** dendro, piñon, trash-fill, 1381v
3 (AD 1400–1450+)	AD 1417	**Hummingbird Pueblo** 2 dendros, piñon, West Kiva, 1404r 2 dendros, piñon, trash-fill, 1418+r dendro, piñon, "North end," 1405r dendro, piñon, "North end," 1465+r **Pottery Mound** dendro, pine, Kiva 6, 1411v dendro, pine, Kiva 6, 1427v dendro, piñon, Kiva 10, 1418v

1450+ (table 3.1). Data from excavation levels were then combined using these three temporal phases, along with spatial considerations, as a guideline. These combined levels provide the basic divisions for analysis in the remainder of this research (table 3.2).

Phase 1, with a mean ceramic date of AD 1286 (see appendix B for calculations), is dominated by black-on-white ceramic types and represents the late thirteenth-century (late Pueblo III) and early fourteenth-century (early Pueblo IV) occupation at Hummingbird Pueblo. It also represents the introduction of Western Pueblo glaze ware into the Lower Rio Puerco area, as well as the transition to local glaze paint production. Since the earliest Western Pueblo glaze-painted pottery is dated at AD 1275 (Eckert 2006b), Phase 1 probably does not date any earlier than this. The earliest glaze-painted pottery in the Rio Grande region has been dated to AD 1313 (Cordell 1975); glaze-paint technology likely did not reach the Lower Rio Puerco area much earlier. As such, AD 1286 may more appropriately be considered a *beginning* date for Phase 1, rather than a *mean* date. The mean ceramic date as calculated for Phase 1 is biased toward an early date due to the substantial number of locally produced white wares recovered. Excavation levels assigned to Phase 1 are only represented at Hummingbird Pueblo, and at least some of these levels may be associated with the stone-robbed roomblock underneath M01 (which dates to Phase 2) described earlier in this chapter. However, the radiocarbon dates clustering around AD 1300 and recovered from the two adobe portions of Hummingbird Pueblo suggest that these roomblocks were established during Phase 1 as well.

Phase 2, with a mean ceramic date of AD 1387, is the best-represented phase in number of excavation levels from Hummingbird Pueblo. This phase also appears to mark the initial occupation of Pottery Mound. Phase 2 may be associated with the early component of Pottery

TABLE 3.2. Excavation levels (Site/Unit/Level/Locus) by phase.

Phase 1	Phase 2	Phase 3
LA578/M02/8–9/1	LA416/30.75N:3.78W/15/NW	LA416/30.75N:3.78W/1/NW
LA578/M02/10–11/1	LA416/30.75N:3.78W/16/NW	LA416/30.75N:3.78W/2/NW
LA578/M02/10/2	LA416/30.75N:3.78W/17/NW	LA416/30.75N:3.78W/3/NW
LA578/M03/1/2	LA578/K01/1/1	LA416/30.75N:3.78W/4/NW
LA578/M03/2/2	LA578/K01/2/1	LA416/30.75N:3.78W/5/NW
LA578/M03/1/3	LA578/K01/3–4/1	LA416/30.75N:3.78W/6/NW
LA578/R02/13/1	LA578/M01/1/1	LA416/30.75N:3.78W/7/NW
LA578/R02/14/2	LA578/M01/2/1	LA416/30.75N:3.78W/8/NW
LA578/R02/15/2	LA578/M01/1/2	LA416/30.75N:3.78W/9/NW
LA578/R02/16/2	LA578/M01/1/3	LA416/30.75N:3.78W/10/NW
LA578/R02/17/2	LA578/M01/3/3	LA416/30.75N:3.78W/11/NW
LA578/R02/18/2	LA578/M01/2/4	LA416/30.75N:3.78W/12/NW
LA578/R02/19–21/2	LA578/M02/1/1	LA416/30.75N:3.78W/13/NW
	LA578/M02/2/1	LA416/30.75N:3.78W/14/NW
	LA578/M02/3/1	LA578/M02/1/1–2
	LA578/M02/4/1	
	LA578/M02/5/1	
	LA578/M02/6–7/1	
	LA578/M02/3/2	
	LA578/M02/5/2	
	LA578/M02/6/2	
	LA578/M02/7/2	
	LA578/M02/8/2	
	LA578/R02/1/1	
	LA578/R02/2/1	
	LA578/R02/4/1	
	LA578/R02/5/1	
	LA578/R02/6–7/1	
	LA578/R02/8–9/1	
	LA578/R02/10/1	
	LA578/R02/11–12/1	
	LA578/R10/2–7/1	

Mound discussed above, as well as the 1381v tree-ring date recovered from trash-fill. Phase 3, with a mean ceramic date of AD 1417, is mostly represented by excavation levels from Pottery Mound and corresponds with the remaining tree-ring dates from that site (1411v, 1418v, 1427v). Hummingbird Pueblo is represented by only one excavation level from Phase 3, which may reflect the tail end of this site's occupation. As all of the stratified trash from the mound beneath the masonry roomblock at Hummingbird Pueblo dates to either Phase 1 or 2, this portion of the site was likely the last to be occupied.

Before moving on to a comparison of material culture between Hummingbird Pueblo and Pottery Mound, the issues of contemporaneity and sample size need to be addressed. First, there is no Phase 1 sample from Pottery Mound available to this research. As such, in the following analyses, I discuss this phase in the southern portion of the study area based upon observations noted by other researchers. Second, Phase 2 is not well represented in terms of excavation levels or sample size at Pottery Mound. Similarly, Phase 3 is not well represented at Hummingbird Pueblo (table 3.2). I do not know if this is due to sampling strategy or occupation differences between the two villages. Although there is probably some temporal overlap between Phases 2 and 3, there is no way to evaluate how much. In the following analyses, I address these issues of contemporaneity and sample size where appropriate and attempt to control for them where possible. With these concerns kept in mind, the chronology shown above allows for the comparison of material culture trends between Hummingbird Pueblo and Pottery Mound, as well as examination of changes in material culture through time within each village.

Discussion and Conclusion

The Lower Rio Puerco district was populated throughout the Pueblo period, although this population was never as dense as other Pueblo regions. During the Pueblo II (AD 900–1175/1200) period, much of the population shifted immediately north of the study area, moving back into the district during the Pueblo III (AD 1175/1200–1300) period. This movement into, and out of, the area reflects the somewhat arbitrary nature of archaeological districts as well as the focus of this research on the Pueblo III and Pueblo IV (AD 1300–1450/1500) periods. Ceramic wares throughout the Pueblo II and Pueblo III periods, however, suggest continuity in two pottery traditions and presumably population. Although there is continuity in pottery manufacture, two distinct traditions developed in the district, which can be identified based on surface treatment, temper choice, and paint type.

These two traditions seem to represent communities of practice as envisioned by Stark (2006). As discussed in chapters 1 and 2, communities of practice are social networks in which potters learn their craft from other potters in their community. As a result of the dynamic nature inherent in communities of practice, there are no perfect "rules" for pottery production and decoration during the Pueblo II (AD 900–1175/1200) and Pueblo III (AD 1175/1200–1300) periods in the Lower Rio Puerco area. White ware vessels *tend* to have either a combination of an unslipped surface, rock temper, and mineral paint or a slipped surface, crushed-sherd temper, and carbon paint. However, as this and other studies in the region (Durand and Hurst 1991; Luhrs 1937; Warren 1982a) have shown, there are many examples of vessels that crosscut these two tendencies. This "messiness" in the ceramic typology of the region reflects the fluidity of the habitus of pottery production, where changes in daily practice occur in response to changes in social and environmental demands.

The nucleation of populations into two villages during the Pueblo IV period (AD 1300–1450/1500), as well as the introduction of glaze ware technology, represents a departure from previous settlement and ceramic patterns. As will be argued in chapter 5, immigrants from the Western Pueblo region introduced glaze technology into the study area. These immigrants moved into an area with a local population who had a long history of residency and their own white ware traditions. The technological switch to glaze ware production within the study area represents one set of decisions made by potters to innovate and adopt strategies as they were faced with the new social demands brought on by aggregation and migration. Understanding the nature of these social demands, and the technological innovations that accompanied them, occupies the remainder of this research.

CHAPTER FOUR

Communities of Practice in the Lower Rio Puerco Area

This chapter shows that a new habitus of pottery production was present in fourteenth-century villages along the Lower Rio Puerco, which consisted of the use of an oxidizing firing atmosphere, application of a well-polished, thick red slip, and use of a glaze paint. After a discussion of the introduction of this new habitus, consideration is given to why it appears at this time; specifically, I consider whether or not local potters adopted new techniques as well as the possibility of immigrant potters making vessels in the region. Arguably, the presence of these new techniques can be divided into three separate communities of practice, two of which reflect transformations in the habitus of local potters, and one of which reflects the habitus of immigrant potters living within the region (chapter 5 argues that this later habitus may reflect more than one immigrant community of practice).

To explore changes in habitus, I recorded various technological traits on locally produced decorated wares from the Lower Rio Puerco area. Recently, archaeologists have recognized the importance of examining technological style, or a suite of technological traits, when attempting to define and understand social boundaries (Gosselain 1992; Hitchcock and Bartram 1998; Sackett 1990; Stark et al. 1995). In technological style, "experience and custom combine to establish a body of information and practice governing the manufacture of pottery vessels . . . resulting in a characteristic final product with a unique range of properties" (Rice 1987:201). In other words, habitus, as discussed in chapter 2, informs potters on the cultural and environmental choices available to them when creating a vessel. Habitus reflects culturally specific ways of doing things, cultural patterns and traditions that are generally unconscious forms of practice. This results in the tendency for potters to combine a suite of production techniques that ends in a technological style. Technological style is complex but more resistant to change than decorative style (Gosselain 1992; Rice 1984). This conservatism is one of technological style's greatest strengths for use in examination of social boundaries (Stark et al. 1995).

A New Constellation of Technological Traits

Prior to identifying a new habitus within the study area, I had to distinguish pottery produced within the study area from pottery produced outside the study area. Following standard procedures established by Anna Shepard (1942, 1965), A. Helene Warren (1981a, 1981b), Judith Habicht-Mauche (1993), Cynthia Herhahn (1995), and Patricia Capone (1995), I paired binocular and petrographic analyses to determine production source through mineralogical analysis of temper. Temper is the nonplastic material that occurs naturally in, or is intentionally added to, clay before forming a pot. For the binocular analysis, all ceramic sherds that were tabulated to ware and type were further divided into temper groups through identification of relative frequencies, average size, and range of sizes of nonplastic inclusions. To substantiate the differences seen between temper groups identified with the binocular microscope, as well as identify the mineralogical composition of each temper group, a subset of sherds was examined using petrographic analysis. This analysis provided more accurate and precise criteria for identifying transparent minerals (Peacock 1970; Rice 1987). On average, two sherds per site from each temper group within each major ceramic type were selected for petrographic analysis, resulting in 178 thin sections (100 from Hummingbird Pueblo, 78 from Pottery Mound). Results of the petrographic analysis were combined with the binocular analysis to more fully describe temper categories (see appendix C for detailed temper descriptions).

The majority (82 percent) of decorated pottery from trash mounds and trash-filled units at Pottery Mound and Hummingbird Pueblo was identified as locally produced within the Lower Rio Puerco area (table 4.1). As discussed in chapter 3, pottery from the study area was characterized by two tempering traditions throughout the Pueblo period. Pottery produced in the northern portion of the study area was tempered with sherd-tempered sherd mixed with a diverse suite of metamorphic and igneous rocks (figure 4.1). The low frequency of any single rock type suggests that these materials are either native to the clay, or a by-product of the production process, and were not intentionally added. Pottery produced in the southern portion of the study area was tempered with a mix of volcanic rocks (Eckert 2001; Voll 1961) (figure 4.2). The range of rocks found in the pottery from the southern portion of the study area matches the range of rocks collected by Elizabeth Garrett from Hidden Mountain (figure 4.3), near Pottery Mound. Pastes with both local temper types range in color from light to dark gray in white wares (Munsell N 5–8/0), and deep red (Munsell 2.5YR 5–6/6–8) to light buff-gray (Munsell 5YR 8/2–4) in glaze wares. All these pastes oxidized to deep red (Munsell 2.5YR 5–6/6–8) in refired sherds (brought to 900°C and held for one hour). Any sherds tempered differently than ones in these two categories were characterized as nonlocal. Nonlocal characterization was further justified if the paste color differed from that described for local wares or if the temper could be sourced to another pottery-producing region.

Once local production was determined, I was able to identify changes in local pottery decoration and technology through time. Decorated wares from the Lower Rio Puerco area

TABLE 4.1. Column percentages of locally produced decorated and utility wares by site and phase (84 percent of total ceramic assemblage).

	Hummingbird Pueblo			Pottery Mound	
	Phase 1	Phase 2	Phase 3	Phase 2	Phase 3
Decorated Wares					
Organic Paint Types					
Loma Fria B/w	62	3	2	1	0
Untyped B/w, organic paint	18	1	0	0	0
Mineral Paint Types					
Socorro B/w	3	0	0	0	0
Untyped B/w, mineral paint	6	0	0	1	0
St. Johns types	4	6	0	0	0
Hummingbird R/b	0	7	0	1	0
Glaze Paint Types					
Heshotauthla, local copy	1	2	0	0	0
Kwakina, local copy	0	1	0	1	0
Pinnawa, local copy	0	<1	0	0	0
Kechipawan, local copy	0	<1	0	0	0
Early Rio Grande Gl/r	5	70	78	67	56
Early Rio Grande Gl/y	0	2	5	7	8
Early Rio Grande Gl/poly	1	6	14	22	29
Intermediate Rio Grande Gl	0	0	0	0	2
Pottery Mound Poly	0	0	0	1	2
Hidden Mountain Poly	0	0	0	1	2
Total decorated wares count	336	1,195	55	177	4,772
Utility Wares					
Plain gray ware	15	46	67	54	60
Indented corrugated ware	69	10	3	0	0
Smeared corrugated ware	15	37	23	33	34
Corrugated smudged ware	1	7	8	13	6
Total utility wares count	831	1,060	39	245	3,417

FIGURE 4.1.
Sherd, igneous rock, and quartz-mica schist temper characteristic of pottery produced in the northern portion of the study area. Both photos x170 magnification: (a) plain light, (b) polarized light.

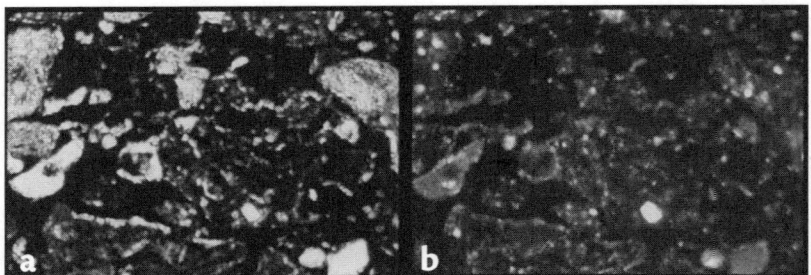

FIGURE 4.2.
Three examples of Hidden Mountain igneous rock temper characteristic of pottery produced in the southern portion of the study area. All photos x170 magnification: (1–3a) plain light, (1–3b) polarized light.

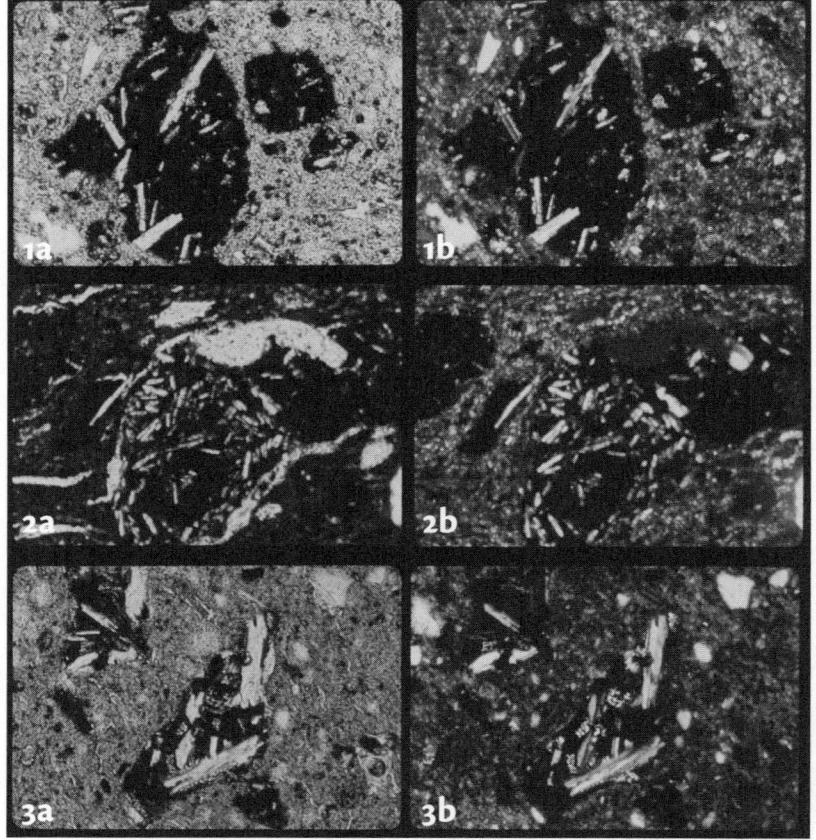

FIGURE 4.3.
Scoria rock sample from Hidden Mountain. Both photos x170 magnification: (a) plain light, (b) polarized light.

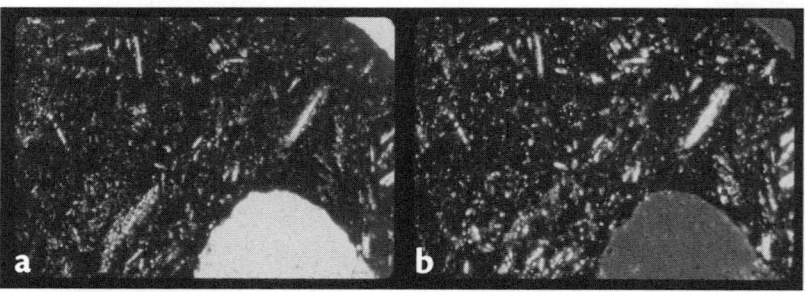

Chapter Four

were typed based upon a range of attributes depending on ware (see appendix A for detailed type descriptions). I considered numerous ceramic attributes when classifying locally produced sherds to type including slip color, surface treatment, glaze texture, glaze color, temper, and design style. Identification of local copies of Western Pueblo glaze ware was employed the most conservatively. Specifically, sherds were identified as being Western Pueblo glaze ware copies only if they were indistinguishable (except for paste color and temper inclusions) from types found on fourteenth- and fifteenth-century sites in the Western Pueblo region. If a local glaze-decorated sherd did not fit these criteria, it was identified as a local variant Rio Grande Glaze Ware. At the time of the original analysis, this did not seem problematic as the Rio Grande Glaze Ware typology recognizes a great deal more variation than the Western Pueblo glaze ware typology. As such, Rio Grande Glaze Ware became a default category and was not meant to imply an association between the Lower Rio Puerco glaze tradition and any particular area in the Rio Grande region. In other words, sherds typed as locally produced Rio Grande Glaze Ware are *not* copies of Rio Grande Glaze Ware.

Even to the untrained eye, changes in pottery production in the Lower Rio Puerco area are obvious, switching from predominately white-slipped wares to red-slipped wares. An examination of percentages of locally produced, decorated ceramic types shows that the majority of sherds in the Phase 1 assemblage from Hummingbird Pueblo (table 4.1) is Loma Fria B/w, a carbon-painted ceramic type. Pottery assemblages from late thirteenth-century sites in the vicinity of Pottery Mound are described as having been mostly Socorro B/w, a mineral-painted type (Warren 1982a). A dramatic shift in new ceramic types (table 4.1) characterizes the Phase 2 decorated ceramic assemblage. At both Hummingbird Pueblo and Pottery Mound, assemblages are dominated (81 percent and 97 percent, respectively) by glaze-painted pottery, which is predominately red slipped. Glaze wares continue to dominate Phase 3 assemblages (97 percent and 99 percent, respectively). The appearance of glaze-painted, red-slipped pottery represents a dramatic change in ceramic production technology without precedent in the study area.

Examination of two specific ceramic attributes (table 4.2) helps to clarify the dramatic technological changes seen to occur over time in the study area. These attributes include firing technology and paint composition. The organic-painted, white-slipped pottery that dominated the Phase 1 assemblage required firing in a reducing atmosphere (Rice 1987). Refiring experiments of a subsample of mineral-painted, white-slipped sherds showed that these types were also fired in a reducing atmosphere. The red-slipped and bichrome-slipped pottery with glaze paint, which comprised the majority of Phase 2 and Phase 3 pottery assemblages, required firing in an oxidizing atmosphere (Rice 1987).

The most striking technological change in fourteenth-century pottery is the switch in paint composition from an organic or mineral paint to a glaze paint (Eckert 2006a; Graves and Eckert 1998; Reed 1949; Shepard 1942). To vitrify, glaze paint requires a firing temperature higher than is normally associated with carbon- or mineral-painted types (Habicht-Mauche 2006:5–6; Rice 1987). Further, there is no continuum in the technology between producing an organic paint and glaze paint (Rice 1987; Vandiver 1990); no matter how hot one fires an organic paint, it will never become a glaze. Glaze paint requires the right combination

TABLE 4.2. Column percentages of attributes that reflect different aspects of technological style on locally produced wares for each site by phase.

Attribute	Hummingbird Pueblo			Pottery Mound	
	Phase 1	Phase 2	Phase 3	Phase 2	Phase 3
Slip Color on Decorated Wares					
white	89	5	2	1	0
red	10	78	78	67	58
bichrome	1	8	14	24	32
yellow/buff	0	9	5	8	9
Paint Type on Decorated Wares					
organic	80	4	2	1	0
mineral	43	14	0	1	1
glaze	7	82	98	98	99
Painted Surface Treatment on Decorated Wares					
self-slip	35	16	25	1	3
thin, washy slip	53	50	56	69	44
thick slip	12	34	18	30	53
Temper Type on Decorated Wares					
mixed igneous rock	11	18	34	82	79
sherd with mixed rock	88	82	66	17	19
untempered	0	0	0	1	2
Temper Type on Utility Wares					
sherd with mixed rock	94	92	90	53	39
mixed igneous rock	6	8	10	47	60

of minerals (silica, alumina, and a flux such as lead or copper) and firing techniques to be produced (Rice 1987:99; Shepard 1956:44–46). Combined, then, slip color and paint type provide evidence of a new suite of technological traits, reflecting a new habitus, being used in the study area starting in the fourteenth century. The social dynamics behind this new habitus require further consideration.

Why the Change of Habitus?

Glaze technology could have been introduced into the Lower Rio Puerco area in one of three ways: local development, diffusion, or immigration. In the Western Pueblo region, where glaze technology was a local development, the transition to glaze paint was a process that included the development of a red-slipped, mineral-painted pottery tradition in the 1100s (Carlson 1970); experimentation with different glaze and subglaze recipes in the 1200s (Huntley 2006); and a continuation of decorative styles throughout the transition from mineral to subglaze to glaze-painted pottery (Carlson 1970; Eckert 2006b; Woodbury and Woodbury 1966). In contrast, glaze production in the Lower Rio Puerco area shows no evidence of such transitions or learning periods, but was introduced into the region as a fully developed technology through either diffusion or immigration.

Distinguishing between diffusion of glaze technology and introduction by immigrants is a bit trickier. Herhahn (2006) has convincingly argued that glaze technology in the Rio Grande region spread mostly through diffusion, although limited migration also occurred. As cultural contact (and transmission) is likely before a migration event (Brown and Sanders 1981), diffusion is a necessary component in arguments supporting migration (Herhahn 2006). This relationship between diffusion and migration makes distinguishing between the two processes especially difficult. One distinction is the degree to which technological knowledge is successfully transmitted to the new area (Herhahn 2006). Lower degrees of similarity would result from diffusion; the knowledge to make glaze paint would have been borrowed, more or less successfully, but the local habitus associated with the production of pottery would already be known. Higher degrees of similarity would result from immigration; the knowledge to make glaze paint would be associated with the immigrants' habitus of pottery production.

Herhahn (2006) examined chemical composition of glaze paint from the Western Pueblo and Rio Grande regions and found a low degree of similarity in glaze recipes between the two areas. She argues that glaze technology transfer occurred mostly through "intergroup interaction and transmission rather than actual migration" (2006:193). Unfortunately, chemical compositional analyses of glaze paint have yet to be performed on any pottery from the Lower Rio Puerco area, making an analysis like Herhahn's currently impossible.

I have argued elsewhere (Eckert 2006a) that glaze technology was introduced into the Rio Grande region through various mechanisms (including diffusion and migration) and that examination on a case-by-case basis is required to understand the situation in any given village. Similar to Herhahn (2006), I argue that a high degree of technological and decorative similarity between local products and those from a donor area provides evidence of immigrants within a village. For example, a substantial proportion of the glaze wares (20 percent) at Tijeras Pueblo in the Albuquerque area is comprised of local copies of Western Pueblo glaze ware (as defined in this study). These copies reflect the presence of immigrants who brought their production techniques (including glaze technology) and decorative traditions with them (Eckert 2006a) from the Western Pueblo region. Furthermore, it was the presence of immigrants that instigated a change in habitus in the Lower Rio Puerco area.

Detecting Immigrants through a Change of Habitus

The thirteenth and fourteenth centuries in the Pueblo Southwest were a time of widespread population movement and settlement reorganization, and the Lower Rio Puerco area was no exception. While many areas in the Southwest were abandoned in the late 1200s (Duff 1998; Lipe 1995), the Lower Rio Puerco continued to be occupied into (at least) the 1400s. These occupants aggregated into two large villages and probably felt the social pressure of newly arrived immigrants moving into the Rio Grande area from both the Western Pueblo and Mesa Verde regions. Although the scenario for immigrants moving into the Lower Rio Puerco area during this period of demographic reorganization makes a certain amount of intuitive sense, evidence for the presence of migrants in the Pueblo Southwest is notoriously difficult to come by (Cordell 1995; Duff 1998). However, there is archaeological evidence for group migrations over much of the Colorado Plateau and into the Rio Grande area (Beal 1987; Cameron 1995; Duff 1998, 2000; Haury 1958; Lindsay 1987; Plog 1979). Much of this evidence implicitly relies on detection of a new habitus as evidence of migration.

Probably the most famous case for migration in the prehispanic Southwest is the site unit intrusion at Point of Pines excavated by Emil Haury (1958). Haury's evidence for migration included various artifact classes that displayed traits "new" to the Point of Pines area, but in many cases similar to the Kayenta area. New traits were evidenced in architectural features, ceramic compositional and design attributes, and more perishable artifacts such as corn and wooden ceremonial objects. Although Haury never used the term, what he was seeing was the habitus that immigrants brought with them into the area—specific ways to build their homes, paint their pottery, and grow their food. Although few doubt Haury's conclusions about Point of Pines, other convincing site unit intrusions have rarely been identified (although see Morris [1938] at Mummy Cave and Bice and Sundt [1972] at Prieta Vista).

The reason for the paucity of site unit intrusions in the Southwest is due to how migration is practiced. Duff (1998) argues that the typical social unit of migration throughout the Pueblo world was most likely relatively small, kin-based groups. Village groups probably separated during migration, moving at separate times along separate paths to potentially separate destinations (Bernardini 2002; Cordell 1995). Most immigrant groups probably joined already established villages or joined with local groups to establish a village. If immigrants were moving in small groups and joining villages occupied by local groups, then there is little reason to expect site unit intrusions.

María Zedeño (1995) examined both technological and decorative ceramic attributes to argue that increased variability during the late thirteenth century in the Grasshopper region of east-central Arizona was the result of changes in the social makeup of local potters. Specifically, she argues that the migration of people into the region dramatically altered patterns of manufacture and circulation. Immigrants into the region brought with them technological knowledge that was new to the region, including use of carbon paint and oxidizing atmosphere. Further, they brought with them their own ideas about how a pot "should" be made (their habitus as viewed here), including the use of sherd temper and specific design styles. Although design style can be copied, Zedeño argues that technological characteristics, such as firing atmosphere and paint recipe, are not as readily copied. As such, the sudden presence of these new characteristics within the region suggests the presence of new potters. The presence of such diverse manufacturing techniques at a single village, Grasshopper Pueblo, is compelling evidence for a multiethnic makeup of the village. Zedeño (1995) argues that her study supports previous research looking at other lines of evidence that have argued for the multiethnic makeup of this village that included immigrants (Crown-Robertson 1978; Ezzo 1991; Reid and Whittlesey 1982; Whittlesey 1978).

Similarly, Stark and her colleagues (1995) examined archaeological evidence for immigration into the Tonto Basin area of Arizona during the thirteenth century. They recognize two masonry types within the area and found that these types correlate with other architectural measures, including residential layout, the ratio of roofed-to-unroofed space, and circulation patterns (1995:225). Although they do not use the term, the correlation of these architectural variables reflects two different habitus for how to build a house. After examining the spatial relations between these architectural styles, Stark and colleagues conclude that immigrants were living among indigenous groups in the Tonto Basin and, in some instances, within village compounds. They argue that differentiation in ethnobotanical remains (specifically mustard and corn pollen) and distribution of locally produced utilitarian pottery support the premise of coresidency in the Tonto Basin.

Three Habitus for Pottery Production in the Lower Rio Puerco Region

Although none of the above migration studies explicitly discuss practice and habitus, this is at the core of what each study is examining. When immigrants moved into a region, they brought with them new social conventions and daily practices. They were forced to change aspects of these practices to accommodate the social conventions of indigenous groups, as well as learn to work with new material to create material culture. Similarly, as indigenous groups were confronted with immigrants, they, too, made changes in their practices. As a result, in a social environment where indigenous and immigrant groups interacted, at least two habitus could be identified. And, although these habitus could be associated with separate groups, changes in both as a result of interaction could also be detected. As the above studies show, what these changes were varied from group to group and situation to situation. However, as outlined by Emil Haury (1958) nearly 50 years ago, when immigrants move into a region there should be a new suite of traits that has no precedent in an area. As outlined by this study, such a new suite of traits reflects the immigrants' habitus for how to "do things."

Similar to Zedeño's (1995) argument for the presence of immigrants in the Grasshopper region, the presence of a new firing atmosphere and paint recipe in the Lower Rio Puerco area lends support to the argument for immigrants in the study area. However, although firing technology and paint recipes are more difficult to copy than design styles, they are not impossible to copy. Although I argue that local potters were learning this new technology from immigrant potters in the study area, local potters also could have traveled elsewhere to learn how to produce glaze wares. To strengthen my argument for the presence of immigrants in the study, I looked more closely at the changes in local communities of practice.

My argument for the transmission of glaze technology into the Lower Rio Puerco area through immigration, rather than diffusion, is strengthened by the association of glaze paint with three separate surface treatments on decorated pottery during Phase 2. Specifically, there is an increase in well-polished slips between Phases 1 and 2 (table 4.2). As discussed in chapter 3, throughout the 1100s and 1200s, potters in the Lower Rio Puerco district could be divided into two communities of practice associated with the northern and southern portions of the study area. Both communities of practice were making white-slipped decorated wares; however, potters in the northern portion of the study area were making pottery with thin, washy slips and sherd temper, while potters in the southern portion of the study area were making pottery with well-polished self-slips and rock temper. These communities of practice are consistent with the two technological styles that dominated the Phase 1 pottery assemblage (table 4.2). During Phase 1, only 12 percent of decorated pottery has a well-polished, thick slip; the remainder of the pottery has either a well-polished self-slip or a thin, washy slip.

With the introduction of glaze paint into the region in the late 1200s or early 1300s, a third community of practice becomes apparent. During Phase 2, 34 percent of decorated pottery at Hummingbird Pueblo, and 30 percent at Pottery Mound, has a well-polished, thick slip. When using the clays selected by Lower Rio Puerco potters, there is no aesthetic reason for the application of a thick slip rather than a self-slip. Either will fire white in a reducing atmosphere, and either will fire red in an oxidizing atmosphere. If both are well polished, the final appearance is almost identical. Application of a slip in this situation is part of the habitus as to how to manufacture a vessel and not a requirement for the vessel's final appearance or function. The application of a well-polished, thick slip dates back to the 1100s in portions of the Western Pueblo and Rio Grande regions, while potters in the Lower Rio Puerco area applied a diverse range of surface treatments throughout their history. The more than twofold increase in the application of this surface treatment—combined with the introduction of a new firing atmosphere, slip color, and paint type—during Phase 2 suggests an influx of new potters into the region.

Although aggregation and immigration clearly transformed indigenous pottery production, local potters were selective in choosing new manufacturing traits. While an oxidizing atmosphere was universally adopted, temper selection continued to vary (sherd or rock). While glaze paint became the dominant choice, surface treatment continued to be diverse (thin, washy slip; well-polished self-slip; or well-polished, thick slip). The end result is that the same two indigenous communities of practice, although transformed, can still be identified in the study area throughout the late 1300s and early 1400s along with a third community of practice associated with immigrants.

To summarize, during the early fourteenth century, a new suite of pottery production techniques appear and come to dominate decorated pottery production in the Lower Rio Puerco. These techniques include the use of an oxidizing firing atmosphere, an increase in the application of a well-polished, thick slip, application of a red slip, and glaze paint. I argue that immigrants who brought their habitus for pottery production with them as they moved into the region introduced this suite of technological attributes into the study area. Although these immigrant potters taught local potters how to produce glaze-painted pottery, local potters were selective about what techniques they adopted. Specifically, local potters adopted an oxidizing atmosphere, glaze paint, and a red slip. However, they chose to continue to practice their finishing techniques and tempering traditions, rather than adopt those of the immigrants.

Haury (1958) argued that the case for immigration could be strengthened if the immigrants' homeland could be determined. In this chapter, I have identified a community of practice that I argue is associated with the presence of immigrants. In the next chapter, I explore evidence concerning the possible origins of these immigrants.

CHAPTER FIVE

Identifying Potential Homelands for Immigrants Living in the Lower Rio Puerco Area during the Fourteenth Century

The last chapter demonstrated that fourteenth-century potters living along the Lower Rio Puerco can be divided into at least three separate communities of practice, two of which reflect transformations in the habitus of local potters, and one of which reflects the habitus of immigrant potters living within the region. Changes in the habitus of each community of practice were the result of immigrants learning to work with new materials and indigenous potters learning to make glaze decoration. Where these immigrants originated requires further consideration. If the homeland(s) of immigrants can be determined, then not only is the argument for immigration into the study area strengthened, but we may gain a deeper understanding of the practice of migration in the prehispanic Pueblo Southwest.

Identification of a homeland can be achieved through an understanding of the process of migration. First, migrants do not move to a new location about which they know nothing (Brown and Sanders 1981); second, once people move into a new region, they often maintain contact with people or places from their homeland; and third, immigrants bring their habitus for how to "do things" with them, a habitus that may be traceable back to their homeland (Beal 1987; Haury 1958). The evidence reflecting these aspects of the migration process suggests that immigrants from the Zuni district of the Western Pueblo region moved into the Lower Rio Puerco area. The evidence for immigration to the study area from the Hopi district of the Western Pueblo region, from the central Rio Grande region, and from the Casas Grandes region will also be considered.

Interregional Contact Prior to Migration into the Lower Rio Puerco Area

Rather than moving to an unknown place with uncertain resources and potentially bad social situations, migrants usually collect information about likely destinations from kin relations and personal contacts (Brown and Sanders 1981; Cadwallader 1992; Duff 1998) in the form of long-distance trade partners, immigrants *to* the potential migrant's community, and recent emigrants *from* the potential migrant's community. As a result of such information gathering, material culture reflecting links between immigrants' homeland and new residence *prior to migration* may be used to identify potential origins (Duff 1998). The best available evidence for such premigration contact in the study area comes from nonlocal ceramic vessels recovered in Phase 1 excavation levels at Hummingbird Pueblo (table 5.1). Production source was determined using the same binocular and petrographic approaches described in the previous chapter.

Through binocular temper analysis of nonlocal pottery sherds, I identify four archaeological districts as potential donor areas for immigrants based on contact prior to migration: the northern and central districts of the Rio Grande region, the Acoma/Zuni district of the Western Pueblo region, and the Mogollon region (see figure 1.1). The majority (53 percent) of nonlocal pottery in Phase 1 excavation levels at Hummingbird Pueblo was produced in the Rio Grande region (see appendix C for detailed description of temper types). Most of this Rio Grande pottery was made with micaceous clay that has residual fragments of quartz-mica schist and gneiss in it (figure 5.1). The vessels made from this clay are utilitarian and are identified as having been produced in the Sandia-Manzano ranges east of Albuquerque in the central Rio Grande district (Warren 1980, 1981c).

Although the presence of micaceous pottery has important implications for participation in Rio Grande exchange networks (Cordell 1998; Habicht-Mauche 1993; Hayes et al. 1981; Warren 1981c), for the immediate analysis, it simply provides evidence for contact with residents of the central Rio Grande area. The remainder of the nonlocal pottery from the Rio Grande region is tempered with tuff, pumice, or ash (figure 5.2). Petrographic analysis on a subset of this temper group showed that texture and composition vary, suggesting that there was not a single production source. This temper group is typical of pottery produced in various portions of the northern Rio Grande district, including the Pajarito Plateau, Santa Fe area, and Española Valley (Habicht-Mauche 1993); pumice temper has also been identified in a low frequency of Chupadero B/w sherds recovered in the Rio Abajo area (Eckert 2007).

In the Phase 1 ceramic assemblage, I identify 17 percent of nonlocal pottery as having been made in the Acoma/Zuni district of the Western Pueblo region. This identification is based upon the hard light-gray to white paste, thick, well-polished orange-red or bright white slip, and sherd temper with few other nonplastic inclusions (Carlson 1970; Colton 1956; Hays-Gilpin and van Hartesveldt 1998; Woodbury and Woodbury 1966). Another 12 percent of nonlocal vessels have a brown sandy paste, are highly burnished on the interior, and are tempered with sand, sherd, or a combination of these materials; as such, I identify these vessels as being produced in the Mogollon region (Hays-Gilpin and van Hartesveldt 1998; Rinaldo and Bluhm 1956).

TABLE 5.1. Column percentages of nonlocally produced decorated and utility wares by site and phase (16 percent of total ceramic assemblage).

Ceramic Type	Temper	Hummingbird Pueblo			Pottery Mound	
		Phase 1	Phase 2	Phase 3	Phase 2	Phase 3
Source = Various Districts in Western Pueblo Region						
Cibola White Ware	sherd	4	1	0	9	7
St. Johns types	sherd	4	0	0	0	0
Utility wares	sherd	17	14	0	73	4
Source = Mogollon District in Western Pueblo Region						
Mogollon Brown Ware	sherd, sand, or combo	12	3	0	0	5
Source = Hopi District in Western Pueblo Region						
Hopi Yellow Ware	untempered	0	0	0	0	12
Source = Acoma/Zuni District in Western Pueblo Region						
Western Pueblo glaze ware	sherd	9	22	33	0	17
Matsaki Polychrome	sherd	0	0	0	0	<1
Source = Northern Rio Grande District in Rio Grande Region						
Santa Fe B/w	sherd and ash/tuff/pumice	2	0	0	0	0
Untyped B/w, mineral paint	ash/tuff/pumice	2	0	0	0	0
Wiyo B/w	ash/tuff/pumice	2	0	0	0	0
Jemez B/w	ash/tuff/pumice	0	<1	0	0	0
Biscuit Ware	ash/tuff/pumice	0	0	0	0	3
Early Rio Grande Glaze	ash/tuff/pumice	0	3	8	0	9
Utility ware	ash/tuff/pumice	1	0	0	0	1
Source = Galisteo Basin in Rio Grande Region						
Galisteo B/w	intermediate igneous	0	<1	0	0	0
Early Rio Grande Glaze	intermediate igneous	0	1	17	0	9
Intermediate Rio Grande Glaze	intermediate igneous	0	0	25	0	3
Source = Central Rio Grande District in Rio Grande Region						
Early Rio Grande Glaze	micaceous clay	0	2	8	0	1
Utility ware	micaceous clay	46	52	8	18	34
Total sherd count		351	796	12	11	545

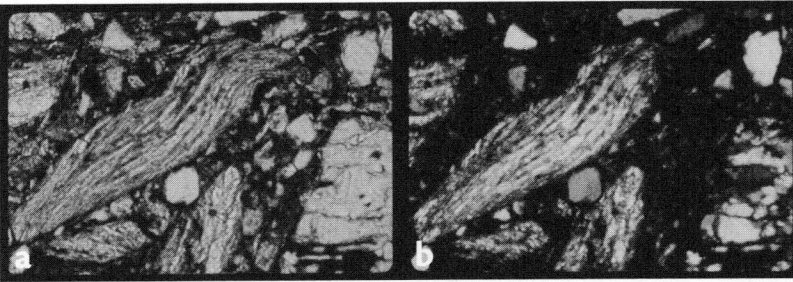

FIGURE 5.1.
Micaceous clay temper characteristic of utility pottery produced in the central Rio Grande district. Both photos x170 magnification: (a) plain light, (b) polarized light.

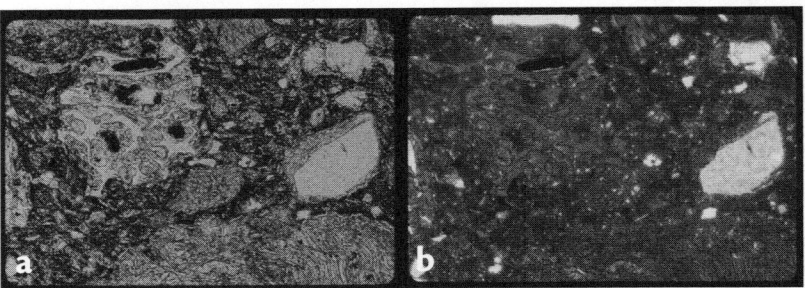

FIGURE 5.2.
Weathered pumice temper, one of numerous igneous tempers characteristic of pottery produced in the northern Rio Grande district. Both photos x170 magnification: (a) plain light, (b) polarized light.

This analysis shows that nonlocal pottery found in Phase 1 excavation levels was produced in the northern and central districts of the Rio Grande region, the Acoma/Zuni district of the Western Pueblo region, and the Mogollon region. By inference, immigrants could have come from any or all of these areas. Evidence of interaction with another region does not necessarily mean immigration from that region; it is simply evidence for potential homeland areas. This is discussed further below.

Interregional Contact after Migration into the Lower Rio Puerco Area

Once people move into a new region, they often maintain contact with people or places from their homeland. For example, descendants of historic Pecos immigrants to Jemez continue to visit the shrines of their homeland (Sando 1982), while descendants of Arizona-Tewa immigrants continue to have close contact with Rio Grande Tewa groups (Stanislawski 1979). The previous chapter showed that immigrants moved into the Lower Rio Puerco area during the late 1200s or early 1300s. Evidence for contact with the homeland, then, could be expected during the mid-1300s and into the 1400s. With these dates in mind, the best available evidence for continued contact with the homeland comes from the nonlocal pottery assemblages from Phases 2 and 3 (table 5.1).

The majority of nonlocal pottery in the Phase 2 (59 percent) and Phase 3 (67 percent) assemblages from Hummingbird Pueblo was produced in the Rio Grande region. During both phases, most (54 percent and 16 percent, respectively) of this Rio Grande pottery was made in the central Rio Grande district; however, some (4 percent and 8 percent, respectively) pottery made in the northern Rio Grande district was also recovered. Nonlocal vessels from the Acoma/Zuni district were also present in Hummingbird Pueblo excavation levels dating to Phases 2 (37 percent) and 3 (33 percent). In the Phase 2 assemblage, I identify only 3 percent of nonlocal pottery as having come from the Mogollon region, while I identify no pottery from this region in the Phase 3 assemblage.

Analysis of nonlocal pottery (table 5.1) during Phase 2 at Pottery Mound is suspect due to the sample size issues raised in chapter 3. With this in mind, no nonlocal pottery was identified from the northern Rio Grande or Mogollon districts during Phase 2. However, 18 percent of nonlocal pottery came from the central Rio Grande district and 82 percent from somewhere in the Western Pueblo region (ceramic types recovered were not district specific). During Phase 3, 13 percent of nonlocal pottery was produced in the northern Rio Grande district, while 35 percent was from the central Rio Grande. Further, 18 percent of nonlocal pottery was made in the Acoma/Zuni district of the Western Pueblo region, 12 percent can be traced directly to the Hopi mesas, and 5 percent was produced in the Mogollon region.

Although no pottery that can be traced to production at Casas Grandes has been found at either Hummingbird Pueblo or Pottery Mound, other lines of evidence suggest that residents of Pottery Mound participated in the Casas Grandes interaction sphere during Phases 2 and 3 (Schaafsma and Riley 1999). Bradley (1999, 2000) argues that Pottery Mound was one of numerous Pueblo villages to participate in a marine shell exchange system that included Casas Grandes as an "active supplier and participant" (1999:224). Considering Paul Minnis and colleagues' (1993) argument that Casas Grandes had tight control over the breeding and distribution of macaws, the presence of a macaw burial at Pottery Mound (Hibben 1975) is further evidence that residents of this village interacted with residents of Casas Grandes. Finally, participation in the Casas Grandes interaction sphere is suggested by the presence of a copper bell recovered during Cordell's 1989 excavations (Unit Summary for Site LA 416, Unit 30.75N/3.78W, NW quadrant, on file, Maxwell Museum, University of New Mexico).

In sum, this analysis shows that portions of the nonlocal pottery found in the Lower Rio Puerco area during Phases 2 and 3 were produced in all three regions—Western Pueblo, Rio Grande, and Mogollon—identified as potential homelands in the previous section. This strengthens the argument that immigrants could have come from at least one of these areas. Further, anecdotal data provide the possibility that some immigrants could have moved into Pottery Mound from as far south as the Casas Grandes region, possibly at a later date than immigrants from more immediate environs. To identify a more specific homeland requires comparison of the immigrants' habitus with the habitus of residents from these regions.

Shared Habitus

When immigrants move, they bring their habitus for how to "do things" with them, a habitus that may be traceable back to their homeland (Beal 1987; Haury 1958). Haury (1958) argued that his evidence for immigration into the Point of Pines site could be strengthened if he could locate the immigrants' homeland. He then identified various artifact classes that displayed traits new to the Point of Pines area, but in many cases similar to contemporaneous material culture in the Kayenta area. Due to this similarity, he argued that the Kayenta area was the most likely homeland for the Point of Pines immigrants. Specifically, then, the argument for migration is strengthened if a new suite of traits in the study area can be identified as the "normal" pattern in another, roughly contemporaneous, region (Haury 1958).

The last chapter argued that a specific suite of technological attributes—oxidizing atmosphere, well-polished, thick red slip, and glaze paint—was new to the Lower Rio Puerco region and was associated with a group of immigrants who had brought a new habitus for pottery production with them. The origins for this new habitus will now be examined as a likely reflection of immigrants from the Zuni district of the Western Pueblo region.

Residents in the Lower Rio Puerco area had contact with residents of the Rio Grande region, the Western Pueblo region, the Mogollon region, and the Casas Grandes region prior to, or after, immigration into the area. Potters in all of these regions made glaze-painted pottery at some point in their history. Thus, examining when glaze ware began to be produced in these areas helps point to where immigrants with this habitus originated.

Although glaze-painted pottery occurred in the Casas Grandes region during the Medio period (AD 1200–1450) (Dean and Ravesloot 1993), the nature of how glaze paint developed or was introduced into the Chihuahua area, as well as the timing of such an event, is still unknown. However, the fact that glaze-painted pottery in the Casas Grandes region is not a red-slipped ware, while glaze wares from the Western Pueblo, Rio Grande, and Mogollon regions are slipped red, suggests that glaze wares from these latter regions are more closely related to glaze-painted pottery in the Lower Rio Puerco area. Until a better understanding of the chronology, recipes, and organization of glaze paint production in the Casas Grandes region is achieved, it is not unreasonable to keep the focus of the discussion on Lower Rio Puerco glaze ware production within the prehispanic Pueblo landscape.

Based on available dates, glaze technology originated in the Western Pueblo region and was introduced into the Lower Rio Puerco area slightly earlier than into the Rio Grande region (figure 5.3) (Eckert 2006b). Glaze technology in the Western Pueblo region developed around AD 1275 (Eckert 2006b). The earliest locally produced glaze-painted vessels in the study area were recovered from Phase 1 excavation levels at Hummingbird Pueblo (see table 4.1). I calculated a mean ceramic date of AD 1286 for Phase 1 (appendix B) but recommended it as a starting date for this phase. Local glaze-painted vessels were also recovered from Phase 2 excavation levels at Hummingbird Pueblo; this phase is associated with a well-provenienced radiocarbon date of AD 1308 ± 50. In the Rio Grande area, the earliest absolute dates associated with locally produced glaze-painted pottery are a group of cutting dates clustered around AD 1313 from Tijeras Pueblo (Cordell 1975:27) and AD 1321r from Arroyo Hondo (Lang 1993). Taken together, these dates suggest that glaze technology was adopted by residents in the Lower Rio Puerco area slightly earlier than in the Rio Grande region. Further, these dates suggest that glaze-producing immigrants came from the Western Pueblo region.

The area of origins for glaze-producing immigrants living in the Lower Rio Puerco area can be further refined. Specifically, the immigrants who brought glaze technology with them were probably from the Zuni area of the Western Pueblo region. Western Pueblo glaze-painted pottery types are divided into three wares (figure 5.3): White Mountain Red Ware,

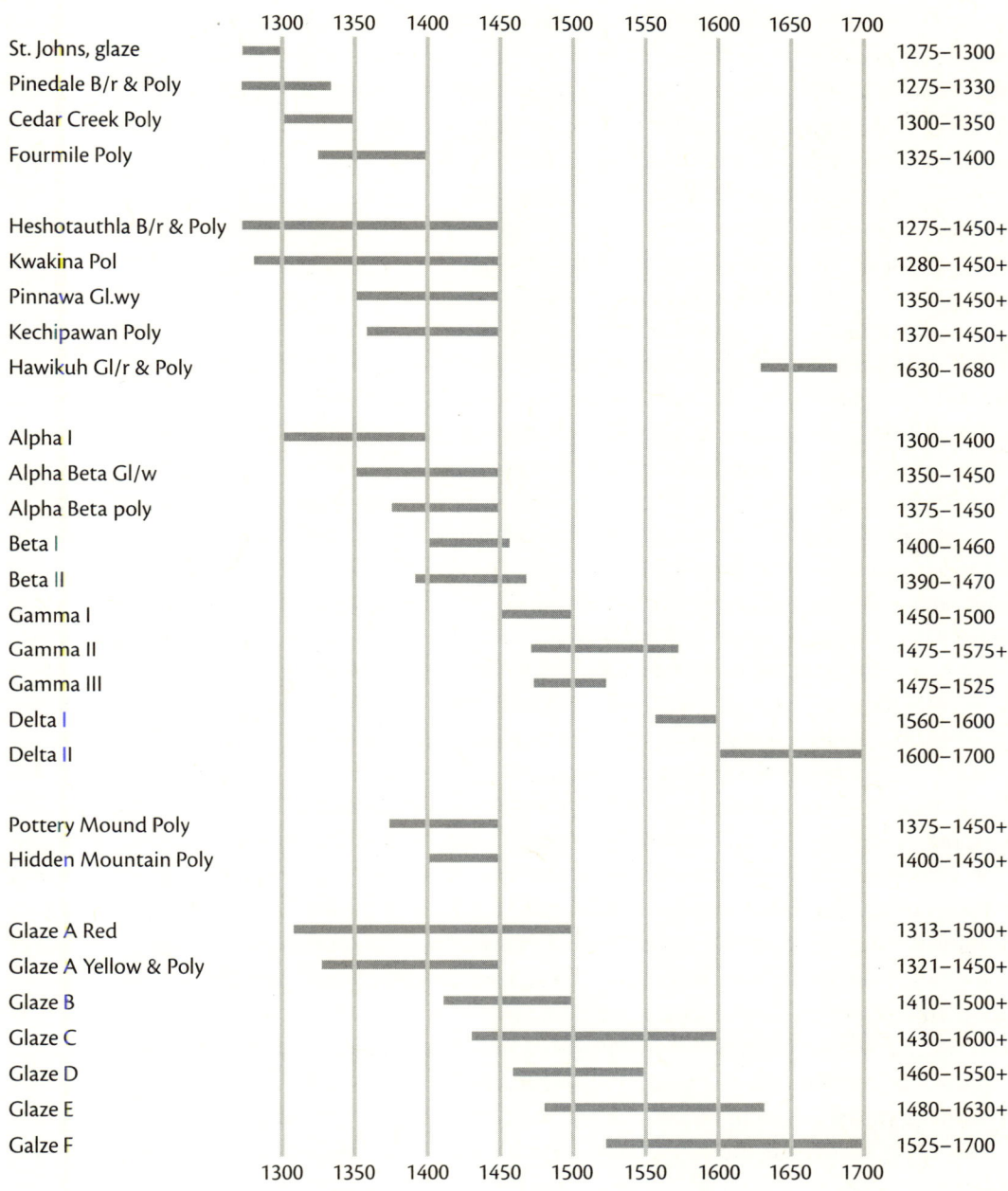

FIGURE 5.3. Timeline showing date ranges of major types in Pueblo glaze wares (after Eckert 2006b).

Identifying Potential Homelands for Immigrants in the Lower Rio Puerco

Zuni Glaze Ware, and Acoma Glaze Ware (Eckert 2006b). White Mountain Red Ware was produced in east-central Arizona, including the Mogollon and Upper Little Colorado areas (Carlson 1970) and includes the ceramic types Pinedale Black-on-red, Pinedale Polychrome, Cedar Creek Polychrome, and Fourmile Polychrome. None of these White Mountain Red Ware types were recorded in the study area.

Zuni Glaze Ware was made in the area surrounding the modern-day Zuni Indian Reservation, specifically from the Upper Little Colorado River immediately to the west of the continental divide in New Mexico (Woodbury and Woodbury 1966). Acoma Glaze Ware was predominantly produced in the area that is now the modern-day Acoma Indian Reservation (Seventh Southwestern Ceramic Seminar 1965). The fourteenth-century glaze-painted ceramic types produced in these two districts are similar and are often assigned the same type name by archaeologists. In the study area, exotic vessels produced in the Western Pueblo region are either Zuni Glaze Ware or Acoma Glaze Ware types rather than White Mountain Red Ware types. Further, *locally* produced copies of Western Pueblo glaze-painted vessels in the study area are consistent with types defined for both Zuni and Acoma glaze wares (Eckert 2006b).

One piece of decorative evidence suggests that at least some immigrants came from the Zuni area specifically. J. J. Brody (1964) noted that the designs on the exterior of most bowls and on the neck of jars from Pottery Mound could be placed into one of three categories: Xs, slashes, or no design (figure 5.4). Bowl exterior and jar neck designs recorded on whole vessels and sherds in this study (see chapter 4) from both Hummingbird Pueblo and Pottery Mound follow the same pattern as those recorded by Brody. The most common designs recorded on locally produced decorated vessels, with the exception of locally produced copies of Western Pueblo glaze wares, were slashes and Xs. Bowls and jars from the same time period produced in both the Rio Grande and Acoma areas are described as having identical exterior designs (Eighth Southwestern Ceramic Seminar 1966; Seventh Southwestern Ceramic Seminar 1965); however, bowls from the Zuni area do not have these designs (Carlson 1970; Seventh Southwestern Ceramic Seminar 1965). In the study area, Xs and slashes were not recorded on nonlocally produced Western Pueblo glaze ware or on local copies of Western Pueblo glaze ware. The absence of these designs on these specific vessels indicates that these vessels are more likely associated with immigrants from the Zuni area than the Acoma area.

More qualitative ceramic evidence also points to a Zuni area, rather than an Acoma area, origins for Western Pueblo glaze ware recovered in the study area. Glaze-painted pottery produced in the Acoma area *tends* to have a relatively more maroon slip, relatively whiter paste, fewer nonplastic inclusions, and a black-glaze line on the exterior of bowl rims; glaze-painted pottery produced in the Zuni area *tends* to have a relatively more orange-red slip, relatively grayer paste, more diverse nonplastic inclusions along with the sherd temper, and only white painted lines on the exterior of bowl rims. These observations are based upon my own research, as well as discussions with Dr. Alfred Dittert. Although possible, such observations have yet to be quantified. However, in the study area, Western Pueblo glaze ware, as well as locally produced copies of Western Pueblo glaze ware, simply *looks* and *feels* like my understanding of pottery produced in the Zuni area: orange-red slip, gray paste, white-paint designs on bowl exteriors, and more diverse nonplastic inclusions.

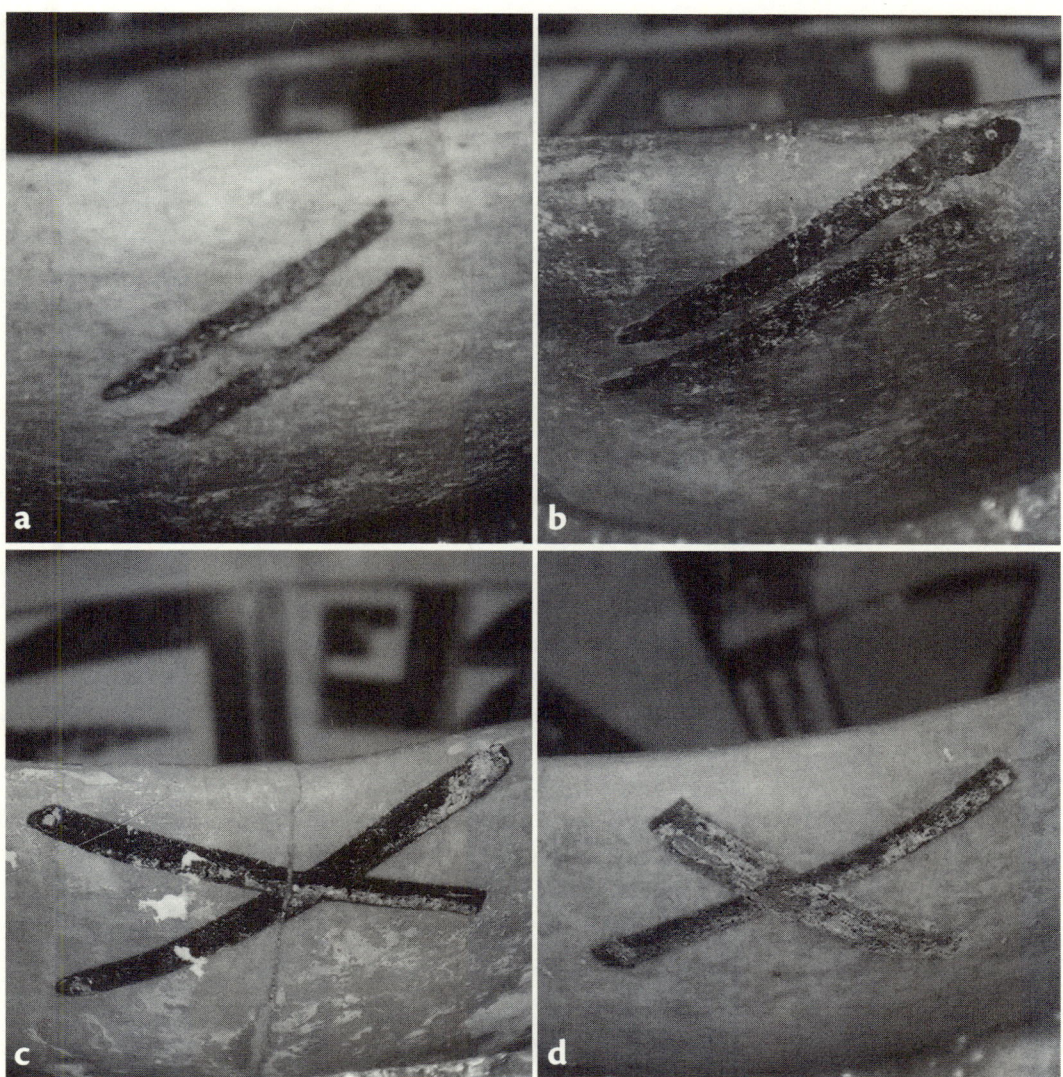

FIGURE 5.4. Photos of exterior designs common to fourteenth-century glaze-decorated pottery produced in the Acoma area, the study area, and the Rio Grande region: (a) San Clemente Polychrome, Maxwell Museum cat.# 87.50.3, (b) Pottery Mound Polychrome, Maxwell Museum cat.# 87.50.4, (c) San Clemente Polychrome, Maxwell Museum cat.# 87.50.18, (d) Pottery Mound Polychrome, Maxwell Museum cat.# 87.50.19. (Images courtesy of the Maxwell Museum of Anthropology, University of New Mexico, photographer Suzanne Eckert.)

Identifying Potential Homelands for Immigrants in the Lower Rio Puerco

I argue that the new habitus for producing glaze-painted pottery that appears in the study area reflects the presence of immigrants from the Zuni area living among indigenous residents of the study area. Our current chronology for the development and spread of glaze paint technology suggests that it originated in the Western Pueblo region and then quickly spread east. Design elements on glaze-painted pottery produced in the Western Pueblo region but recovered from Hummingbird Pueblo are consistent with design elements on vessels produced in the Zuni area during this period. Further, Western Pueblo copies produced at Hummingbird Pueblo share these same design elements, again pointing to Zuni as the origin of this habitus.

Immigrants Living at Pottery Mound

Evidence for immigrants from the Zuni district is much stronger at Hummingbird Pueblo than at Pottery Mound. One reason for this difference is that Hummingbird Pueblo contains a Phase 1 ceramic assemblage while Pottery Mound does not. However, another reason is the lack of both Western Pueblo glaze ware and copies of Western Pueblo glaze ware in Pottery Mound's Phase 2 ceramic assemblage (table 5.1), even though glaze-painted pottery was being produced at the village during this same period. This absence may reflect differences in the ethnic makeup of immigrants at Hummingbird Pueblo and Pottery Mound, with few to no immigrants from the Zuni area having lived at the latter village. However, another explanation should also be considered.

Western Pueblo immigrants may have initially moved to the Hidden Mountain site, a late thirteenth- and early fourteenth-century village located approximately 6 km from Pottery Mound (see chapter 2). Although ceramic type descriptions are unavailable, this site is recorded as having early glaze-painted pottery on its surface (Marshall and Walt 1984; ARMS site files). Disparate social groups are suspected of having lived in this village, and then possibly to have settled Pottery Mound (Marshall and Walt 1984). If this were the case, then potters at Pottery Mound would have been familiar with glaze technology prior to the settlement of the village and may have already developed their own local types. Specifically, the color combinations and design elements of Hidden Mountain Polychrome (discussed in the next chapter), a ceramic type exclusively recovered from Pottery Mound, are reminiscent of pottery produced in the Zuni area but laid out in a different fashion. Unfortunately, detailed data from the Hidden Mountain site are currently unavailable, and without such data, the role this site played in immigration into the study area cannot be evaluated.

Anecdotal evidence suggests that there was a migration from the Hopi mesas to Pottery Mound (Hibben 1975; Vivian 1961). Currently, three lines of evidence support this model. First, 12 percent of the nonlocal pottery recovered from Phase 3 excavation levels at Pottery Mound can be traced directly to the Hopi mesas. Hopi pottery was also recorded on the Hidden Mountain site (ARMS site files). Whether or not the presence of this pottery at these two villages represents contact with a donor area, continued contact with the homeland after migration, or simply exchange between two unrelated groups of people is impossible to evaluate without further data. If the presence of Hopi pottery does represent only exchange networks, the nature of these networks was unusual on the Pueblo social landscape since Hopi Yellow Ware is normally not found in such high quantities so far from the Hopi mesas (Hays-Gilpin, personal communication 2002).

Second, various researchers have commented on the similarity of Hopi designs and ones found on pottery and kiva murals at Pottery Mound (Crotty 1987; Vivian 1961; Voll 1961). Although pottery designs can be copied, it seems unlikely that Hopi designs would be heavily incorporated into ceremonial paintings without their associated ritual knowledge. Ritual specialists living at Pottery Mound could have learned aspects of the Hopi ritual system in a variety of ways: they may have traveled to the Hopi region to learn ceremonies; they may have been immigrants who originally learned their knowledge on the Hopi mesas; or they may have been taught ritual practice by an immigrant from the Hopi area.

Third, and finally, some of the locally produced glaze-painted vessels with Hopi designs are untempered (see table 4.2). This pattern is not present in the pottery from Hummingbird Pueblo. The clays from the Hopi mesas are of excellent quality and do not require tempering. The same cannot be said of the clays from the Lower Rio Puerco area. The low frequency of untempered vessels at Pottery Mound may indicate that Hopi immigrants attempted to continue their manufacturing traditions using local clays. All of these data are merely suggestive of a migration from Hopi; however, the possibility should not go unnoted.

A Few Words Concerning Casas Grandes

There is also evidence of ties between residents of Casas Grandes and Pottery Mound. First, as discussed above, marine shell, a copper bell, and at least one macaw burial are present at Pottery Mound—a suite of material culture specifically associated with participation in the Casas Grandes interaction sphere (Bradley 1999, 2000; Minnis 1988; Schaafsma and Riley 1999; Whalen and Minnis 2001). Second, some researchers (Hibben 1967, 1975; Young 1994) have noted Mesoamerican influence on the iconography present in the kiva murals at Pottery Mound. For example, Hibben noted that the horned/plumed serpent in Kiva 7 bore a striking resemblance to horned/plumed serpents on Ramos Polychrome from the Medio period at Casas Grandes. Third, and finally, as is the case with Hopi Yellow Ware discussed above, Ramos Polychrome can be untempered (Di Peso et al. 1974).

At first blush this evidence seems similar to that presented above for immigrants from Hopi; however, I am currently hesitant to argue that immigrants from Casas Grandes had moved into the study area. Although this hesitation could be due to the lack of Casas Grandes pottery in the study area, the lack of Lower Rio Puerco pottery at Casas Grandes (Di Peso et al. 1974; Douglas 1992), the very low frequency of Casas Grandes material culture at Pottery Mound, or because Mesoamerican influence in Southwest iconography has been noted as early as the Classic Mimbres period (AD 1000–1150) and therefore may not represent direct contact between the painters of Pottery Mound murals and Casas Grandes residents (Brody 1977), my hesitation does not stem from any of these arguments. My hesitation is due primarily to the observation that the new habitus for pottery production identified in the study area cannot be traced to the Casas Grandes region.

Although individual ceramic attributes, such as glaze paint and untempered clay, are present in the Casas Grandes region, the *suite* of new attributes identified in the study area cannot be traced to this region. Although sherd-tempered, red-slipped, glaze-painted pottery was produced in numerous archaeological districts in the Pueblo Southwest during the time period under question, including the study area, it was not produced in the Casas Grandes region. Similarly, although yellow-slipped, untempered pottery with a Sikyatki design style was produced on the Hopi mesas (albeit without the glaze paint or red-slipped bowl exteriors found within the study area), such a combination was never produced in the Casas Grandes region.

The presence of three material culture classes at Pottery Mound that have strong links with Casas Grandes begs the question as to why no Casas Grandes pottery has been identified in the study area. Whatever the nature of the contact between residents of Pottery Mound and the Casas Grandes region, it appears to have been very different than the interaction between residents of Pottery Mound and other Pueblo peoples. Contact between Casas Grandes and the study area needs to be understood in more depth, as Casas Grandes could have been a source of prestige goods or ritual knowledge or a direction for migrants *from* Pottery Mound to move to as that village was abandoned. Participants in the Casas Grandes interaction sphere may represent a specific subset of Pottery Mound residents—such as a single ritual group or gender—when compared with participants who interacted with other Pueblo villages. However, I do not currently see evidence for a new habitus that can be traced specifically to the Casas Grandes region in the study area and so do not believe that immigrants from this region lived at Pottery Mound.

Rio Grande Residents or Immigrants?

Finally, there is no reason that immigrants from Rio Grande villages were not present at Hummingbird Pueblo or Pottery Mound. However, evidence for such a migration is a bit more difficult to detect due partially to the nature of archaeological research in the region and due partially to the geography of the study area. Because of its close proximity to villages along the central and lower Rio Grande, along with a fairly broad definition of Rio Grande Glaze Ware, many past researchers have considered both Hummingbird Pueblo and Pottery Mound to be Rio Grande villages (Crotty 1987; Eckert and Cordell 2004; Marshall and Walt 1984; Voll 1961). As discussed in the previous chapter, this affected how pottery was categorized in this research.

The archaeological regional category of the study area as part of (or not part of) the Rio Grande may or may not reflect the prehispanic residents' perception of themselves. Whether or not they considered themselves to be part of any communities along the Rio Grande, ceramic evidence suggests that they were participating in Rio Grande exchange networks. Considering the dynamic nature of settlement during this period in the study area, along with the ceramic evidence for sustained contact between residents of the study area and the Rio Grande region, there is no reason not to believe that at least some people from the Rio Grande area could have moved to either Hummingbird Pueblo or Pottery Mound. Whether or not these new residents should be considered "immigrants" requires a better understanding of how villages along the Rio Puerco were (or were not) incorporated into communities along the Rio Grande.

Discussion and Conclusion

In this chapter, I have provided several lines of evidence to argue for the coresidency of local and immigrant groups in the Lower Rio Puerco area. Such coresidency is not surprising considering the extensive amount of population movement during this period in Pueblo prehistory (Cameron 1995; Cordell 1995; Ezzo and Price 2002; Spielmann 1998a). Although various regions were identified as possible homelands, I argue that at least some of the immigrants at Hummingbird Pueblo came specifically from the Zuni area in the Western Pueblo region. More anecdotal evidence suggests that there may also have been a migration of people from the Hopi mesas to Pottery Mound.

Although we can be confident that immigrants from Zuni, Hopi, or elsewhere moved into Lower Rio Puerco villages because of a perception that their new situation would be somehow better than their old, the specifics of this perception can probably never be known. The thirteenth century was one of environmental uncertainty, with some regions of the American Southwest being more drastically affected by the great drought of 1275 than other regions (Ahlstrom et al. 1995; Dean and Robinson 1979; Dean et al. 1985). The thirteenth and early fourteenth centuries also appear to have been a time of social uncertainty across the Pueblo landscape with new ritual features being adopted and then given up, new villages being built only to be left within a generation, an increase in interpersonal violence, and entire archaeological districts being abandoned (Bernardini 1998; Cameron 1995; Duff 1998; Kintigh 1985; LeBlanc 1999).

Although some migrants may have been moving over the Pueblo landscape in an attempt to flee potentially volatile social or environmental situations, other migrants may have been moving toward an obviously more prosperous social situation. Specifically, Duff (2002) has argued that residents of "ceremonially poor" villages may have attempted to recruit ritual specialists away from their village of residence. Such a move would potentially enhance the prestige of residents who were able to recruit these specialists, as well as the prestige of the specialists. Such a scenario may help explain the similarity in designs from Hopi and Pottery Mound kiva murals.

The evidence for immigration into the study area presented here is complex, with some evidence being stronger than other evidence. However, there is enough data combined to suggest that multiple ethnic groups resided together, for a time, within Hummingbird Pueblo and Pottery Mound. The specific makeup of these groups, in terms of number of individuals from different archaeological districts, may never be known. What is important is that villages in the Lower Rio Puerco area, like many other villages in both the Western Pueblo and Rio Grande regions, were composed of newly aggregated populations with potentially very diverse histories. This diversity may have resulted in social tensions concerning social norms, such as how to build a house, how to make and decorate pottery, what to eat and when, calendric events, how to perform ceremonies, and how to interact. Faced with these tensions, residents, both old and new, would have had to negotiate various aspects of social behavior. They would have been more willing to give up some aspects of their histories, while tightly holding on to other aspects.

While many aspects of negotiated behavior are not detectable in the archaeological record, how pottery was produced and decorated is. Combining the information from the previous and current chapter, a broad account of how the pottery assemblage within the study area came to be can be outlined. Sometime in the late 1200s or early 1300s, immigrants from the Zuni area moved into the newly established village of Hummingbird Pueblo (as well as possibly the Hidden Mountain site). Immigrant potters brought with them knowledge of glaze paint technology, as well as a tradition of thick slips, sherd temper, and oxidizing atmosphere. Sometime in the early 1300s, the Hidden Mountain site was abandoned and residents of this village established the village of Pottery Mound. Soon after, Hopi immigrant potters brought their pottery production technology with them as they moved into this village.

Zuni and Hopi immigrant potters interacted with local potters, and this interaction changed the habitus of all the potting communities involved. Zuni and Hopi potters learned to work new clays, giving up (in the Hopi instance) untempered vessels. These immigrants also learned to work with local pigments to create color combinations reminiscent of their homeland (discussed in more detail in the next chapter). Local potters learned glaze technology and adopted oxidizing atmosphere and new design elements, at the same time holding on to their diverse finishing techniques (self- and washy slips). One of the dramatic changes in ceramic production by local potters was the transition to glaze technology by the entire Lower Rio Puerco population. The adoption of glaze technology by local residents cannot be explained by the presence of immigrants alone.

In the study area, changes in pottery production that resulted in glaze-painted vessels becoming the dominant decorated ware represent both the influx of new ceramic producers as well as modifications in local technology. The change to glaze technology in the Lower Rio Puerco area represents individual and aggregate decisions by immigrant and local potters. Because habitus is a set of day-to-day practices (and not ideas) that unfold within specific contexts, these practices can transform as demands change, or as environmental or cultural conditions change. During the Pueblo IV period, the habitus of ceramic production and decoration transformed rapidly, reflecting changes in cultural conditions. The remaining chapters in this volume examine factors that encouraged potters in the Lower Rio Puerco area to modify their local traditions to produce glaze-decorated pottery to the exclusion of all other decorated types.

CHAPTER SIX

Communities of Identity in the Lower Rio Puerco Area

In chapter 4, different communities of practice were identified in the ceramic production tradition of the Lower Rio Puerco area. Rock temper and a self-slip on decorated wares were identified with potters who had a history in the southern portion of the study area. Sherd temper and a diversity of surface treatments (including a thin, washy slip and self-slip) were identified with potters who had a history in the northern portion of the study area. In chapter 5, changes in technological style were examined to help detect the presence of immigrants in the study area and to identify their region(s) of origin. Potters from the Zuni area were identified based upon differences in firing atmosphere, paint technology, and surface treatment. Anecdotal evidence led to speculation that potters from the Hopi district may also have immigrated to Pottery Mound. I argue that these communities of practice reflect different combinations of immigrant and indigenous social groups who were living together within local villages. In this and the next chapter, I move away from technological analyses and focus on decorative analyses to identify communities of identity.

The Relationship between Communities of Practice and Communities of Identity

I assume that communities of practice in the prehispanic Southwest were composed of multiple kin-based groups. Ethnographic evidence shows that the learning context of Southwestern pottery production is groups of related women (Shepard 1956), and archaeological data show that this was probably also true in the past (Crown and Wills 1995; Rautman 1997; Weigand 1977). Young potters learned their craft from older female relatives who not only taught them how to manufacture a vessel, from clay preparation to final firing, but also taught them the acceptable range of variation in choices at each step in the production process. As such, these young women learned their family's habitus, which accompanied them throughout their lives. This habitus would not only guide them concerning how to make a vessel, but also guide what form any necessary change in the process would take. The material result of this social process would be communities of practice similar to those identified in the previous chapters.

In the previous two chapters, different communities of practice were associated with different indigenous and immigrant groups. I assume that these groups were composed of multiple families. This chapter examines whether these communities of practice were also communities of identity. As outlined in chapter 1, communities of identity are social networks in which potters share a group identity. This identity could be based on a variety of social processes, including a shared migration history, religion, or kinship. Unlike communities of practice, communities of identity are based entirely on social perception and therefore they may or may not correspond to communities of practice; however, it is within a community of identity that a potter will signal her social boundaries.

By examining the relationship between technological and decorative style in this chapter, I identify communities of identity by exploring whether or not potters within each community of practice were using their products to emphasize social boundaries based on different histories and geographic origins. Ceramic types in the study area seem to reflect an emphasis on social boundaries, through visual clues on pottery, between groups with different migration histories. As such, there is a relationship between communities of practice and communities of identity in fourteenth-century villages along the Lower Rio Puerco.

A contradiction arises with this argument: if historic social boundaries were being maintained and emphasized through visual clues on pottery, then the adoption of glaze technology and red slips by local residents needs to be more adequately explained. White ware and glaze ware are more visually different than the variation among glaze ware types and would have provided more distinct visual clues if emphasis on such social boundaries was a priority. To examine this contradiction, the possibility that glaze technology was adopted as part of a larger ritual system is explored and accepted in the next chapter.

This contradiction may be explained if decorative attributes associated with different local and immigrant groups identified in this chapter were used primarily to signal information to members *within* each group and not to emphasize differences *between* groups. Such signaling resulted from different potter communities within a village making different choices based upon their daily social demands. The end result consisted of a site-wide assemblage of decorated vessels that shared glaze paint decoration but could also be divided into various suites of decorative and technological attributes.

The Role of Decorative Style in Signaling Social Boundaries

Throughout Pueblo prehistory, ceramic vessels served important utilitarian functions in cooking, storage, and food service. Consequently, they were conspicuous in their use in a variety of social contexts and could play an important role in cultural transmission from one generation to the next. The decisions made in pottery decoration could have served to signal group membership at a variety of levels. For example, designs on the interior of bowls may have been meant to be viewed only by those who ate from those bowls, thus signaling family members about important aspects of lineage membership; while designs on the exterior of bowls may have been meant to be viewed by people from across a plaza space, perhaps signaling another lineage that everyone was a member of the same ritual society. Such signaling would create daily reminders of group membership and the social interactions appropriate to such membership, such as who could be called upon for what social obligations, who was and was not part of the potential marriage pool, and what allegiances could be expected in times of social stress.

In a village the size of Pottery Mound or Hummingbird Pueblo, residents would have known who were members of which families and would have been aware of each family's history. Visual clues on pottery did not create social boundaries between such families and groups of families. These visual clues, however, could have been used to emphasize such boundaries by incorporating design elements that reminded viewers of unique family histories, or they could have been used to blur such boundaries by incorporating signs that stressed village membership. Of course, multiple signs could have been incorporated into a design—ones that emphasized family history and ones that emphasized village membership. In an extreme case of solidarity, one would expect all pottery within a village to have identical designs. In an extreme case of individuality, one would expect each potter to decorate her vessels with completely unique designs. The patterning in the Lower Rio Puerco ceramic assemblage falls between these two extremes. An analysis of decorative style provides a clearer understanding of where this patterning lies along the continuum.

I argued that the technological styles defined in the last chapter may have reflected only unconscious decisions on the part of potters and, correspondingly, on the type of social boundary (communities of practice) being detected. However, the expression of social boundaries can be patterned on several scales in material culture (Hitchcock and Bartram 1998:48). Technological style may incorporate both conscious and unconscious decisions (Stark 1998, 2006). If potters were using their wares to help emphasize social boundaries between groups with distinct histories, then aspects of technological style may have been used as part of this discourse. In this chapter, technological and decorative style are used to examine active attempts at social boundary maintenance, whether they are to emphasize or blur those boundaries. In this context, decorative style refers to the characteristic patterns of pottery embellishment that result in a unique set of visually represented design attributes (Rice 1987). Decorative style can be indicated through such attributes as "design layout, motifs, motif fillers, interaction of motifs in a design, and overall decorative artistry" (Crown 1994:78).

Much debate has occurred over the past four decades as to how to define and interpret style (see Hegmon 1995 for an excellent review). Ceramic sociology studies of the 1960s and early 1970s (Deetz 1965; Hill 1970; Longacre 1970; Plog 1978, 1983; Whallon 1968) argued that similarity in ceramic style was the result of social interaction and shared production and learning contexts. For example, Dean Arnold (1989) found that, among the Ticul of Mexico, the relationship between style and behavior lies within a household learning context. Potters learn their craft as children through imitation and practice, rather than through direct teaching. As such, technological and stylistic knowledge was thought to have been passed down along kin-based lines and to reflect kin-based groups.

Studies such as Arnold's led researchers to argue that stylistic similarity was a passive reflection of interaction intensity. However, a contemporary study (Friedrich 1970) found that the relationship between production context and stylistic similarity is far from perfect; the shared production/learning context may be reflected in some manufacturing aspects but not in others. In the village of San José in Michoacán, Mexico, Margaret Friedrich (1970) found that some design attributes reflected intensity of social interaction between potters, while other design attributes did not. A potter's selection of different attributes relied on personal preference, intensity of interaction with other potters, and ease of reproduction (some design attributes are easier for a potter to copy than others).

Subsequent work has supported Friedrich's findings, showing that learning contexts, and resulting patterns in material culture, are not always straightforward (DeBoer 1990; Hardin 1984; Longacre 1991). Scott MacEachern (1998) found that technological and stylistic patterning did not correlate well with geographic location (or ethnic identity) in the Mandara Mountains of Cameroon and Nigeria. In this area, as in the Ticul case study, potters learn their craft primarily from their mothers or other female relatives. The "messiness" in ceramic patterning results from women moving in and out of communities as they marry and divorce. Regardless of where they live, women continue to make pottery using the same techniques, morphologies, and decorations. Further, they pass this knowledge on to their daughters, who often marry out of the community they grew up in.

A more active role for style is outlined by art history and information exchange theory; both approaches argue that decorative style imparts important cultural meaning to those who view it (Conkey and Hastorf 1990; Costin 1998; Hodder 1982; Wiessner 1983; Wobst 1977). This meaning, however, varies from group to group (Shennan 1989). Differences in styles are thought to reflect different social or cultural identities (Graves 1994; Hayashida 1999; Hegmon 1995; Wobst 1977). Different social groups who wish to maintain their separate identities may consciously choose to emphasize difference by promoting group membership with an "emblematic," or decorative, style (Wiessner 1983). On the other hand, decorative style may convey less specific meanings, such as by providing daily reminders of the social structure through culturally loaded symbols or by providing important cues to people in specific social contexts (Goffman 1974).

After studying several classes of material culture among the Baringo of Kenya, Ian Hodder (1977, 1979b) argued that artifacts that call attention to social boundaries must carry some form of stylistic message. Further, stylistic messaging is especially emphasized in situations where there is tension between groups (Hodder 1979b). These groups may be divided along gender, ethnicity, or socioeconomic status. Or, as in the case of potters in Taricá, Peru, style may be used to mark differences between individual potters wanting to identify vessels that they produced (Donnan 1971). In the case of pottery, messaging will probably occur most commonly on vessels that are used during public occasions. For example, Warren DeBoer and James Moore (1982) found that among the Shipibo-Conibo of Peru, the most diverse forms of style occurred on pottery used during public festivals.

Recent critics of ceramic sociology and information theory suggest alternative approaches to examining style that integrate competing theories (Dietler and Herbich 1998; Hegmon 1998; Hodder 1990; Sackett 1986; Stark 1998). Specifically, Dietler and Herbich (1998:245) have argued for an approach that incorporates aspects of structure (material culture conforms to cognitive structures that underlie all cultural practice), agency theory (material culture is a medium of active communication between cultural participants), and the French school of *technologie* (choices are made at all stages in the production of material culture). They argue that these approaches are not contradictory explanations of material culture but are only partial explanations. Dietler and Herbich (1998) use practice theory as a means to bridge the gap between various approaches, providing a more holistic understanding of style and how it articulates with material culture and social behavior.

Dietler and Herbich (1998) applied their integrative approach to their study of pottery production, style, and social boundaries among the Luo of western Kenya (discussed in chapter 1). Although they were able to define micro-styles between different potter communities, these micro-styles were not meant to be expressions of identity between such communities. Potters could identify their vessels but could not explain the rules by which such identifications were made. In other words, micro-styles were created through habitus, which guided potters' perceptions of the acceptable range of variation in choices at different stages of the production process. The resulting micro-styles could change at any point in the process as new environmental or cultural demands were placed upon the potters, and these changes could have unintended consequences in other domains of social practice.

The potential information provided by decorative style has made it an important focus of study for archaeologists (Conkey and Hastorf 1990). In the last decade, two substantial studies of ceramic decorative style in the prehispanic Southwest have provided guidelines for researchers pursuing stylistic studies in the same area: Patricia Crown's (1994) examination of Salado Polychrome and Michelle Hegmon's (1995) examination of black-on-white pottery from the Kayenta and Mesa Verde regions.

Crown (1994) used a diverse suite of analytical tools to examine the appearance, distribution, and eventual disappearance of Salado Polychrome during the 1300s and 1400s. She concludes that the ware was associated with the spread of the Southwestern Regional Cult, an ideology and ritual system that integrated disparate social groups. Along with examining the distribution, production source, organization of production, pottery technology, vessel form, context, and use, she also examined design and design content on Salado Polychromes (1994:55–98, 131–76). After a detailed analysis of design including layout, symmetry, balance, motifs, quality of execution, irregularities, and general style, she determined that Salado Polychrome designs were remarkably uniform over a wide area of production and distribution. What regional variation she did find in the frequency of some characteristics she attributed to personal preferences by potters. Crown's research is important not only for its contribution to understanding the Salado phenomena, but also for providing an excellent example of how informative a multivariate approach to analysis of pottery can be, and how analysis of style plays an important role in that approach.

Hegmon (1995) focused on early black-on-white pottery produced in the Kayenta and

Mesa Verde regions. By examining both the structure of style, as well as measurements of stylistic similarity and diversity, she found differences between her two study regions in terms of distribution of painted pottery, patterns of design style, design structure, and design attributes. She argued that these differences were the result of the different role of style in each region. Hegmon's work is notable not only for its application to the study of ceramic style in the Southwest, but for the broad theoretical and analytical approach that she applied to style.

Some archaeologists have turned to practice theory as a means of understanding how style articulates with social boundaries (Hegmon 1998; Lightfoot et al. 1998; Stark 2006). As discussed in chapters 1 and 2, practice theory allows archaeologists to conceive of social boundaries as behavior with material consequences. People reproduce their social boundaries through daily practice; daily practice is structured by basic organizational principles; and these basic organization principles are expressed through habitus (Stark 2006). Decorative style, as an aspect of habitus, is one medium in which potters could negotiate social boundaries on a variety of scales through a variety of visual clues. New social demands may be expressed through changes in habitus, which could include changes in these visual clues.

There are many different ways potters within a community of practice could be associated—through kinship, a shared history, exchange alliances, or ideology (Habicht-Mauche and Nelson 2006; Stark 2006). All of these ways can crosscut one another, and all could be expressed on pottery. The issue pertinent to this study is the relationship between decorative style and the communities of practice identified in the last chapter. If, as I assume, decorative style reflects the signaling of multiple scales of social boundaries, then this relationship can be explored. I associate communities of practice with groups who had different migration histories into Hummingbird Pueblo and Pottery Mound and explore whether or not these communities of practice were also communities of identity—an identity based, in part, on a shared social history and region of origin.

I recognize different communities of identity by examining the relationship between ceramic types and technological styles. Specifically, I examine the relationship between two technological attributes (temper choice and surface treatment) and decorated types. If decorated pottery was used to emphasize social boundaries between groups with different migration histories, technological attributes should consistently co-occur on vessels identified as specific decorated types. If, however, decorated pottery was used to blur such social boundaries, then technological attributes should crosscut decorated types.

Decorative Style in the Lower Rio Puerco Area

The glaze-decorated pottery of the Lower Rio Puerco area is distinctive in terms of both slip color combinations and design styles. Following Crown (1994) and Hegmon (1995), I discuss decorative attributes—design style, slip color, and iconic motifs—that relate to the intentional signaling of social boundaries within the study area. For this analysis, I examined 41 whole and partial vessels, including 7 jars and 34 bowls. Ten vessels were recovered from Hummingbird Pueblo (figure 6.1) and 31 from Pottery Mound (figures 6.2–6.5). All vessels were collected by Frank Hibben during his years of excavation at each site and are curated at

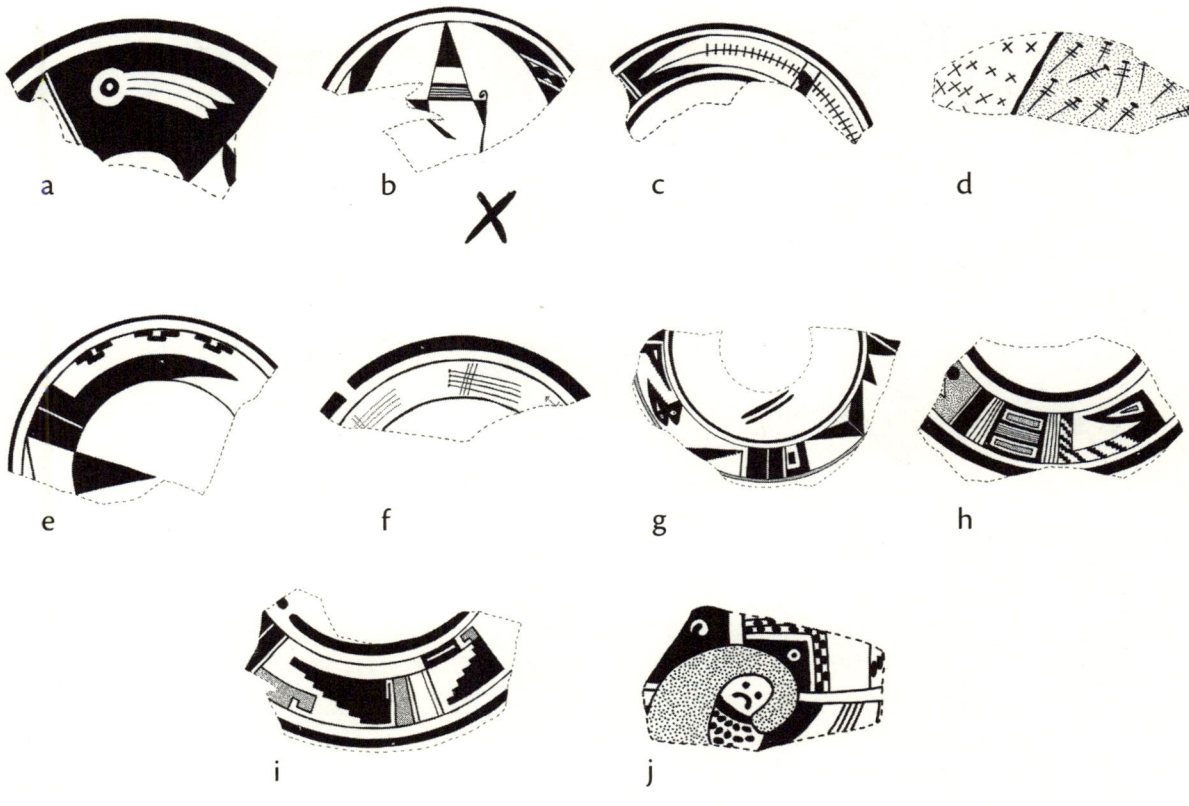

FIGURE 6.1. Partial vessels recovered from Hummingbird Pueblo: a, f, j, San Clemente Polychrome bowls; b, c, d, Agua Fria Glaze-on-red bowls; e, Cieneguilla Polychrome bowl; g, h, i, Pottery Mound Polychrome jars. NOTE: stippled area is red on original vessels.

the Maxwell Museum, University of New Mexico, Albuquerque. Proveniences for the vessels were not specific and included unknown, burials, rooms, and sampling trenches with no noted cultural association. There was no cache of vessels, nor did a majority of vessels come from a single burial or room. As such, although the sample size is small, there is no reason to believe that the assemblage is not fairly representative of vessel design styles from the two sites. In addition, over 6,000 decorated sherds were examined from Hummingbird Pueblo and Pottery Mound. Proveniences included trash middens as well as trash-filled rooms and kivas.

DESIGN STYLE

Patricia Crown (1994) has argued that examination of style, defined as "the constant form, and sometimes constant elements, qualities, and expression, in the art of an individual or group" (Schapiro 1953:287), permits comparison within and between ceramic types. The occurrence of a specific style across space and time indicates some form of interaction between

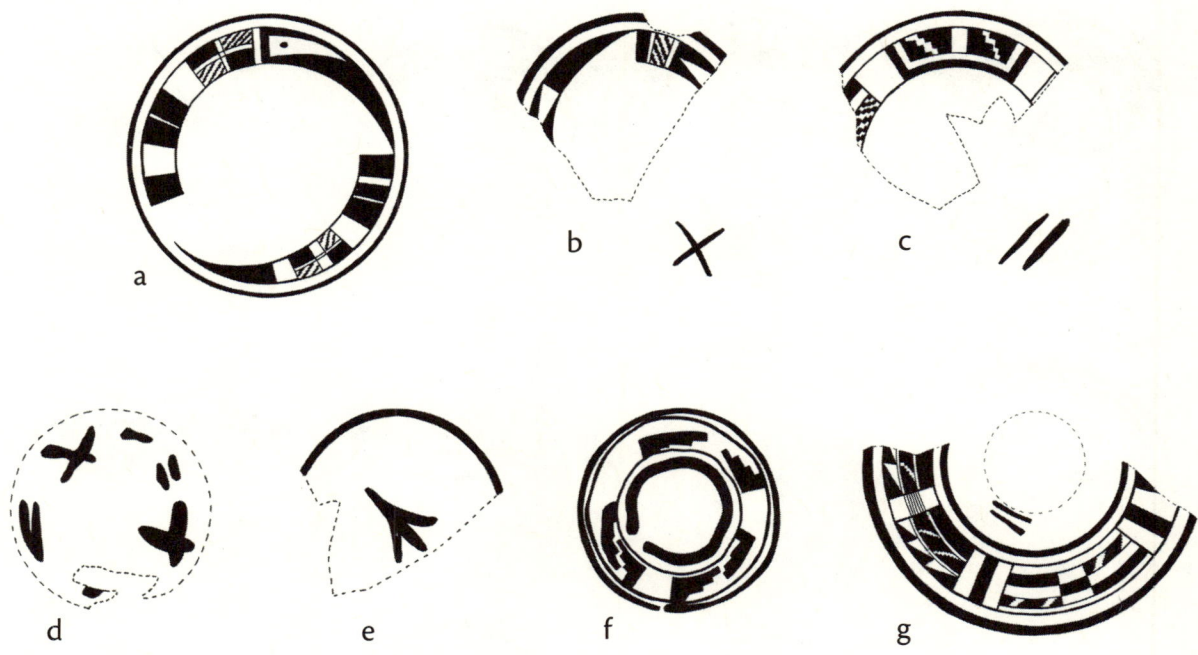

FIGURE 6.2. Agua Fria Glaze-on-red vessels recovered from Pottery Mound: a, b, c, bowls; d, e, small bowls; f, small jar; g, jar.

groups spanning this spatial and temporal range. Aspects of design style—such as balance or the number of times a motif is repeated—may reflect the habitus by which a prehispanic Pueblo potter ordered her designs (Brody 1977; Crown 1994; Greenberg 1975; Moulard 1984; Shepard 1954). If this habitus were different among immigrant and local groups living in the Lower Rio Puerco area, then differences in style would reflect these different social groups. Obviously, design style cannot be recorded on most sherds, thus, identifying design styles in the study area was based solely upon analysis of whole and partial vessels. Four design styles can be identified.

(1) The *Heshotauthla* style (Seventh Southwestern Ceramic Seminar 1965) has designs laid out in a thin band, normally divided into quarters, around a circular open base. The Heshotauthla style is often incorporated under the Pinedale style. Unlike the Pinedale style, however, the Heshotauthla style almost never has hatched motifs (for a fuller discussion, see Eckert 2006b). Designs are geometrics, often with more painted surface than unpainted, incorporating solids, eyes, and negative lightning. Examples of the Heshotauthla style include figures 6.2a, 6.2b, 6.2c, 6.2g, 6.3b, 6.3f, 6.3h, and 6.5d.

(2) The *Rio Grande Glaze A* style (Brody 1964) has been recognized as an outgrowth of the Heshotauthla style (Seventh Southwestern Ceramic Seminar 1965; Snow 1989; Warren 1980).

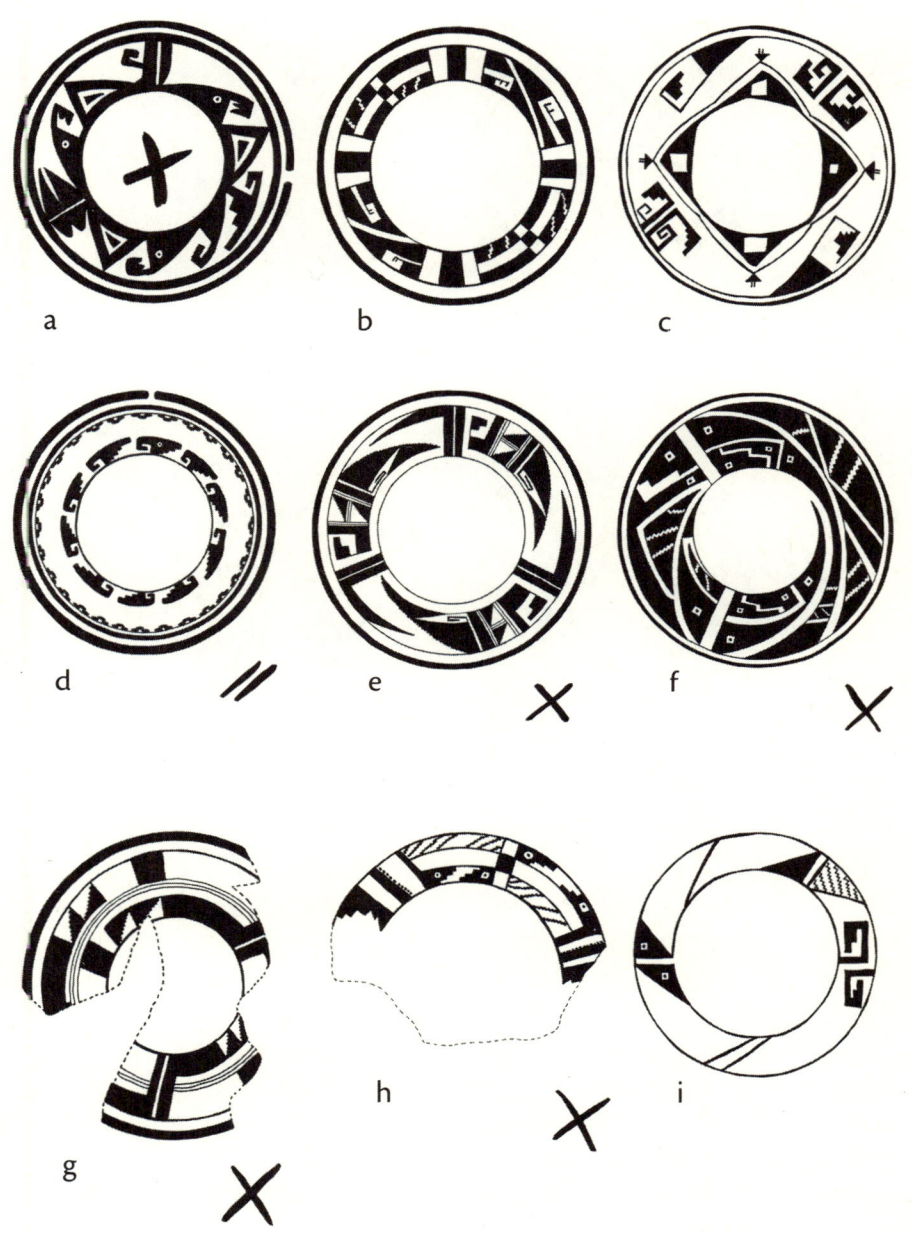

FIGURE 6.3. San Clemente Glaze-on-polychrome bowls recovered from Pottery Mound.

Communities of Identity in the Lower Rio Puerco Area

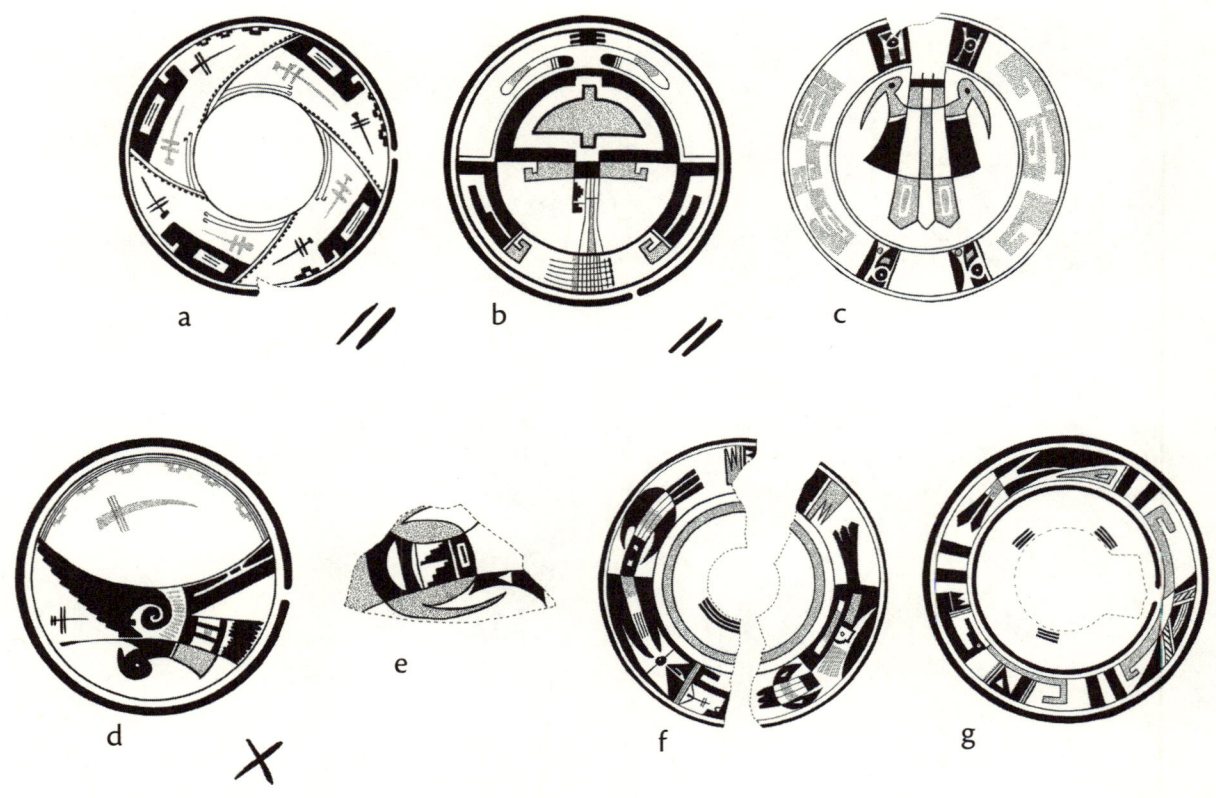

FIGURE 6.4. Pottery Mound Polychrome vessels recovered from Pottery Mound: a, b, c, d, e, bowls; f, g, jars. NOTE: stippled area represents red paint on original vessels.

Designs are laid out in one or two bands—normally divided into two, three, or four sections—around a circular open base. Sometimes a simple element is painted in the center of a bowl, but the design is unrelated to the band; designs in bands are normally geometrics. Although similar to the Heshotauthla style, the Rio Grande Glaze A style is more "open." The Heshotauthla style often creates a negative effect through the use of more solid than open space. The Rio Grande Glaze A style, on the other hand, incorporates either equal amounts of solid and open space, or more open than solid space. Examples of the Rio Grande Glaze A style include figures 6.1c, 6.1e, 6.2f, 6.3a, 6.3c, 6.3d, 6.3e, 6.3g, 6.3i, 6.4a, 6.5a, and 6.5e.

(3) The *Sikyatki* style (Brody 1964; Colton 1955; Fewkes 1973) has dynamic designs, an asymmetrical layout, and a focus on the center of the vessel. A band may encircle the center design but will include only simple elements. Common design elements include highly conventionalized feathers and birds, as well as other representational icons. Examples of the Sikyatki style include figures 6.1g, 6.1h, 6.1i, 6.4b, 6.4c, 6.4d, 6.4e, 6.4f, and 6.4g.

FIGURE 6.5. Miscellaneous decorated bowls recovered from Pottery Mound: a, Cieneguilla Polychrome; b, Pinnawa Glaze-on-white; c, d, Cieneguilla Glaze-on-yellow; e, Glaze C Glaze-on-yellow; f, Glaze C Glaze-on-polychrome; g, h, Hidden Mountain Polychrome. NOTE: stippled area represents red paint on original vessels.

(4) *Atypical* style was assigned to vessels that do not appear to have been painted in any common style defined by Southwestern archaeologists. Many of these vessels have styles similar to Heshotauthla or Rio Grande Glaze A style, except that geometric aspects of the design are connected, but outside, the banded design field and dip into the bowl center. Examples of an atypical style include figures 6.1a, 6.1b, 6.1d, 6.1f, 6.1j, 6.2d, 6.2e, 6.5b, 6.5c, 6.5f, 6.5g, and 6.5h.

These four styles are typical on Pueblo IV decorated pottery, and the first three are associated with specific archaeological districts. The Rio Grande Glaze A style developed in the glaze-producing districts of the Rio Grande region; the Heshotauthla style developed in the Acoma/Zuni district of the Western Pueblo region; and the Sikyatki style developed in the Hopi district of the Western Pueblo region. All four design styles are well represented on the whole and partial vessels from the Lower Rio Puerco area (table 6.1) with Heshotauthla style recorded on 19 percent (n = 7), Rio Grande Glaze A style recorded on 28 percent (n = 10), Sikyatki style recorded on 25 percent (n = 9), and an atypical style recorded on 28 percent (n = 10) of vessels.

SLIP COLOR

Due to its high visibility, one important decorative attribute that may have signaled group identity in the prehispanic Pueblo Southwest is slip color (Crown 1994; Douglas 1982; Graves and Eckert 1998; Kintigh 1998; Plog 2003). The most common slip color (47 percent, n = 17) on whole and partial vessels recovered from the Lower Rio Puerco area (table 6.1) is a combination of yellow-buff (Munsell 7.5YR 6–7/6–8) and red (Munsell 10R 4/4–8). On bowls, this combination always occurs with yellow-buff on the interior and red on the exterior. On jars, this slip combination occurs with red slip around the neck and lower half of the vessel and yellow-buff slip around the shoulders of the vessel. The second most common slip color on whole and partial vessels is red (25 percent, n = 9). Other slip colors include bright white, yellow (10YR 8/4–6), and yellow-gray (10YR 6–7/2–4). These latter two colors may be variations or misfired versions of the yellow-buff. Based on the sherd data, the most common slip color produced through the Pueblo IV period in the study area was red, followed by the yellow-buff and red slip combination (table 6.2). The difference between the most common slip color on whole vessels (polychrome) compared to sherds (red) may be a reflection of a small sample size of whole vessels. There may also be a temporal bias in the whole vessels, with Phase 3 (where polychrome slips are most prevalent) being overrepresented.

Slip color did not seem to be commonly used to signal distinct social groups in the public domain as, regardless of the interior color of the bowl, most vessels look identical on the exterior with a red slip. This suggests that if slip color was used to signal group identity below the level of the village, it was only signaling people in the immediate vicinity of the bowl (possibly eating out of it). However, a small percentage of vessels have distinctive exterior slip colors (tables 6.1 and 6.2), which may have been a means of signaling some form of group membership at a distance. Specifically, bowls with a yellow-buff, light buff, or white exterior would have stood out visually from the majority of bowls with a red slip on the exterior.

TABLE 6.1. Design attributes recorded for whole and partial vessels from Hummingbird Pueblo and Pottery Mound.

Figure Reference	Production Provenience	Ceramic Type	Form	Design Style	Interior Slip Color	Exterior Slip Color
Hummingbird Pueblo						
6.1a	local	San Clemente Poly	bowl	atypical	white & red	red
6.1b	local	Agua Fria Gl/r	bowl	atypical	red	red
6.1c	local	Agua Fria Gl/r	bowl	Glaze A	red	red
6.1d	local	San Clemente Poly	bowl	atypical	red	red
6.1e	local	Cieneguilla Poly	bowl	Glaze A	yellow	yellow
6.1f	local	San Clemente Poly	bowl	atypical	yellow-buff	red
6.1g	local	Pottery Mound Poly	jar	Sikyatki	none	yellow-buff & red
6.1h	local	Pottery Mound Poly	jar	Sikyatki	none	yellow-buff & red
6.1i	local	Pottery Mound Poly	jar	Sikyatki	none	yellow-buff & red
6.1j	local	San Clemente Poly	bowl	atypical	yellow-buff	red
Pottery Mound						
6.2a	local	Agua Fria Gl/r	bowl	Heshotauthla	red	red
6.2b	local	Agua Fria Gl/r	bowl	Heshotauthla	red	red
6.2c	local	Agua Fria Gl/r	bowl	Heshotauthla	red	red
6.2d	local	Agua Fria Gl/r	bowl	atypical	red	red
6.2e	local	Agua Fria Gl/r	bowl	atypical	red	red
6.2f	local	Agua Fria Gl/r	jar	Glaze A	none	red
6.2g	local	Agua Fria Gl/r	jar	Heshotauthla	none	red
6.3a	local	San Clemente Poly	bowl	Glaze A	gray-yellow	red
6.3b	local	San Clemente Poly	bowl	Heshotauthla	yellow-buff	red
6.3c	Albuquerque?	San Clemente Poly	bowl	Glaze A	gray-yellow	red
6.3d	Albuquerque?	San Clemente Poly	bowl	Glaze A	white	red
6.3e	local	San Clemente Poly	bowl	Glaze A	yellow-buff	red
6.3f	local	San Clemente Poly	bowl	Heshotauthla	yellow-buff	red
6.3g	local	San Clemente Poly	bowl	Glaze A	yellow-buff	red
6.3h	local	San Clemente Poly	bowl	Heshotauthla	red	white & red
6.3i	local	San Clemente Poly	bowl	Glaze A	yellow-buff	red
6.4a	local	Pottery Mound Poly	bowl	Glaze A	yellow-buff	red
6.4b	local	Pottery Mound Poly	bowl	Sikyatki	yellow-buff	red
6.4c	local	Pottery Mound Poly	bowl	Sikyatki	yellow-buff	red
6.4c	local	Pottery Mound Poly	bowl	Sikyatki	yellow-buff	red
6.4e	local	Pottery Mound Poly	bowl	Sikyatki	yellow-buff	red
6.4f	local	Pottery Mound Poly	jar	Sikyatki	none	yellow-buff & red
6.4g	local	Pottery Mound Poly	jar	Sikyatki	none	yellow-buff & red
6.5a	local	Cieneguilla Poly	bowl	Glaze A	yellow-buff	yellow-buff
6.5b	Zuni	Pinnawa Gl/w	bowl	atypical	white	white
6.5c	local	Cieneguilla Gl/y	bowl	atypical	yellow	yellow
6.5d	local	Cieneguilla Gl/y	bowl	Heshotauthla	yellow-buff	yellow-buff
6.5e	Galisteo	Glaze C Gl/y	bowl	Glaze A	pale yellow	pale yellow
6.5f	Galisteo	Glaze C Poly	bowl	atypical	pale yellow	pale yellow
6.5g	local	Hidden Mountain Poly	bowl	atypical	red	white
6.5h	local	Hidden Mountain Poly	bowl	atypical	red	white

Communities of Identity in the Lower Rio Puerco Area

TABLE 6.2. **Slip color combinations for common local pottery types, Phases 2 and 3 percentages (counts in parentheses) combined.**

Slip Color Combination	Ceramic Types	% (n)
white slip	Loma Fria B/w, Socorro B/w, Untyped B/w, Pinnawa Gl/w (local copy), Kechipawan Polychrome (local copy)	1 (84)
red slip	Early Rio Grande Gl/r (including Agua Fria Gl/r), St. Johns B/r and Polychrome, Heshotauthla Gl/r and Polychrome (local copies)	62 (3771)
yellow to yellow-buff slip	Early Rio Grande Gl/y (including Cieneguilla Gl/y)	7 (423)
on bowls, yellow-buff slip on interior and red slip on exterior; on jars, red slip on neck and base, yellow-buff slip on shoulder	Early Rio Grande Gl/poly (including San Clemente Polychrome), Pottery Mound Polychrome	26 (1609)
on bowls, bright white slip on interior and red slip on exterior; on jars, red slip on neck and base, bright white slip on shoulder	Kwakina Polychrome (local copy)	0 (19)
on bowls, red slip on interior, white slip on exterior; no recorded cases on jars	Hidden Mountain Polychrome	2 (104)
light buff slip	Hummingbird Buff Ware	2 (111)

ICONIC MOTIFS

After Crown (1994:134), I use "icons" to mean any images with formal similarities to a referent. Specific icons can be identified on pottery from the Lower Rio Puerco area. I do not attempt to interpret these images here, but rather am looking to see if certain icons co-occur or if some icons never occur together. However, I do recognize that naming such images "serpents" and "clouds" automatically dictates a certain interpretation. I use these terms as a way to remain consistent with previous research (Adams 1991; Crotty 1990; Crown 1994; Fewkes 1973; Graves and Eckert 1998; Hays-Gilpin 1996; Hays-Gilpin and Hill 1999). Although other icons may be identified on individual vessels, I focus on what appear to be the most common in the assemblage as a whole.

Of the 36 locally produced whole vessels examined, 89 percent (n = 32) had recognizable icons (table 6.3). The most common icons are lightning/snakes (39 percent, n = 14), eyes (25 percent, n = 9), and birds (25 percent, n = 9). Butterflies were only recorded on pottery produced outside the study area (n = 2). Co-occurrence clearly exists: eyes and lightning/snakes occur together on 17 percent (n = 6) of the vessels; birds and feathers occur together on 11 percent (n = 4) of the vessels.

TABLE 6.3. Icons recorded for whole and partial vessels from Hummingbird Pueblo and Pottery Mound (* denotes nonlocally produced vessel).

Figure Reference	Serpent	Mask	Eye	Star	Lightning	Bird	Feather	Butterfly	Dragonfly	Cloud	Track
6.1a				X						X	
6.1b						X					
6.1c											
6.1d							X				
6.1e									X		
6.1f										X	
6.1g						X					
6.1h	X										
6.1i		X									
6.1j	X		X		X						
6.2a	X		X		X						
6.2b					X						
6.2c					X						
6.2d			X								
6.2e											X
6.2f											
6.2g					X						
6.3a			X	X		X					
6.3b					X						
6.3c*								X			
6.3d*			X			X				X	
6.3e						X					
6.3f	X		X		X						
6.3g											
6.3h			X		X						
6.3i	X		X		X						
6.4a									X	X	
6.4b		X				X	X		X		
6.4c						X	X				
6.4d						X	X		X	X	
6.4e		X									
6.4f						X	X		X		
6.4g		X			X	X					
6.5a						X					
6.5b*		X									
6.5c											
6.5d					X						
6.5e*								X			
6.5f*											
6.5g	X		X		X						
6.5h	X		X	X	X						

Communities of Identity in the Lower Rio Puerco Area

TABLE 6.4. Icons recorded on sherds from Hummingbird Pueblo and Pottery Mound.

Ceramic Type	Serpent	Mask	Eye	Star	Lightning	Bird	Feather	Dragonfly	Cloud
White wares	—	—	—	—	—	—	—	—	—
St. Johns types	—	—	—	—	—	—	—	—	—
Western Pueblo glaze ware, local copies	—	—	20	—	9	—	—	—	—
Early Rio Grande Gl/r	2	2	32	5	89	15	1	6	9
Early Rio Grande Gl/y	—	1	10	—	23	1	1	—	6
Early Rio Grande Gl/poly	—	—	19	2	39	4	—	—	2
Intermediate Rio Grande Glaze	—	—	2	1	—	1	—	1	1
Hummingbird R/bf	—	—	1	—	1	—	—	—	—
Pottery Mound Polychrome	—	1	5	—	3	2	—	1	1
Hidden Mountain Polychrome	—	—	4	—	4	1	—	—	—

Four patterns are important to note concerning the distribution of icons on sherds in the study area. First, because only one icon usually appeared on any given sherd, the co-occurrence of icons could not be examined. Second, no icons were recorded on white wares, which were produced in the Pueblo III and early Pueblo IV period (table 6.4). Third, icons were rare on other nonglaze types (including St. Johns and Hummingbird Red-on-buff). Fourth, and finally, no icons were restricted to a particular Pueblo IV glaze ware type (table 6.4). In other words, iconic representation became much more common on Pueblo IV pottery in the Lower Rio Puerco area and was associated with glaze ware production. This suggests that icons may not have been related to signaling group membership, but may have been associated with the introduction of a new ritual system, as has been suggested for other contemporary ceramic wares in other regions of the American Southwest and northern Mexico (Crown 1994; VanPool 2003). This subject is explored further in the next chapter.

CERAMIC TYPES

Archaeologists use the concept of type, defined as a group of ceramic vessels that consistently show the same methods of manufacture and decoration, to identify spatially restricted and temporally persistent traditions of pottery production (Colton 1943, 1953; Colton and Hargrave 1937). There is a long tradition of defining ceramic types in the American Southwest, with the result that these categories are well established in the literature (Carlson 1970; Colton 1956; Eckert 2006b; Habicht-Mauche 1993; Hays-Gilpin and van Hartesveldt 1998; Kidder and Shepard 1936) and help make comparisons of ceramic assemblages between sites and regions possible (Mills 1993). For this study, types are useful in that they provide a sense of the *overall* combination of design attributes as well as reflecting the diversity of the ceramic assemblage as a whole.

TABLE 6.5. Percentage of locally produced Pueblo IV pottery types recovered from Phases 2 and 3 at Hummingbird Pueblo and Pottery Mound.

Decorated Ware	Hummingbird Pueblo		Pottery Mound	
	Phase 2	Phase 3	Phase 2	Phase 3
Western Pueblo Glaze Ware, Local Copies				
Heshotauthla types	3	0	0	<1
Kwakina Polychrome	2	0	1	<1
Pinnawa Gl/w	<1	0	0	<1
Kechipawan Polychrome	<1	0	0	0
Rio Grande Glaze Ware				
Early Rio Grande Gl/r	73	79	67	56
Early Rio Grande Gl/y	3	6	7	8
Early Rio Grande Gl/poly	8	15	22	29
Intermediate Rio Grande Glaze	0	0	0	2
Lower Rio Puerco Types				
Hummingbird R/bf	10	0	1	<1
Pottery Mound Polychrome	<1	0	1	2
Hidden Mountain Polychrome	0	0	1	2
Total sherds for each phase	1,074	55	177	4,754

Among the whole vessels examined, three ceramic types were common (see table 6.1; see appendix A for detailed type descriptions): Agua Fria Glaze-on-red (Gl/r), San Clemente Polychrome, and Pottery Mound Polychrome each comprise 28 percent of the locally produced types. The remainder of types includes Cieneguilla Glaze-on-yellow (Gl/y) and Polychrome (11 percent) and a type defined for the first time in this research, Hidden Mountain Polychrome (5 percent). Agua Fria Gl/r, San Clemente Polychrome, and Cieneguilla Gl/y and Polychrome are all early Rio Grande Glaze Ware types that date to the fourteenth and fifteenth centuries. Agua Fria Gl/r is commonly found on sites throughout the central and southern districts of the Rio Grande region, while Cieneguilla Gl/y and Polychrome are restricted more to sites in the central Rio Grande district. San Clemente Polychrome is found, in small amounts, on sites in the central and southern portions of the Rio Grande region. Hidden Mountain and Pottery Mound Polychrome are types that appear to be restricted mostly to the study area, although sherds of Pottery Mound Polychrome have been reported from sites in the central and southern portions of the Rio Grande region (Hayes et al. 1981).

There is a greater variety of locally produced ceramic types evidenced in the sherds than in the whole vessels (table 6.5; see appendix A for description of types). The most common types of locally produced pottery are early Rio Grande Gl/r (including, in part, Agua Fria

Gl/r) and early Rio Grande Glaze-on-polychrome (Gl/poly; including, in part, San Clemente Polychrome).* Lesser amounts of other ceramic types include locally produced white ware types, local copies of Western Pueblo glaze ware, Rio Grande Gl/y (including Cieneguilla Gl/y), Intermediate Rio Grande Glaze Ware types, and types produced only in the Lower Rio Puerco area including Pottery Mound Polychrome, Hummingbird Red-on-buff, and Hidden Mountain Polychrome. As with the whole vessels, the variety of types present at both sites suggests that pottery may have signaled different levels of social boundaries because of visual clues such as color combinations and specific icons.

Of interest to the current analysis is that each of these types reflects different decorative styles as seen through different combinations of slip color, design style, and, in some instances, icons. For example, Hidden Mountain Polychrome is defined by a red-slipped interior, a bright white–slipped exterior, and the focus of design on a band on the exterior (an atypical design style). In addition to the bright white slip, serpent, eye, and lightning icons are common on this type (see tables 6.3 and 6.4), while birds and feathers are not. Visually, Hidden Mountain Polychrome vessels would have been strikingly different from all other pottery produced in the Lower Rio Puerco area, even at a distance. Not only is the use of a bright white slip uncommon in the study area, but its application on the exterior of bowls only occurs on this pottery type. Further, the focus of a glaze-painted design on the exterior of bowls would also have been distinct.

An example of a pottery type that was not as visually distinct as Hidden Mountain Polychrome, but still represents a unique combination of slip color, design style, and icons, is Pottery Mound Polychrome. This type is defined by a Sikyatki design style, the co-occurrence of bird and feather motifs, and the combination of yellow-buff and red slip color. Visually, the exterior of Pottery Mound Polychrome vessels is identical to the majority of pottery produced in the study area—that is, red slipped with either no design or a simple design such as Xs or slashes. As such, only people within the immediate vicinity of the bowl (such as those being served from it or eating out of it) would see the unique set of design attributes that define this pottery type. If this suite of decorative attributes was used to signal a social boundary, it would have been on a different level than those attributes found on Hidden Mountain Polychrome.

The co-occurrence of these design attributes—specific slip colors, icons, and design styles—may represent the emphasis on social boundaries between specific groups within the Lower Rio Puerco area. However, what these groups were—immigrants and local residents, different groups of immigrants, different groups of local residents, or possibly ritual societies—requires examination of technological styles associated with these suites of design attributes. As technological attributes were not (and in many instances could not be) recorded on the whole vessels, such an analysis requires examination of the sherd assemblage. The

---

*Pottery Mound Polychrome and San Clemente Polychrome both have the yellow-buff and red slip color combination. Since these two types are distinguished largely upon design style (impossible to see on most sherds) and the use of red filler in design motifs on Pottery Mound Polychrome, some sherds typed as San Clemente Polychrome were probably part of Pottery Mound Polychrome vessels. This is the nature of identification of sherds but should be kept in mind in this analysis.

following section explores the social boundaries between communities of identity through examination of whether suites of design attributes, as represented by ceramic types, co-occur with technological traits.

Identifying Social Boundaries:
The Relationship between Technological and Decorative Styles

In the previous chapters, technological attributes were examined to detect the presence of different communities of practice in the Lower Rio Puerco area. I established that variation in technological attributes reflected different social groups, including immigrant and indigenous, living within the study area. The two technological attributes examined in this section—temper and surface treatment—were selected based upon this previous analysis. Rock temper and self-slip on decorated wares were identified with potters from the southern portion of the Lower Rio Puerco area. Sherd temper and various surface treatments, mostly thin, washy slip or self-slip, were identified with potters from the northern portion of the study area. Immigrant potters from the Zuni district used sherd temper and thick slips, while immigrant potters from the Hopi district manufactured pots with no temper. Hopi Yellow Ware from Pottery Mound also indicates that potters from the Hopi Mesas used either a well-polished self-slip or a well-polished thick slip as surface treatment on their vessels.

In this section, I argue that communities of practice identified in the previous chapters were often also communities of identity. My argument is based upon an examination of the relationship between technological styles and suites of design attributes. If suites of design attributes (reflected in pottery types) were used to emphasize social boundaries between groups with different migration histories, decorated types and technological attributes should consistently co-occur on vessels. For example, if the distinctiveness of Hidden Mountain Polychrome was used to emphasize potters' unique history from the Zuni district, then one would expect this type to be exclusively tempered with sherd and have a well-polished self-slip. If, on the other hand, Hidden Mountain Polychrome was produced by various potters, regardless of their migration history, then one would expect the pottery type to vary in terms of both temper and surface treatment. I found a co-occurrence of technological attributes on *some* pottery types, suggesting that certain decorated ceramic types were used to emphasize group identity associated with different habitus, which in turn reflect different migration histories and regions of origin.

During the first half of the 1300s, represented by Phase 2 in this study, two decorated ceramic types at Hummingbird Pueblo co-occur with distinctive temper choice and surface treatment (table 6.6). Local copies of Western Pueblo glaze ware and Hummingbird Red-on-buff are always tempered with sherd and have a thick slip (table 6.6). These two types are also visually distinctive in terms of their slip colors. Local copies of Western Pueblo glaze ware are the only types produced during this period that have a bright white slip. Similarly, Hummingbird Red-on-buff has a distinctive buff-colored slip unlike any other type produced throughout the region. However, this type does not have glaze paint, but rather a matte red paint. I suggest that these two types were produced by immigrants from the Zuni district,

TABLE 6.6. Row percentages of decorated types by technological attributes for major decorated types by phase.

	Northern Portion of Study Area		Acoma/ Zuni	Southern Portion of Study Area			Hopi	
Temper	sherd	sherd	sherd	rock	rock	rock	none	TOTAL COUNT
Surface	self-slip	thin slip	thick slip	self-slip	thin slip	thick slip	thick slip	
Phase 2 (early 1300s) Hummingbird Pueblo								
Western Pueblo glaze copies	—	—	100	—	—	—	—	45
Early Rio Grande Gl/r	6	39	22	20	2	11	—	840
Early Rio Grande Gl/poly	4	20	36	9	—	31	—	77
Hummingbird R/bf	—	—	100	—	—	—	—	90
Phase 3 (late 1300s/early 1400s) Pottery Mound								
Western Pueblo glaze copies	—	—	100	—	—	—	—	19
Early Rio Grande Gl/r	—	31	4	10	27	28	1	1413
Early Rio Grande Gl/poly	—	9	—	—	34	55	2	1208
Pottery Mound Polychrome	—	—	5	—	30	64	2	106
Hidden Mountain Polychrome	—	—	100	—	—	—	—	103

and their descendants, and were used to help emphasize the social boundary between themselves and other groups already living in Hummingbird Pueblo. Local copies of Western Pueblo glaze ware were very similar to vessels made in the Zuni district. Hummingbird Red-on-buff, on the other hand, incorporates new color combinations that reflect design choices made by immigrant potters in a new social context where emphasizing their unique migration history may have been a priority.

I detected no other social boundary, such as the one defined for Zuni immigrants, in the Phase 2 Hummingbird Pueblo assemblage. The majority of decorated types during the early 1300s is early Rio Grande Gl/r (including Agua Fria Gl/r). Numerous combinations of temper and surface treatment were recorded for this early type. Similarly, early Rio Grande Gl/poly (including San Clemente Polychrome) had a wide range of technological variation. These two types appear to have been produced by various communities of practice and were not used as a means to emphasize differences between these communities. Due to sample size issues discussed previously, the Phase 3 (late 1300s/early 1400s) Hummingbird Pueblo and Phase 2 (early 1300s) Pottery Mound assemblages were not analyzed.

Three decorated ceramic types at Pottery Mound co-occur with temper choice and surface treatment in the late 1300/early 1400 ceramic assemblage, represented by Phase 3 in this study (table 6.6). The first two types, local copies of Western Pueblo glaze wares and Hidden Mountain Polychrome, are tempered with sherd and have a thick slip (table 6.6). During Phase 3, these two types are the only ones to incorporate a bright white slip. As at Hummingbird Pueblo during Phase 2, these types reflect the emphasis placed on a unique migration history by Zuni immigrants. The third pottery type, Pottery Mound Polychrome, is usually tempered with rock and has a thick slip. Although not as strong a pattern, this tends to be true for Early Rio Grande Gl/poly (including San Clemente Polychrome) as well. Pottery Mound Polychrome comprises less than 3 percent of the decorated sherd assemblage at Pottery Mound, but it comprises 24 percent of the whole vessel assemblage. I believe this disparity is the result of an archaeological typology that results in some sherds of Pottery Mound Polychrome being identified as Early Rio Grande Gl/poly—an important issue that cannot be rectified in this study but should be addressed in future research at the site.

None of the communities of practice I identified in previous chapters had a habitus that included a combination of rock temper and a thick slip; in other words, Pottery Mound Polychrome and some examples of Early Rio Grande Gl/poly appear to be produced using a new habitus. Based upon the incorporation of the Sikyatki design style and a yellow-buff slip, Hibben (1975) and Charles Voll (1961) have argued that Pottery Mound Polychrome was produced by immigrants from the Hopi mesas. Three other lines of evidence help support their speculation as well as explain the combination of rock temper and thick slip on these vessels. First, slipped vessels produced in the Hopi district also have a well-polished, thick slip. Second, a low percentage of Pottery Mound Polychrome is untempered; untempered pottery is common on the Hopi mesas but is not really technologically feasible using the clays in the study area. I suggested in the last chapter that the presence of locally produced untempered vessels may reflect Hopi immigrant potters experimenting with local clays. Third, and finally, when Hopi potters found that they could not work with local untempered clay, they may have turned to local potters for advice. As a result, they would have incorporated rock temper when preparing their clays.

Similar to the early 1300s ceramic assemblage at Hummingbird Pueblo, the majority of decorated types during the late 1300s and early 1400s at Pottery Mound is Rio Grande Gl/r (including Agua Fria Gl/r). Again, all possible combinations of temper and surface treatment were recorded for this type, reflecting numerous habitus for pottery decoration. Pottery Mound potters do not appear to have used Rio Grande Gl/r to emphasize differences between them.

The co-occurrence of technological style (as reflected in temper group and surface treatment) by decorative style (as reflected in ceramic type) is stronger for some pottery types than for others. I believe this is the result of at least four aspects of human behavior. First, ceramic types are classifications created by archaeologists to answer specific research questions and are not "real" in the minds of the potters painting them. I defined my types to reflect a suite of decorative attributes, but my understanding of the multiple habitus for decorating pottery in the study area is imperfect. Second, some ceramic types defined in this study were made longer than others; as a result, those types might be expected to have more decorative and technological variation.

Third, what archaeologists define as different pottery types may have been used by residents of the Lower Rio Puerco area in different social contexts to signal different information. For example, Zuni district immigrants may have been the only people to produce Hidden Mountain Polychrome, while potters from different areas (including the Zuni district) may have produced early Rio Grande Gl/r. Zuni immigrants may have used Hidden Mountain Polychrome in social contexts where signaling affiliation with their specific migration history was important and used early Rio Grande Gl/r in social contexts where village membership was more important to emphasize.

Fourth, the use of a specific temper type and surface treatment reflects *tendencies* of potters. These tendencies may change through time, as families move across the landscape and are faced with new social situations and new environments (e.g., changes in raw material). For example, white ware pottery from the Lower Rio Puerco area produced during the late twelfth and thirteenth centuries *tends* to be divisible by archaeologists using surface treatment and temper choice into a northern and southern tradition. However, this pattern is not perfect. Throughout time, some families who lived in the northern portion of the study area may have chosen to move to the southern portion, and vice versa. Such moves would have potentially changed social allegiances and networks, and potters may have chosen to decorate their pottery to reflect their new social situation. However, this change in decoration may or may not have corresponded with a change in temper choice and surface treatment. Such behavior would result in *tendencies* for a relationship to exist between a decorative style and a technological style.

Conclusion

Some potters in the Lower Rio Puerco area chose to use their products to emphasize a social identity that reflected their unique migration history. However, different potter communities were reaffirming such social boundaries on at least two different levels. During the early 1300s at Hummingbird Pueblo, and the late 1300s/early 1400s at Pottery Mound, immigrant potters from the Zuni district used white and buff slips that would have been noticeably different from the more typical red slip pottery, even at a distance. Vessels slipped in white or buff could have signaled the potter's identity from across a room, kiva, or plaza space. Because of this public distinctiveness, the scale of social boundary maintenance emphasized by these slip colors would reasonably have been below the scale of the village, but above the scale of the immediate family—possibly at the scale of the lineage, sodality, or other social grouping that divided villages between immigrant and local groups. Additionally, these vessels may have been used in events when a specific family was hosting a meal, as a reminder to the guests of their hosts' unique heritage.

During the late 1300s/early 1400s at Pottery Mound, some potters chose to decorate the interior of their bowls with a yellow-buff slip, unique design style, and specific icons. I argue that at least some of these potters came from the Hopi district. Only people within the immediate vicinity of a bowl would notice the decoration on the interior. As such, the interior of bowls would have been signaling group affiliation to people who were probably members of the same intimate social group. Decorations on the interior of the vessels may have served to remind members of their group obligations and reaffirm their group's unique heritage.

Despite the diversity of pottery traditions in the Lower Rio Puerco ceramic assemblage, it should not be forgotten that the majority of pottery produced in the study area during the fourteenth and early fifteenth century was glaze painted and red slipped. The adoption of glaze paint and red slips may reflect an atmosphere in which diverse groups of people—including Western Pueblo immigrants and indigenous groups from both the northern and southern portions of the study area—were attempting to socially integrate. One important mechanism of social integration is a shared ritual system. The next chapter examines the nature of ritual practice in the Lower Rio Puerco area and discusses how residents of this area negotiated new social boundaries within the arena provided by a new ritual system.

CHAPTER SEVEN

Social Integration and Ideology

A New Ritual System along the Lower Rio Puerco

In the previous chapter, we saw that different suites of technological and decorative attributes on glaze-decorated pottery reflect communities of identity with different migration histories living together in the Lower Rio Puerco villages. These groups included immigrants (and their descendants) from the Western Pueblo region and indigenous groups with different local histories in the north and south of the study area. Although these groups decorated their pottery somewhat differently, they all produced vessels with glaze paint and red slip. Because of the similarity of decoration on bowl exteriors, we saw that emphasizing boundaries between groups with different social histories was not always a priority.

This chapter argues that potters at Pottery Mound and Hummingbird Pueblo adopted the Western Pueblo tradition of glaze-decorated pottery during the fourteenth century for socio-religious reasons. Specifically, I link glaze-painted pottery with a larger suite of characteristics associated with a new ritual system that focused on social integration and community well-being (Adams 1991; Crown 1994). Social dynamics during the period under examination were affected by disparate groups living together in close proximity and in higher population densities than any previous period (Adams and Duff 2004). As such, residents of the Lower Rio Puerco villages would have had to find mechanisms to cope with the tensions associated with these new social conditions. Ritual has been argued to be a successful means of social integration in such situations (Adams 1991; VanPool and VanPool 2003). After examining ritual developments in the Pueblo Southwest generally during the fourteenth century, I identify a new suite of ritual characteristics (including glaze-painted pottery) in the Lower Rio Puerco area. In the next chapter, I discuss more fully the ritual implications of this new suite of characteristics.

Post-1300 Ritual Developments in the Pueblo Southwest

The development of new ritual systems generally, and the origin of the katsina ritual specifically, during the fourteenth century has received considerable attention in the last 20 years of Southwest archaeological research (Adams 1991; Carlson 1982; Crown 1994; Duff 2002; Ferg 1982; Graves and Eckert 1998; Schaafsma 1980; Schaafsma and Schaafsma 1974; Spielmann 1998b; Vivian 1994). E. Charles Adams (1991) examined the distribution of the Fourmile ceramic style, mask iconography (on pottery, kiva murals, and rock art), rectangular kivas, and enclosed plazas to understand the development of the katsina ritual. Drawing mostly on data from the Western Pueblo region, he argues that sometime during the late 1200s and early 1300s, katsina ritual developed in the Upper Little Colorado River area. It then rapidly spread throughout much of the Pueblo world. He believes a second version of katsina ritual developed in the late 1300s in the Hopi area and spread throughout much of the Western Pueblo region and portions of the Rio Grande region, replacing the earlier version. Adams's argument for a specific geographic origin of katsina ritual is problematic due to his lack of understanding and examination of similar contemporaneous developments in the Rio Grande region; however, his documenting of a new suite of material culture that appears during the late 1200s in the Western Pueblo region is an important contribution to our understanding of the development of katsina ritual.

Schaafsma has detailed iconographic changes in rock art and the implications these changes have for new ideological developments in the Rio Grande region (Schaafsma 1980, 1981, 1992, 1994, 2000; Schaafsma and Schaafsma 1974). Sometime after AD 1300, rock art in the Rio Grande area underwent sudden stylistic and content changes (Schaafsma 1980:26). This new style, the Rio Grande Rock Art Style, is notable for its elaborate representations of masked beings that have been interpreted as katsinas. Schaafsma argues that this style evolved out of the Jornada Mogollon Rock Art Style, which developed in the area southeast of the Rio Grande area. There are similarities in ceramic designs between the two regions as well (Stewart et al. 1980). The most problematic aspect of Schaafsma's work is dating the rock art. She provides a beginning date of AD 1325 for the Rio Grande Rock Art Style based on similarities with ceramic designs (Schaafsma and Schaafsma 1974). Adams (1994:115) has argued that the style may have a beginning date as late as the 1400s based on similarities with kiva mural depictions. What is important from Schaafsma's work is that sometime after AD 1300, a new ideology developed or was introduced into the Rio Grande area, and this new ideology appears to have moved into the region from the south.

Crown (1994) has argued for the existence of a pan-Southwestern Regional Cult, of which katsina ritual is but a part. By examining stylistic, compositional, and technological data from Salado Polychrome pottery, Crown tested four models of production and distribution of these ceramic types. She argues that the Pinedale design style represents a regional belief system that developed throughout much of the Pueblo Southwest during the 1300s (Crown 1994:214–17). The multiple archaeological contexts in which vessels with a Pinedale style are found suggest that the style was not restricted in function nor related to a specific social group. Crown interprets the birds and snakes present on this style to represent water, earth, weather, and fertility. She believes these relate to a Southwestern earth/fertility cult that coalesced from earlier traditions during the large-scale migrations of the late 1200s and early 1300s. This cult was mainly concerned with fertility and group well-being.

Some researchers (Graves 1996; Potter 2000; Spielmann 1998b) have focused on the role of communal feasting in the fourteenth-century Pueblo ritual system. Based on the depictions of decorated pottery from kiva murals as well as an increase in vessel sizes between thirteenth- to fourteenth-century bowls in sites from the Rio Grande area, Katherine Spielmann (1998b) argues that an integral part of the new ritual system adopted in this region during the 1300s included an emphasis on communal feasting, as well as on water-related ritual activities. William Graves (1996) found similar evidence for feasting in the Salinas area and further argues that one village hosted large-scale feasts more often than other villages based on the higher frequency of imported glaze-decorated bowls at this site. Based on an increase in fauna that was conducive to community hunting techniques and large-scale collection, James Potter (2000) has argued that communal feasting became an important aspect of ritual and social integration in the post-1275 Zuni region.

These researchers all view feasting as an important integrative mechanism during the fourteenth and fifteenth centuries; however, archaeological evidence for feasting in the Zuni area appears to have focused on intravillage integration, while feasting in the Rio Grande region also had an intervillage component. Although the preferential hosting of large feasts by some Rio Grande villages may reflect the potential for prestige enhancement and self-aggrandizement by individuals within those villages (Spielmann 1998b), feasting also appears to have provided a social environment in which religious beliefs could be reaffirmed and various formal and informal social networks could be maintained.

Archaeologists concerned with fourteenth-century ritual systems have noted that ritual practice appears to differ by region, and often by village, suggesting that the new ritual system was diverse (Duff 2002; Eckert and Cordell 2004; Graves and Eckert 1998; Spielmann 1998a). Specifically, Duff (2002) explored the development of ritual in the Upper Little Colorado River region. He sees ritual in this region as incorporating different practices and sodalities that developed among various social groups and within separate villages. The result was a region with an eclectic mix of ritual practice and numerous ritual specialists who could be recruited by other villages for their unique esoteric knowledge.

To summarize, throughout the Pueblo Southwest ideological systems seem to have undergone a change sometime around AD 1300. This "new" ideology was seen in the emergence of a masked iconography on a variety of media, changes in ceramic decoration including a suite of icons focused on group well-being, the adoption of the rectangular kiva in some areas, and community feasting. This system probably did not develop in any one region, or was represented by any one ceramic or architectural type, but, as Crown (1994) suggests, was the result of concepts and social concerns shared throughout the greater Pueblo region. Different subsets of concepts could have been selectively adopted and combined to fit the specific needs of individual communities or villages (Eckert and Cordell 2004). The results would not have been a uniform religion, but a group of shared ideas and practices worked and reworked.

Post-1300 Ritual Developments in the Lower Rio Puerco Area

In this section, I identify changes in the ritual system practiced by residents living in the Lower Rio Puerco area during the fourteenth and fifteenth centuries through identification of a new suite of ritual characteristics. In an attempt to cope with disparate social groups and relatively high population densities in newly established villages, residents of the study area appear to have adopted aspects of the new ritual practices that were sweeping over portions of the Pueblo Southwest during this period (Adams 1991; Crotty 1987; Crown 1994; Kenagy 1986; Schaafsma 1980, 1981, 1992, 1994, 2000; Spielmann 1998b). Based on ethnographic analogy and previous work by other archaeologists, Crown (1994) has outlined material expectations for the association of pottery with the spread of a new ritual system. These expectations include association of pottery with a single burial ritual, production of pottery as mortuary furniture, production of pottery for ritual consumption, differential distribution of pottery in ritual contexts, imagery indicative of a religious ideology, and independent evidence for the spread of new ritual. Due to the various roles pottery can play in multiple contexts as well as the evidence for a new ritual system sweeping over the Pueblo Southwest during the period under examination, Crown's expectations (with the exception of production of pottery for ritual consumption and differential distribution of pottery in ritual contexts, for which there are currently not enough data to examine) should be considered in light of the adoption of glaze-decorated pottery in the Lower Rio Puerco study area.

ASSOCIATION OF GLAZE-DECORATED POTTERY WITH A SINGLE BURIAL RITUAL AND PRODUCTION OF GLAZE-DECORATED POTTERY AS MORTUARY FURNITURE

If glaze-decorated pottery was associated with a new ritual system that required specific burial practices, then the pottery may be associated with a specific mortuary treatment (Crown 1994). No burial data are available from Hummingbird Pueblo; however, an unpublished burial report (Hibben 1993) from Pottery Mound describes 41 burials recovered from the Duck Unit group. These burials were all located in dense trash-fill immediately north of the roomblock that comprises the northeast corner of the main mound (see figure 3.3). At the time of excavation (1979–1986), this area was being eroded by the Rio Puerco. Data recorded for each burial vary in detail.

Burials that contain glaze-decorated pottery cannot be segregated from other burials by gender, age, alignment of body, treatment, or associated grave goods. Of the 41 burials described, 17 had glaze-decorated pottery. Of these 17 burials, burial practices varied widely. Adult females, adult males, and infants were buried with glaze-decorated pottery.

Some bodies were wrapped in reed matting or leather and cotton, while other bodies did not appear to have been wrapped. When recorded, glaze-decorated pottery was placed in various locations within a grave, including over the head, over the left shoulder, at the small of the back, on the knees, on the arms, and below the pelvis. Burial alignments also varied, including east, west, northeast, southeast, northwest, and southwest. Finally, nonceramic grave goods in burials that also had glaze-decorated pottery varied but included stone tools, clay effigies, stone effigies, corncobs (placed within bowls), blue corn pollen, pipes, bone awls, beads, turquoise, and prayer sticks. These data suggest that glaze-decorated pottery was not associated with a highly specific burial practice.

Similarly, glaze-decorated pottery was not produced specifically as mortuary furniture. I recorded use wear on 60 percent of the whole glaze-decorated vessels associated with burials. This use wear includes scrapes on the bottom of bowl interiors, well-worn bowl exteriors and jar bases, and repair holes. The extensive amount of glaze-decorated sherds recovered from trash contexts further supports the idea that this pottery was manufactured for uses above and beyond that of mortuary furniture.

IMAGERY INDICATIVE OF A RELIGIOUS IDEOLOGY

As indicated in the previous chapter, all of the icons identified in this study were on glaze-decorated pottery; no icons were identified on the white wares produced in the region during the late 1200s and early 1300s (table 7.1). The introduction of a new suite of icons associated with glaze-decorated pottery indicates the presence of a new iconic system in the Lower Rio Puerco area during the 1300s. The most common icons recorded on sherds include eyes, snakes/lightning, and birds, with more than one incident of serpents, masked figures, stars, feathers, clouds, and dragonflies also being recorded. Most of these icons are known ethnographically to represent water and were used in fertility ceremonies (Crotty 1995; Dutton 1963; Kenagy 1977; Parsons 1996).

Crown (1994) found a similar iconic system to exist on Salado Polychrome, a ceramic type contemporaneous with glaze-decorated wares but produced to the southwest of the study area near the Arizona–New Mexico border. Based on the ethnographic literature, she argued that this iconic system reflected a concern for fertility, weather control, and community well-being. She further argued that this iconic system was associated with the spread of the Southwestern Regional Cult, an ideology and ritual system that integrated disparate groups. In the study area, all these common icons crosscut most glaze-decorated ceramic types (see table 6.4). In other words, potters, regardless of their group affiliations as identified in the previous chapter, were choosing from the same suite of motifs. This suggests that these icons were not related to signaling group identity based on migration histories in Lower Rio Puerco villages, but rather may have been associated with concepts of universal concern, such as rain, fertility, or group well-being.

This new iconic system on pottery is also present on kiva murals at Pottery Mound, further supporting the idea that a new ritual system, of which glaze-decorated pottery was but a part, was introduced into the study area. Iconic motifs on kiva murals are more detailed than those on pottery, allowing researchers to identify birds to species (Emslie and Hargrave

TABLE 7.1. Number of occurrences of icons by ceramic type as recorded on sherds.

Ceramic Type	Serpent	Mask	Eye	Star	Lightning/Snake	Bird	Feather	Dragonfly	Cloud
White wares	—	—	—	—	—	—	—	—	—
St. Johns types	—	—	—	—	—	—	—	—	—
Western Pueblo glaze ware types	—	—	20	—	9	—	—	—	—
Early Rio Grande Gl/r	2	2	32	5	89	15	1	6	9
Early Rio Grande Gl/y	—	1	10	—	23	1	1	—	6
Early Rio Grande Gl/poly	—	—	19	2	39	4	—	—	2
Intermediate Rio Grande Glaze	—	—	2	1	—	1	—	1	1
Lower Rio Puerco R/b	—	—	1	—	1	—	—	—	—
Pottery Mound Polychrome	—	1	5	—	3	2	—	1	1
Hidden Mountain Polychrome	—	—	4	—	4	1	—	—	—

1978), specific ceremonial personages (Crotty 1987, 1995; Vivian 1994), and the use of specific ritual paraphernalia including decorated pottery, prayer sticks, spears, shields, and animal skins (Hibben 1975; Walt 1981). Such detail has led numerous researchers to suggest that katsina ritual was practiced at Pottery Mound.

Although a part of the Southwestern Regional Cult as defined by Crown (1994), katsina ritual is specifically focused on masked dancers believed to be katsina spirits. Adams (1991) associated the spread of katsina ritual in the 1300s with the adoption of masked iconography and the Fourmile design style on pottery. Kiva murals at Pottery Mound, as well as ceramic iconography from both Pottery Mound and Hummingbird Pueblo, portray masked figures. Adams (1991) considers the Sikyatki design style identified on Pottery Mound Polychrome and kiva murals as related to, and possibly a type of, the Fourmile style. Similarly, both Crotty (1987, 1995) and Vivian (1994) recognize the masked dancers portrayed on Pottery Mound murals as part of katsina ceremonialism. The similarities between many of these portrayals of masked dancers and modern Pueblo katsinas argue strongly in favor of the presence of the katsina ritual at Pottery Mound. How katsina ritual articulated with other social processes at Pottery Mound will be explored presently.

INDEPENDENT EVIDENCE FOR THE SPREAD OF A NEW RITUAL SYSTEM

Patricia Crown (1994) argued that evidence for the spread of a new ritual system could also be found in evidence independent of pottery. Independent evidence for the spread of a new ritual system into the Lower Rio Puerco area comes from both architectural and faunal data. In terms of architecture, Adams (1991) associated the spread of katsina ritual in the 1300s with the adoption of the enclosed plaza space and the rectangular kiva. The maps presented in chapter 3 from Pottery Mound and Hummingbird Pueblo show that both sites have multiple plazas; however, only Hummingbird Pueblo has well-defined, partially enclosed plazas. Enclosed, partially enclosed, and open plazas are features common to large sites throughout the Pueblo Southwest and Casas Grandes region (Cordell 1997). These features probably served as the focus of ceremonial activities within large villages during various eras. The adoption of a specific type of plaza space cannot be associated with the spread of a specific ideology, nor the production of glaze-decorated pottery during the 1300s. However, the presence of plaza spaces at both villages reflects a new community space in the study area and implies a ritual system that, at least in part, could have consisted of public ceremony (Ruscavage-Barz 1999).

Adams (1991) also associated the spread of katsina ritual with the adoption of the rectangular kiva. Prior to AD 1250, the rectangular kiva was predominantly found in the Mogollon region of the American Southwest. Starting sometime in the late 1200s, the rectangular kiva became the predominant kiva form in villages throughout the Western Pueblo region (Adams 1991; Adler 1989; Cordell 1997; Lipe 1989). Rectangular kivas have also been identified in the Rio Grande region at some sites established in the late 1200s (Biella 1979; Cordell 1975; Kidder 1958). Because rectangular kivas are often incorporated into a roomblock, rather than as freestanding structures, identification of these ceremonial rooms often requires excavation. As such, only two rectangular kivas have thus far been identified at Hummingbird Pueblo based on the presence of flagstones, a bench, and a ventilator. Both of these structures are smaller than similar structures identified at Pottery Mound. At Pottery Mound, 15 freestanding rectangular kivas have been identified, along with one freestanding round kiva (Hibben 1955, 1966, 1975). The rectangular kiva represents a new ceremonial structure in the Lower Rio Puerco area during the 1300s; prior to this time, kivas in the study area were round. Further, similar designs on murals in these kivas and glaze-decorated pottery suggest that the two were associated (Adams 1991) and may have been adopted together as part of a new ritual system.

Another source of ritual data independent of pottery in the study area comes from the faunal assemblage. Various researchers have noted the importance of birds in modern Pueblo ritual, especially feathers from raptors and perching birds (Bunzel 1992; Dutton 1963; Ladd 1963; Parsons 1925; Stephen 1936). Although some archaeologists have argued that most wild birds were hunted, at least in part, for food (Emslie 1981; Harris 1976), Potter (1997) and Charmion McKusick (1981, 1982; Creel and McKusick 1994) have pointed out that there appears to have been very little consumption of most bird species among prehistoric Pueblos; this includes turkey, whose primary importance may have been feathers for ritual paraphernalia such as prayer sticks (Ladd 1963). However, turkey is consumed by some modern Pueblo groups (Gnabasik 1981), as are other ground-dwelling species of birds such as grouse and quail (Neusius 1985). In the archaeological record, birds and feathers are portrayed on rock art (Schaafsma 1980), but never in a hunting context; however, birds are portrayed on Classic period (AD 1000–1150) Mimbres bowls in both hunting and ritual contexts (Munson 2000; Shaffer and Gardner 1997; Shaffer et al. 1996). Birds portrayed on

Table 7.2. Summary of bird taxa from Phase 1 Hummingbird Pueblo.

Scientific Name	Common Name	NISP	% NISP	MNI	% MNI
IDENTIFIED REMAINS		**9**	**19**	**3**	**100**
Class Aves	**Birds**	**9**	**19**	**3**	**100**
Order Anseriformes	Swans, Geese, Ducks	1	2	1	33
Anas sp.	Ducks	1	2	1	33
Order Galliformes	Gallinaceous Birds	8	17	2	67
Family Phasianidae	Grouse, Quails, and Allies	1	2	1	33
Callipepla sp.	Quail	1	2	1	33
Subfamily Meleagridinae	Turkeys	7	15	1	33
Meleagris gallopavo	Turkey	7	15	1	33
UNIDENTIFIED REMAINS		**38**	**81**	**n/a**	**n/a**
Class Aves	**Birds**	**38**	**81**	**n/a**	**n/a**
	indeterminate birds	4	8	n/a	n/a
	small birds	5	11	n/a	n/a
	medium birds	4	8	n/a	n/a
	large birds	25	53	n/a	n/a
TOTAL AVES REMAINS		**47**	**100**	**3**	**100**

kivas murals at Pottery Mound—including raptors, roadrunners, parrots, turkeys, waterfowl, and hummingbirds—are always shown in a ritual context, either sitting on or around masked dancers; there are no portrayals of birds being consumed for food on these murals (Crotty 1990; Emslie and Hargrave 1978; Hibben 1975).

Faunal data (tables 7.2–7.4), combined with ethnographic accounts and kiva mural depictions, suggest that residents of the Lower Rio Puerco area began to incorporate feathers from various bird species into ritual during the 1300s. Wild birds (as opposed to turkey) never comprise more than 1 percent of the total faunal assemblage at Hummingbird Pueblo and Pottery Mound (see appendix D for summary of entire faunal assemblage). This suggests that if they were hunted for food, they were not relied upon as a subsistence source. A breakdown of bird bone by species and phase helps illuminate the types of birds and feathers collected by Lower Rio Puerco residents. During the late 1200s (Phase 1 in table 7.2) at Hummingbird Pueblo, there are no perching birds or raptors in the avifauna assemblage. During the early 1300s (Phase 2 in table 7.3) at Hummingbird Pueblo and the late 1300s (Phase 3 in table 7.4) at Pottery Mound, raptors make up the majority of wild bird species, however perching and waterbird bones are also present in trash middens. All of these birds were available, at least seasonally, in the immediate vicinity of the Lower Rio Puerco valley (Emslie 1981), and so changes in exchange networks cannot account for the lack of raptor species in Phase 1. These data, combined with the ethnographic and kiva mural data described above, suggest that the

TABLE 7.3. Summary of bird taxa from Phase 2 Hummingbird Pueblo.

Scientific Name	Common Name	NISP	% NISP	MNI	% MNI
IDENTIFIED REMAINS		210	69	8	100
Class Aves	Birds	210	69	n/a	n/a
Order Anseriformes	Swans, Geese, Ducks	2	1	1	12
Anas sp.	Ducks	2	1	1	12
Order Falconiformes	Vultures, Hawks, Falcons	19	6	3	38
Indeterminate Falconiformes	Hawks, Falcons	11	4	n/a	n/a
Family Accipitridae	Eagles, Hawks	4	1	3	38
Buteo swainsoni	Swainson's Hawk	1	0	1	12
Buteo jamaicensis	Red-Tailed Hawk	2	1	1	12
Buteo lagopus	Rough-Legged Hawk	1	0	1	12
Order Galliformes	Gallinaceous Birds	187	61	4	50
Family Phasianidae	Grouse, Quails, and Allies	5	2	1	12
Callipepla sp.	Quail	5	2	1	12
Subfamily Meleagridinae	Turkeys	84	27	3	38
Meleagris gallopavo	Turkey	93	30	3	38
Order Passeriformes	Perching Birds	2	1	n/a	n/a
Indeterminate Passeriformes	Unidentified Perching Birds	2	1	n/a	n/a
UNIDENTIFIED REMAINS		95	31	n/a	n/a
Class Aves	Birds	95	31	n/a	n/a
	indeterminate birds	4	1	n/a	n/a
	small birds	1	0	n/a	n/a
	medium birds	23	7	n/a	n/a
	large birds	67	22	n/a	n/a
TOTAL AVES REMAINS		305	100	8	100

collection of nonfood bird species began during Phase 2 in the study area, possibly in association with new ritual practices adopted at this time.

However, although the bird assemblage from Pottery Mound appears to be more diverse than the one from Hummingbird Pueblo, this is likely the result of sample size differences between the two sites, as five times the amount of fauna per cubic meter of excavation was identified at Pottery Mound when compared to Hummingbird Pueblo (table 7.5). Further, there were no identified wild bird species in the Phase 3 Hummingbird Pueblo assemblage or the Phase 2 Pottery Mound assemblage, but this is also probably a reflection of sample size rather than meaningful patterning. As bird bone is relatively uncommon, it is no surprise that it was not recovered from these two poorly represented phases.

TABLE 7.4. Summary of bird taxa from Phase 3 Pottery Mound.

Scientific Name	Common Name	NISP	% NISP	MNI	%MNI
IDENTIFIED REMAINS		**526**	**38**	**27**	**100**
Class Aves	**Birds**	**526**	**38**	**27**	**100**
Order Anseriformes	Swans, Geese, Ducks	4	0	1	4
Anas sp.	Ducks	4	0	1	4
Order Falconiformes	Vultures, Hawks, Falcons	27	2	3	3
Indeterminate Falconiformes	Hawks, Falcons	1	0	n/a	n/a
Family Accipitridae	Eagles, Hawks	21	1	1	4
Indeterminate Accipitridae	Eagles, Hawks	2	0	n/a	n/a
Accipiter sp.	Hawk	1	0	n/a	n/a
Buteo sp.	Hawk	17	1	n/a	n/a
Buteo lagopus	Rough-Legged Hawk	1	0	1	4
Family Falconidae	Falcons, Caracaras	5	0	2	7
Indeterminate Falconidae	Falcons, Caracaras	1	0	n/a	n/a
Falco sparverius	American Kestrel	4	0	1	4
Order Gruiformes	Cranes, Rails, and Allies	2	0	1	4
Family Gruidae	Cranes	2	0	1	4
Grus sp.	Crane	2	0	1	4
Order Galliformes	Gallinaceous Birds	448	33	18	67
Family Phasianidae	Grouse, Quails, and Allies	31	2	1	4
Callipepla sp.	Quail	30	2	n/a	n/a
Callipepla gambelii	Gambel's Quail	1	0	1	4
Subfamily Meleagridinae	Turkeys	417	30	17	63
Meleagris gallopavo	Turkey	417	30	17	63
Order Columbiformes	Pigeons, Doves	8	1	1	4
Family Columbidae	Pigeons, Doves	8	1	1	4
Zenaida macroura	Mourning Dove	8	1	1	4
Order Strigiformes	Owls	2	0	1	4
Indeterminate Strigiformes	Unidentified Owl	2	0	1	4
Order Piciformes	Woodpeckers	1	0	1	4
Family Picidae	Woodpeckers	1	0	1	4
Indeterminate Picidae	Unidentified Woodpecker	1	0	1	4
Order Passeriformes	Perching Birds	34	2	1	4
Indeterminate Passeriformes	Unidentified Perching Birds	26	2	n/a	n/a
Family Corvidae	Jays, Magpies, Crows	8	1	1	4
Indeterminate Corvidae	Unidentified Jays, Crows	6	0	n/a	n/a
Corvus corax	Common Raven	2	0	1	4
UNIDENTIFIED REMAINS		**840**	**61**	**n/a**	**n/a**
Class Aves	**Birds**	**840**	**61**	**n/a**	**n/a**
	indeterminate birds	5	0	n/a	n/a
	small birds	31	2	n/a	n/a
	medium birds	48	3	n/a	n/a
	large birds	756	55	n/a	n/a
TOTAL AVES REMAINS		**1366**	**99**	**27**	**100**

TABLE 7.5. Recovered artifact types and cubic meters of excavation by phase.

Site	Phase	Total Cubic Meters of Excavation	Pottery Count per Cubic Meter	Identified Fauna Count per Cubic Meter	Bird Count per Cubic Meter
Hummingbird Pueblo	1	1.9	1,167	901	47
Hummingbird Pueblo	2	5.6	2,225	1,241	305
Hummingbird Pueblo	3	0.2	422	496	0
Pottery Mound	2	0.5	94	65	0
Pottery Mound	3	7.0	8,199	5,874	1,366

SUMMARY

Much of the above data suggest that glaze-decorated pottery was adopted as part of a new ritual system in the Lower Rio Puerco region. There is independent architectural and faunal evidence for the spread of a new ritual system into the study area that is contemporaneous with the adoption of glaze-decorated pottery by local residents. Specifically, the initial appearance of the plaza and the adoption of the rectangular kiva suggest new forms of ritual space that could be associated with new ceremonial practices. Further, the increased collection of wild birds, probably for the use of their feathers, suggests a new suite of ritual paraphernalia. Finally, the icons present on glaze-decorated pottery are related to both the images on Pottery Mound kiva murals, as well as the iconic system associated with the spread of the Southwestern Regional Cult, including katsina ritual.

The Nature of Ritual in the Lower Rio Puerco Area

Residents of the Lower Rio Puerco area adopted a new ritual system similar to developments witnessed at the same time in other portions of the Southwest. This new ritual system was associated with specific material culture including glaze-decorated pottery slipped in a new range of color combinations, a new iconic system including masked figures, plaza space, rectangular kivas, and the use of a wide range of wild birds. Scholars most commonly argue that the new ideological developments that spread across the Pueblo Southwest during the 1300s were adopted as a means of socially integrating newly aggregated or aggregating communities (Adams 1991, 1994; Anderson 1951; Crown 1994; Schaafsma 1981, 1994; Schaafsma and Schaafsma 1974).

The data presented in the last section suggest that aspects of the Southwestern Regional Cult, concerned with controlling fertility and group well-being, were adopted in the Lower Rio Puerco area during the 1300s. One part of this cult, katsina ritual, was associated specifically with the introduction of masked iconography. Among the ethnographic Pueblos, katsina ritual effectively integrates members within a community by establishing important ceremonial relationships that crosscut kin groups (Connelly 1979:61; Titiev 1944:129), organizing groups to work on community projects (Washburn 1980:44), and enforcing proper social behavior (Adams 1991:157–58).

As with ethnographic Pueblo groups, aspects of katsina ritual, or the Southwestern Regional Cult in general, may have helped to integrate disparate social groups in the study area during the fourteenth century. First, the use of the plaza space for public ceremonies would have allowed larger groups of people to participate, either as performers or observers, in ceremonies than kivas would have. Second, the adoption of glaze-decorated pottery by all residents of the study area would have helped to crosscut kin-based social groups by providing visual clues that everyone was a member and believer in the same ritual system. Third, and finally, the newly adopted iconic system suggests that the associated ritual system was concerned with fertility and weather control. These would have been universal concerns to agriculturalists in the Southwest, regardless of individual migration history or kin affiliation.

The view of katsina ritual as social integrator has been challenged (Plog and Solometo 1997); this challenge can be expanded to include other fourteenth-century ideological developments. Rock art evidence from the southern Rio Grande suggests that katsina ritual in that area was associated with warriors (Schaafsma 2000; Schaafsma and Schaafsma 1974). Depictions of katsina-like figures carrying shields along with sun, bear, or star motifs are common (Schaafsma 1980:243–99). These icons are associated with war in modern Pueblo traditions (Schaafsma 1980:297–98). War motifs, although consistent in the archaeological record throughout the Southwest, appear far more frequently in the Rio Grande region (Schaafsma 1980). Some have speculated that the greater number of sociolinguistic groups in the modern Rio Grande region also existed in the past, which may explain the stronger emphasis on warriors in this area when compared to the Western Pueblo region (although modern day Zuni and Hopi both have warrior societies, see Parsons [1939] and Titiev [1944]). Communities in the Rio Grande area had to interact with disparate social groups while attempting to gain access to available resources. Katsina warriors could represent a response to the threats perceived by these groups when dealing with other peoples (Plog and Solometo 1996). However, the dichotomy of "us" versus "them" may have served to bind disparate groups within a village in the face of an external enemy, resulting in the integration of groups within a village but the segregating of groups between villages (Schaafsma 1994).

Three lines of evidence from the study area suggest that the new ritual system adopted in the Lower Rio Puerco villages may not have been as socially integrative as in some other contemporaneous villages. First, although all residents of the study area were producing glaze-decorated pottery, some decorative aspects on glaze-painted vessels continued to emphasize social boundaries between groups with different migration histories. Second, Crotty (1990) found that there is no central theme in the kiva murals of Pottery Mound. While murals at Kuaua and Gran Quivira consistently express egalitarian values and a concern for subsistence, murals at Pottery Mound express themes that range from elaborately dressed dancers to military capability to exhibition of valuable possessions. She argues that the display of material wealth reflected in the Pottery Mound murals was the result of rival lineages within the village vying for social and political dominance.

Third, multiple plazas and kivas at Hummingbird Pueblo and Pottery Mound may reflect a ritual practice in these villages that was less centralized than that of other contemporaneous villages. If kivas and plazas were the focus of socially integrative ritual during the Pueblo IV period (Adam 1991; Lipe 1989), then room-to-kiva (Lipe 1989; Steward 1937) and room-to-plaza ratios can be used as one proxy for measuring village social integration. I examined such ratios for Hummingbird Pueblo, Pottery Mound, and other Pueblo IV sites in the Rio Grande and Western Pueblo regions (table 7.6). Data from other sites were controlled in that I selected sites that we are fairly certain of in terms of room and kiva count, were of similar size to Pottery Mound and Hummingbird Pueblo (100–500 rooms), and dated to approximately the same time period (AD 1300–1500).

Both Pottery Mound and Hummingbird Pueblo have among the lowest room-to-plaza ratios. Pottery Mound is ranked second only to Nuvakwewtaqa. However, the plazas at Nuvakwewtaqa may not have been contemporaneous (Bernardini and Brown 2004); if such were the case, that village's ratio at any given time would be higher. Hummingbird Pueblo ranks third with Rowe Ruin. Although such an analysis is currently meaningless for Hummingbird Pueblo, where location of kivas is still uncertain, calculating a room-to-kiva ratio for Pottery Mound is probably fairly accurate. Pottery Mound has the lowest room-to-kiva ratio, suggesting that kivas may not have played the same role in integration at Pottery Mound as at other Pueblo IV sites. Kivas at Pottery Mound were possibly used to integrate smaller social units (such as clans or sodalities), while kivas at other sites were integrating larger social units (such as the entire village or a moiety). Combined, room-to-kiva and room-to-plaza ratios along with ceramic and mural data suggest that aspects of social integration associated with this new ritual system in the Lower Rio Puerco may have been weakly developed compared to other contemporaneous regions that used plazas for village-wide ceremonies.

The previous chapter showed that certain decorative attributes on glaze-painted pottery were used to emphasize social boundaries between groups with different migration histories. This chapter demonstrates that glaze-decorated pottery was adopted as part of a new ritual system and may have been used to help integrate disparate social groups by signaling village-wide participation in this system. This complex, and seemingly contradictory, patterning in the ceramic assemblage reflects the complexity of fourteenth-century potters' identity.

On the one hand, the social makeup of the Lower Rio Puerco population consisted of disparate social groups with unique migration histories. These migration histories would have been reflected in the daily practice of residents in any number of ways. Groups with different social histories may have had different linguistic traditions. Different migration histories may have been incorporated into oral traditions describing the origins of different family groups. Origins in different regions may have been reflected through a different habitus practiced by each group—a different way of doing numerous daily activities from making tools to forming a ceramic vessel to building or remodeling a roomblock. Further, ideological differences concerning the ritual cycle, marriage practices, or social etiquette may also have divided groups. At the same time, different migration histories would have potentially been the source of important exchange networks, marriage pools, and esoteric knowledge. These differences would only have become important sources of identity once disparate groups

TABLE 7.6. Room-to-kiva and room-to-plaza ratios for Pottery Mound, Hummingbird Pueblo, and contemporaneous sites in the Rio Grande and Western Pueblo regions.

Site Name Site Number	Period	Room No.	Kiva No.	Room: Kiva	Plaza No.	Room: Plaza	References
Lower Rio Puerco District							
Pottery Mound LA 416	1350–1500	200	10	20	4	50	Eckert and Cordell 2004
Hummingbird Pueblo LA 578	1300–1450	200	?	?	3	67	Ibid.
Western Pueblo							
Puerco Ruin AZ Q:1:22	1250–1350	125	2	62	1	125	Kintigh 1996
Calabash LA 1331	1200–1350	367	2	183	1	367	Roney 1996
Nuvakwewtaga Chavez SE AZ O:4:1 (ASU)	1250–1380	196	1+	196	4	49	Bernardini and Brown 2004
Nuvakwewtaga Chavez SW AZ O:4:1 (ASU)	1250–1385	398	1+	398	3	133	Ibid.
Tsa'akpahu NA 1039	1300–1450	300	1+	300	4	75	Adams et al. 2004
Kookopngyamu NA 1019	1300–1400	250	3	83	3	83	Ibid.
Central Rio Grande							
Tijeras Pueblo LA 581	1262–1395	250	2	125	1	250	Eckert and Cordell 2004
La Bajada Ruin LA 7	1300–1450	500+	4	125	5	100	Ibid.
Bullman Pueblo LA 713	1200–1400	100	1	100	?	?	Ibid.
Pueblo del Encierro LA 70	1200–1500	230	9	25	3	77	Ibid.
Kuapa LA 3443 and 3444	1200–1400	400+	9	44	3	133	Ibid.
Rio Abajo							
Cerro Indio Pueblo LA 287	1300–1400 1600–1680	100+	1	100	1	100	Lekson et al. 2004
Sevilleta Pueblo LA 774	1300–1450 1600–1680	150+	3	50	2	75	Ibid.
Northern Rio Grande							
Rowe Ruin LA 108	1275–1400	200	1	200	3	67	Snead et al. 2004
Arrowhead Ruin LA 251	1325–1540	105	2	52	1	105	Ibid.
Arroyo Hondo LA 12	1300–1345 Component I	1,000+	6	167	10	100	Creamer 1993
Arroyo Hondo LA 12	1370–1415 Component II	200	1	200	3	67	Ibid.
Forked Lightning LA 672	1275–1400	150	7	21	Multiple	—	Ibid.
Pindi LA 1	1275–1400	175	2	87	2	87	Ibid.

began to live together. Although some aspects of social practice may have been negotiable, other aspects would not have been. Potters, and their associated social groups, would have wanted to reaffirm their identity by keeping core practices that reflected "who they were." Part of this reaffirmation would have been visual reminders on pottery.

On the other hand, regardless of their migration history, residents of both villages in the Lower Rio Puerco area were struggling with the same issues: how to negotiate their identity within the new social context of aggregation and immigration, environmental concerns stemming from being agriculturalists in an arid environment, keeping the cosmos in balance, and daily domestic concerns over sickness, childbirth, marriage, and death. These are all concerns that are manipulated through ceremonies and ritual. Residents of both villages appear to have readily adopted a new ritual system, aspects of which were focused on integrating diverse groups of people (Adams 1991; Crown 1994; Spielmann 1998b). By focusing on the shared concerns of all residents and incorporating different ceremonial practices into a whole, this new ritual system would have provided an arena for participants to negotiate new and old social identities. By producing pottery with the same suite of icons, similar colored slips, and glaze paint, potters from diverse backgrounds would have been able to promote a visual sense of unity and oneness.

Although the newly adopted ritual system may have provided mechanisms for social integration, aspects of that ritual system in the Lower Rio Puerco area could also have been a source of social tension. As discussed above, numerous kivas and plazas at both sites suggest that multiple ritual societies may have been present in each village, while kiva murals at Pottery Mound suggest that competition between ritual groups may also have been emphasized. If this were the case, then ritual practice would not only have been a place to reaffirm village-wide membership and unity, but would also have been an arena in which competition between identities and ideologies played out. This conflict in the social order—diverse identities versus village unity—is explored in greater detail in the next chapter.

CHAPTER EIGHT

Pottery and Practice in Fourteenth-Century Villages along the Lower Rio Puerco

The relationship between social boundaries, migration, and ritual is multilayered. These social dynamics interact with one another to create a rich, complexly patterned material culture. This material culture reflects the habitus of people living their daily lives and attempting to negotiate the various obligations of each of these dynamics. Evaluation of architectural, ceramic, and faunal data from the Lower Rio Puerco area indicates that fourteenth- and fifteenth-century social dynamics were affected by both aggregation of the local population at Hummingbird Pueblo and Pottery Mound, as well as immigrants moving into the area from at least the Western Pueblo region, as well as possibly from the south.

While pottery was used in daily routine to signal members within groups who shared a migration history, it was also part of a newly adopted ritual system that focused on village-wide social integration. However, while this new ritual system provided mechanisms of coalition so that diverse groups could live together, this new system also had aspects that emphasized competition between these social groups. I turn now to a summary of various themes presented throughout this book concerning the nature of the fourteenth- and fifteenth-century social landscape in the Lower Rio Puerco area, as well as provide suggestions about future research.

Migration

I have argued that immigrants moved into both Hummingbird Pueblo and Pottery Mound. I suggest that some of these immigrants were from the Zuni district in the Western Pueblo region, while others may have been from the Hopi mesas, northern Mexico, or both. This case study raises at least two implications concerning migration in the American Southwest that require further data to substantiate: the size of the immigrating group in relation to local groups, and the transfer of technological knowledge between immigrant and local groups.

First, this study proposes that social dynamics within Lower Rio Puerco villages were affected by both aggregation of local groups as well as the presence of immigrants living within these aggregated villages. Another factor that affects social dynamics within a village is the relative size of an immigrant group compared to the indigenous one (Neuberger 1977). I have argued that local residents of the Lower Rio Puerco area adopted a new ritual system during the fourteenth century, possibly introduced by immigrants from the Western Pueblo region. To suggest that a large group immigrating from the west resulted in the dominance of this new ritual system is tempting. However, an understanding of historic Pueblo groups makes the argument for a small, but ritually powerful, group of immigrants living within each village as likely an argument (Duff 1998). Data to evaluate immigrant group size at either village is currently lacking but may be potentially seen in future analyses of domestic features and intrasite patterns of various artifact types.

Second, one of the dramatic changes associated with the movement of immigrants into the study area was the transition to glaze technology by the entire Lower Rio Puerco population. This transition included the application of glaze paints, use of an oxidizing firing atmosphere, and decoration with new iconic motifs. The change to glaze technology represents individual and aggregate decisions by immigrant and local potters to transform their habitus of pottery production to meet the new social demands of living with disparate groups in a large village. The social process behind this transformation is currently unclear: application of new iconic motifs *could* have been copied from other pottery or *could* have been taught by an immigrant potter; pottery from different potter groups *could* have been fired together, or firing episodes *could* have been segregated by production group; glaze paint recipes *could* have been shared or *could* have been strictly controlled by Western Pueblo immigrants. Studies on glaze composition (Habicht-Mauche and Nelson 2006; Huntley 2006), design execution (Van Kueren 2006), and symmetry (Washburn 1983, 1992, 1999) could provide insights into such questions.

Glaze-Decorated Pottery and Communities of Identity

As prehistoric potters decorated their vessels, they created "communities of identity." These communities of identity likely reflected the more conscious aspects of habitus. When the habitus of one group is placed alongside the habitus of another, as would be the case with immigrants and indigenous groups living together, issues of *who we are* and *how things are done* come to the forefront of concern. These two issues may be entangled, in that how one decorates a pot or builds a dwelling is a direct reflection of who one is (in terms of kin, migration history, ritual practice), and vice versa.

The co-occurrence of specific decorative and technological attributes reflects the use of glaze-decorated pottery to emphasize social boundaries between groups with distinct migration histories. However, because the majority of decorated pottery within the region would have looked identical from a distance, I argue that potters were primarily emphasizing membership *within* each group and not emphasizing differences *between* groups. Social groups defined by distinct migration histories would have played an important role in a potter's identity. In turn, this identity could have affected such aspects of daily life as defining potential marriage and exchange partners, access to natural and sociopolitical resources, and who could be called upon in times of economic need. Because groups with different migration and social histories lived together, identity based on such histories would also have helped to define the social incompatibilities and tensions within a village. As such, potters would have had to negotiate between a desire to reaffirm their specific heritage, while at the same time attempting to "get along" with their fellow residents through participation in village-wide social dynamics.

Fourteenth-Century Pueblo Social Organization along the Lower Rio Puerco

This study has identified social groups living in the Lower Rio Puerco area during the Pueblo IV era that had different migration and social histories, including immigrants most likely from the Western Pueblo region, along with the presence of a new ritual system in the region that had both integrative and divisive aspects. The coalition of various groups into two large villages in the Lower Rio Puerco area during the late thirteenth and fourteenth centuries would have led to fundamental shifts in notions of who and what defined a community, how social interactions were negotiated on a variety of levels, and how ritual practice articulated with these other social dynamics. These developments required that transformations in group identity, social organization, and growth of power structures be negotiated. Such transformations occur through daily attempts by both immigrants and indigenous groups to reproduce their social order in the changed context of aggregation and interaction.

The demographic upheaval and social turmoil of the thirteenth and fourteenth centuries resulted in various traditions coming into contact and, as Pueblo ethnography and ethnohistory have shown, various communities choosing different combinations of social mechanisms to integrate their villages. These mechanisms can be seen in the social organization of modern groups. Clans provide an important means of unifying otherwise unrelated kin groups among the modern Hopi; these clans provide the basic unit for much ritual knowledge and ceremonial obligation (Eggan 1950; Fox 1967; Titiev 1944). Clans exist among the modern Tewa but do not dominate social divisions (Hawley 1937). Rather, clans in Tewa villages are divided into summer/winter moieties with religious societies. Membership in a moiety and religious society helps to crosscut family ties by providing social relations associated with ritual obligations (Hawley 1937; Parsons 1974).

These two groups—the Hopi and the Tewa—are at the opposite ends of what has come to be known as "the Keresan Bridge" (Fox 1967; Lange 1958; Plog 1978). In between these two extremes are the Keres, for whom this bridge is named. While the Rio Grande Keres have lineages and clans, they use nonkinship groups (sodalities and associations) to fill political duties. Other historic Pueblo groups divide themselves dually and along clan lines to different degrees, with a tendency for clans to be stronger among the Western Pueblos and moieties to be stronger among the Rio Grande Pueblos (Fox 1967). In all instances, membership in ritual groups and the obligations these groups entail help to crosscut kin-based social boundaries.

Two facets of Pottery Mound's material culture have been used to indicate that a dual organizational system functioned at the village: the fact that the glaze-decorated pottery assemblage from Pottery Mound can be divided into two common types (red slipped and bichrome slipped) and the presence of two large kivas (Hibben 1966; Voll 1961). However, I am cautious of this interpretation without further supporting data. In terms of the pottery, different slip combinations were associated in this study with social groups identifying separate migration histories, and not with a dual division within the site. A correlation between the icons found on specific pottery types and within specific kivas would be informative; however, a systematic identification of mural icons from the original murals (and not reproductions) has yet to be done.

As for the two large kivas (one round and one rectangular), Hibben (1966) interpreted these as "moiety" kivas. Among modern Eastern Pueblo groups with either one or two large kivas, a dual division functions at some level (Dozier 1970). Such dual division is absent among the modern Hopi and Zuni (see Eggan 1950 for a discussion of evidence for "remnants" of such division at Zuni). However, no modern Eastern Pueblo village has an additional 14 kivas alongside the big kiva, as is the case at Pottery Mound. Pottery Mound has the lowest room-to-kiva ratio when compared to contemporaneous Pueblo sites or to Casas Grandes in northern Mexico. The disparity between Pottery Mound's ratio and modern room-to-kiva ratios is even greater than the one between Pottery Mound and contemporaneous sites (Lipe 1989), although caution should be taken in making such a comparison as sustained contact with the Spanish may have driven the use of many kivas underground among historic groups.

If a dual division organization did exist at Pottery Mound, it was functioning differently than seen among modern Pueblo groups. The residents of this village may not have incorporated a dual division in their ritual system, but may have had a ritual system that crosscut clan groups similar to the modern Zuni (Ladd 1979). Alternatively, residents of Pottery Mound may have had a dual division that was combined with other systems of organization. Overall, Pottery Mound may have been a focus of ritual experimentation, possibly with a unique blending of Western Pueblo, Rio Grande, and northern Mexican organizational systems.

Regardless of the socioreligious organization present in the fourteenth-century Lower Rio Puerco area—clans, moieties, or some other system—it is doubtful that the complexities of such a system were fully established prior to the formation of villages late in the thirteenth century. Prior to this time, the population of the Lower Rio Puerco area was dispersed across the landscape in small residential sites. Further, residents in the north and south of the study area appear to have been involved in different regional and interregional networks. However, as immigrants and indigenous groups aggregated into Hummingbird Pueblo and Pottery Mound, village members would be faced with the daily decisions and obligations of living in a village with residents of diverse backgrounds (Johnson 1982). Further, immigrants would not have had access to as large a kin-based network as had been available to them in their traditional homeland. This would have led to reliance on non-kin, possibly other immigrants with similar regions of origin, or possibly a local group with which they had good relations.

In the daily practice of relying on non-kin for traditionally kin-based relations and obligations, the seeds of fictive kin groups or other social structures (sodalities, moieties) could have been founded. Similarly, local groups living together in a large village would have found daily access to social networks that would once have required more time and effort. Informal social networks would have developed in villages based on age, gender, language, or other common aspects that would have helped meet the daily needs of individuals faced with a new suite of social concerns. These informal networks, based on daily practice as well as more formal relations, would have helped to define social organization in newly established villages.

Glaze-Decorated Pottery and Village-Wide Ritual Practice

The region-wide adoption of glaze technology suggests that pottery production groups within villages interacted so that a common collection of ideas on how to decorate a vessel was shared throughout the study area. The adoption of glaze-decorated pottery was likely associated with the adoption of a broader suite of attributes related to a new ritual system. In an attempt to cope with disparate social groups and relatively high population densities within villages, residents of the Lower Rio Puerco area appear to have adopted a ritual system that focused on village integration and community well-being (Adams 1991; Crown 1994; Spielmann 1998b).

An important aspect of the socioreligious system adopted in the Lower Rio Puerco area during the fourteenth century involved the katsina religion. Masked figures on kiva murals at Pottery Mound, and on the occasional sherd at both villages, suggest that at least a portion of this new religious system included katsina ritual. If the adoption of glaze-decorated pottery is associated with the katsina religion in the study area (as suggested by masked icons appearing on vessels), then the universal adoption of glaze technology throughout the region suggests that all residents of both villages practiced the katsina religion. However, how the katsina religion articulated with other ritual practices in the region is unclear.

Among modern Western Pueblo groups, the katsina religion is primarily concerned with rainmaking and community well-being, while among modern Eastern Pueblos katsina religion is more concerned with medicine (Eggan 1950). Further, katsina membership varies from group to group. For example, among the Tewa the katsina religion is organized by moiety and membership is restricted, while among the Hopi participation is tribe-wide but organized by clan (Dozier 1970; Titiev 1944). Further, among some groups, katsina ritual is a reflection of village history and an outline of what order families joined the village; as such, katsina ritual is an important aspect of immigrant community dynamics (Ferguson 1989; Kroeber 1917; Ladd 1979; Parsons 1939; Titiev 1944). Organization at Hummingbird Pueblo may have been more along the organization of modern Zuni, where all adult males are members of ceremonial organizations, which "cut across kinship and clan boundaries" (Ladd 1979:484; see also Ferguson 1989; Kroeber 1917; Parsons 1939); while organization at

Pottery Mound may have divided clans into sodalities or moieties. Or the organizational systems may have been reversed or may have been completely different.

Regardless of the organizational nature of the katsina religion in the study area, overall, three specific aspects of the new ritual system in the Lower Rio Puerco area would have helped to integrate disparate social groups living together. First, the plaza space provided an arena where participants in ceremonies could have publicly displayed their belief in the new ritual system. Second, the adoption of glaze-decorated pottery by all residents living along the Lower Rio Puerco provided visual clues that everyone was a member and believer in the same religion. Third, and finally, a shared suite of icons provided visual reminders that this religion focused on universal concerns. Despite the apparent integrative qualities of this new ritual system, architectural data and kiva mural images suggest that this system may not have been as socially integrative as in other contemporaneous Pueblo villages. For example, multiple plazas and kivas may reflect ceremonial divisions that competed for prestige within each village.

Seeds of Social Tension in the New Ritual System

The complexities of the Pueblo IV ritual system helped to integrate disparate kin groups in Lower Rio Puerco villages but, by their very nature, these complexities would also have created new means by which to segregate the population. Although among modern day pueblos, ritual societies have members from various kin groups; the ritual knowledge and paraphernalia are also often owned by a specific lineage. This could easily have been the case in the prehispanic past, where scholars have postulated that ritual specialists were recruited by specific villages to come and live (Duff 2002; Eggan 1950; Whiteley 1986). During good times the complexities of ritual would have worked to keep harmony in a village. However, during periods of social stress brought on by any number of internal or external factors, the ritual system may have added another layer of tension to an already divided community prone to factionalism (Brugge 1969; Dozier 1966; Fenton 1957; Kimmel 1981; Siegal and Beals 1960; Stewart 1984; Titiev 1944; Whiteley 1988). If these tensions could not be overcome, then the resulting social conflict could have led to violence or the fissioning of the village population.

Access to ritual knowledge is not centralized among modern day Pueblo villages; different clans, lineages, or moieties control different aspects of the overall body of knowledge. However, much ritual knowledge—and the sodalities and societies that are created around it—is ranked (Brandt 1994; Ware and Blinman 2000). As such, the social groups that control different knowledge are also ranked in ritual importance (Ladd 1979; Titiev 1944). In some instances, there is nothing subtle about this ranking, and it overlaps with political control. For example, among Rio Grande Keresan groups, curing societies exert control over political life (Ware and Blinman 2000:384), and this hierarchy is reaffirmed through ritual performance. Communal ritual helps to mask social and cultural tensions (Turner 1968), often by conveying messages about the immutability of social and cosmic order (Rappaport 1979). In the case of Pueblo groups, part of this social order is ranking of ritual knowledge, and the authority of this hierarchy is reaffirmed through ritual performance and its associated symbols (Potter and Perry 2000:64).

A ritual system ranked on the basis of ritual knowledge could easily have existed in the Pueblo IV Lower Rio Puerco area and may well have extended to the social groups who owned such knowledge. Ranking may have been based on migration order into a village, or it may have been based upon access to esoteric knowledge, including prestige gained by owning ritual knowledge from distant locations (Bradley 2000; Helms 1979). Two combined pieces of evidence suggest that access to certain ritual knowledge played an important role in village hierarchies at both Pottery Mound and Hummingbird Pueblo. First, a new suite of ritual attributes identified in chapter 9, presumably from the Western Pueblo region, was adopted throughout the study area during the fourteenth century. Second, as discussed in chapter 7, Pottery Mound kiva murals incorporate numerous aspects of Hopi imagery. The presence of Hopi imagery at Pottery Mound may be particularly telling of a ranked ritual system, as the modern day Hopi are especially focused on the order of clan migration onto the Hopi mesas as a means of ranking clans and their ritual knowledge (Eggan 1950; Titiev 1944).

The seemingly widespread acceptance of various aspects of Western Pueblo ritual, despite few actual Western Pueblo immigrants, in the study area suggests that one important component of the newly adopted ritual system may have been its very "otherness," its association with distant lands or foreign knowledge. If this were the case, then individuals within a lineage or sodality could have gained recognition through successful trips to "the West" or "the South" to bring back ritual paraphernalia from distant locations. Actual immigrants from "the West" or "the South" with ritual knowledge may have gained prestige by their very origins. Prestige gained by separate individuals could ultimately have been combined to bring overall prestige to their lineage or sodality.

Although the new ritual system may have included practices that crosscut kin-based social groups, this crosscutting may not have been strong enough to overcome the various concerns of the specific individuals and separate immigrants groups who settled in the region. If ritual knowledge were ranked, some members of a village would have had a higher stake in maintaining the socioreligious structure that developed. Ranking of ritual knowledge would have created a tension between notions of equality and hierarchy. The practice by potters of signaling a common belief and participation in a shared ritual system by similar decoration on the exterior of their bowls, while continuing to signal social boundaries between groups with different migration histories on the interior, may reflect this tension between incorporation and segregation that has been noted in modern Pueblo society (Brandt 1994). Imagery on kiva murals at Pottery Mound that appears to portray rival lineages vying for social (and religious?) dominance more dramatically reflects such possible tensions (Crotty 1990). The complete abandonment of the region suggests that the particular combination of ritual activities adopted by the residents of the area was eventually unable to overcome other sources of tension. Possibly, this tension was the result of factionalism enhanced by the very ritual system meant to integrate the community. Other sources of tension could have resulted from warfare (LeBlanc 1999), environmental stresses brought on by a dry period at about AD 1450 (Cordell 1980), attraction to "greener pastures," or some combination of these factors.

We do not know where the residents of the Lower Rio Puerco villages emigrated to when they left the area; however, some speculations can be made. Nonlocal pottery came from both the Western Pueblo and Rio Grande regions, providing potential migrants with information about both of these areas. In the case of Pottery Mound, some village residents possibly moved to the Hopi mesas. Hibben (1975) noted that Acoma elders recognize specific ritual aspects on the Pottery Mound kiva murals; however, it is impossible to know if that is a result of migration to Acoma from Pottery Mound. The ritual prestige and knowledge gained from contact with the Western Pueblo region may have resulted in some ritual specialists from the Lower Rio Puerco area being recruited by Rio Grande villages. If factionalism was a problem at both sites, then there is no reason to believe that all residents of both villages migrated to the same regions, or for the same reasons. Some residents may have gone west, while others went east, and still others went south. Some residents may have been recruited for their ritual knowledge; others may have fled a bad situation toward a socioreligious system that looked more promising. The end result was the same; the villages of the Lower Rio Puerco area were abandoned.

Conclusion

Various forms of material culture in the Pueblo IV period along the Lower Rio Puerco drainage have been evaluated in this study. Using practice theory as an interpretive framework, I identified a set of processes, beginning with immigration and ending with abandonment, that have significant implications in understanding integration and socioreligious organization. I have told a story of migration and integration in the study area that includes the development of a complex ritual system composed of various elements of a more pan-Southwestern cosmology and ideology. This ritual system had mechanisms for integration and segregation, inclusion and exclusion, inherent in its structure. The system appears to have been successful for a while in that both Pottery Mound and Hummingbird Pueblo were probably occupied for at least four generations. Ultimately, though, the villages were abandoned.

This story is not unique to the villages of the Lower Rio Puerco area. Many small towns were established during the late 1200s and early 1300s—some probably by aggregating indigenous groups, some by immigrants, and others by a combination of such social groups. Most of these small towns were short lived. Mechanisms of integration in these early Pueblo IV villages did not seem to function as well as mechanisms of integration practiced by villages established in the Protohistoric period, many of which continue to be occupied to the present. The early Pueblo IV period was probably marked by the movement of kin groups between various villages, working and reworking different aspects of ritual, social organization, and political structure until a system was created that included a combination of inclusion and exclusion. We see the descendants of these "successful" systems among modern Pueblo groups, however much they have transformed over 500 years.

The relationship between migration, ritual, community identity, and material culture is a complex one. It is the result of decisions made by individuals in an attempt to navigate the multiple social dynamics of daily living. The early Pueblo IV period was one of social, political, and ideological uncertainty. Not until the Protohistoric period did many groups begin to "settle" down and define the regional identities that exist today (Duff 2002). Part of this identity would have been the formalization of a ritual system (Ware and Blinman 2000). Prior to the Protohistoric period, many villages were established that created different combinations of ideology and ritual to cope with the social stress brought on by disparate groups living together. For as many villages as were successful in this endeavor, there were at least as many villages that were not successful. These latter villages, as well as the ones that eventually became the villages of today, are what we must investigate if we are to truly understand the complexities of human behavior.

APPENDIX A

Pueblo III and Pueblo IV Pottery Types Produced in the Lower Rio Puerco Region

This section describes the Pueblo III and Pueblo IV pottery types *produced* in the Lower Rio Puerco region and presents the data used in the chapter 3 seriation (see tables A1, A2 and A3 beginning on page 117). Because the Lower Rio Puerco area is located at the junction of various ceramic traditions, the ceramic typology is more diverse than other regions of the Southwest, especially during the Pueblo IV period. Both Western Pueblo and Rio Grande ceramic types were produced in the Lower Rio Puerco area, and what follows is a description of the local variants of those types. Pottery produced in numerous other regions of the Southwest was recovered in the study area; however, no detailed descriptions of these types are offered here as such descriptions have been published elsewhere by researchers working in those various regions.

Pottery was determined to be locally produced based upon paste and temper characteristics. Pottery produced in the Lower Rio Puerco area was characterized by two tempering traditions. Pottery produced in the northern portion of the study area was tempered with sherd-tempered sherd mixed with a diverse suite of metamorphic and igneous rocks assumed to be native to the clay. Pottery produced in the southern portion of the study area was tempered with a mix of igneous rocks. Pastes from both portions of the study area range in color from gray to black in utility wares, light to dark gray in white wares, and deep red to light buff-gray in glaze wares. All pastes oxidized to a deep red in refired sherds.

To help understand the description of ceramic types presented, a variety of terms should be defined as they are used here. The matrix of a vessel is called the paste and the inclusions are called the temper. A slip is a watered-down clay applied to cover irregularities in the vessel surface before the vessel is fired and may be thin and washy or thick and well polished. Self-slips were also observed on pottery from the study area. Various types of paint were used to decorate pottery in the region; in this study, these paint types were distinguished through visual examination. Some paints are dull and often even with the vessel surface (a matte paint) while other paints are shiny, bumpy, and glasslike (a glaze paint). Glaze paints are a combination of specific minerals (including lead) that have been fired to relatively high temperatures. Matte paints are produced from a wider range of materials, including organic and mineral. Organic paints often have blurry edges with a watery appearance and are usually a flat black with no surface relief (having completely soaked into the clay body). Mineral paints are usually dense, may be crackled or blistered, and have hard edges. They often sit up on the surface of the vessel and range in color from red to brown, reddish-brown, and warm black. A special case of mineral paint is kaolin paint, which produces a white color. Through refiring experiments, matte paints in the study area were often found to be a combination of mineral and organic materials, which usually produce a brown color that is soaked into the clay body. The edges may be somewhat blurry, but parts of the paint may sit up on the surface of the vessel or be crackled.

Design layout describes the overall positioning of decoration on a vessel: for example, decoration can be banded, which means it runs parallel to the rim. Design elements are the breakdown of individual decorations within the overall design: triangles, dots, and squares are all design elements. Filler describes the contents of the design elements such as solid, opened, or hatched lines. Finally, a design style (the most common four in the study area are described in chapter 6) describes the combination of the last three variables (layout, elements, and filler). For example, a Heshotauthla design style has a banded layout; steps, lines and dots are common elements; and the filler is solid, never hatched.

Utility Ware

Utility ware recovered from the Lower Rio Puerco area was typed based upon surface treatment. Surface treatments most commonly recorded include Plain, Indented Corrugated, Smeared Indented Corrugated, and Corrugated with a Smudged interior. Based upon the high percentage of utility sherds with soot, utility pottery is assumed to have been used primarily for cooking. Paste texture for locally produced utility pottery was coarse to very coarse; paste color was often masked by soot but ranged from gray to black. Paste normally oxidized to a deep red in refired sherds. Locally produced utility wares were tempered with either sherd and mixed rock assumed to be native to the clay or with a suite of igneous rocks sourced to the Hidden Mountain area in the southern portion of the study area.

Plain Gray. No coils are present on the vessel body, however the base of the neck is usually corrugated or banded. The vessel surfaces have been smoothed but are not polished. The clay body is white to light gray, occasionally with a slightly darker core.

Indented Corrugated. This type has fingernail-indented coils, generally 4–9 mm wide, usually diagonally patterned across the coils. These indentations can occur on just the neckband with a plain body or plain corrugated body, or on the entire vessel. The clay body is light to dark gray, sometimes with a darker core.

Smeared Indented Corrugated. This type has indented corrugations that have been partially scraped, but the coils are still visible. Obliteration can occur on just the neckband or on the entire vessel. The clay body is light to dark gray, sometimes with a darker core.

Indented or Smeared Corrugated, Smudged. This type is the same as the Indented Corrugated or Smeared Indented Corrugated described above, except there is a black, burnished interior. Polish on the smudged interior ranges in quality from streaky to very smooth and shiny. The clay body is light to dark gray, sometimes with a darker core.

White Wares

Decorated white wares from the Lower Rio Puerco area were typed based upon a range of attributes (e.g., surface treatment, design, and paint type). Most decorated bowls in the Lower Rio Puerco area are assumed to have been used for food service, while decorated jars were used for storage. Paste texture for locally produced pottery was moderately coarse to fine; paste color normally ranged from light to dark gray in white wares. Paste normally oxidized to a deep red or light buff in refired sherds.

Loma Fria B/w. Loma Fria B/w is the most common Pueblo III white ware type recovered from the northern portion of the study area and into the Middle Rio Puerco region. DATE RANGE: AD 1200–1275. SLIP/SURFACE TREATMENT: thin, washy slip to gray false slip that may be slightly crazed; decorated surfaces always polished, bowl exteriors may or may not be polished. PAINT: carbon or carbon/mineral mix. TEMPER: crushed sherd-tempered sherd with mixed rock. DESIGN LAYOUT: varies greatly, but is similar to Galisteo B/w. DESIGN ELEMENTS: can be similar to Reserve B/w, Puerco B/w, Escavada B/w, Santa Fe B/w, Galisteo B/w, and even Red Mesa B/w; design usually rectilinear, stepped, or barbed (no curvilinear elements); negative elements common; thin and thick parallel lines not unusual.

Socorro B/w. Socorro B/w is the most common Pueblo III white ware type recovered from the southern portion of the study area and into the Rio Abajo region. DATE RANGE: AD 1200–1400. SLIP/SURFACE TREATMENT: usually unslipped, surface is light gray to dark blue-gray; surface uniformly smoothed but may be unpolished or polished to a velvety matte luster. A slipped version of this type has also been recorded in the Lower Rio Puerco region, sometimes as Unnamed Mineral Painted White Ware. PAINT: well-controlled mineral paint; distinctive crazing common, but generally more granular in appearance; often subglazed; usually black, sometimes brown in study area. TEMPER: mixed igneous rock, may have some crushed sherd mixed in. DESIGN LAYOUT: often bands of balanced mixture of opposed hatched and solid designs. DESIGN ELEMENTS: primarily opposed solid and hatched designs; hatched design areas are balanced with solid design areas; oblique fine-lined hatching most common, sometimes longitudinal hatching; occasionally opposed solid designs similar to some Puerco B/w elements. COMMENTS: vessel walls are often quite think and hard, and sherds will usually ring when struck; vitrification is often visible in the wall; designs are usually well executed.

White Mountain Red Ware

White Mountain Red Ware describes the red-slipped pottery produced and distributed in east-central Arizona and west-central New Mexico from the Pueblo II through the Pueblo IV period. Only one type of White Mountain Red Ware was identified as being locally produced in the Lower Rio Puerco area: St. Johns Black-on-red (B/r) and Polychrome. This type appears to be the first locally produced red-slipped pottery in the area. Paste texture for locally produced White Mountain Red Ware was moderately coarse to fine; paste color normally ranged from light gray to light buff-gray in this ware. Paste normally oxidized to a deep red or light buff in refired sherds.

St. Johns B/r and Polychrome. St. Johns B/r and Polychrome were only recovered in bowl form in the study area, although jars of this type have been reported from other regions. DATE RANGE: AD 1175–1300. SLIP/SURFACE TREATMENT: evenly slipped and polished; slip is red to orange. PAINT: mineral; bowl interiors have a black to brown matte paint; bowl exteriors have a white paint. TEMPER: crushed sherd-tempered sherd with mixed rock. DESIGN LAYOUT: balanced mixture of opposed or interlocking hatched and solid elements. DESIGN ELEMENTS: primarily opposed solid and hatched designs, including curvilinear scrolls, rectilinear bands, and interlocking barbs; hatched design areas are balanced with solid design areas; designs tend to be tight and busy with elements close together; framing line; broad-lined geometrics on exterior of bowls. COMMENTS: in the Lower Rio Puerco region, St. Johns may be confused with Heshotauthla. St. Johns has matte paint, hatched elements, and/or wide white lines on the exterior of bowls. Heshotauthla is always glazed, has no hatching, and has fine white lines on the exterior of bowls.

Zuni/Early Acoma Glaze Wares

Zuni Glaze Ware types were an outgrowth of early White Mountain Red Ware matte-painted types, including St. Johns B/r and Polychrome. These glaze-painted types are most commonly produced and distributed from the Upper Little Colorado River area in the west to the El Morro Valley in the east. Not much is known about the Acoma Glaze Ware types, but current understanding suggests that the early types share traits with the Zuni Glaze Ware types. Locally produced versions of these Western Pueblo types have a moderately coarse to fine paste. Paste color ranged from light gray to light buff-gray in these types, oxidizing to a deep red or light buff in refired sherds.

Heshotauthla Gl/r and Polychrome (aka Heshotauthla B/r and Polychrome). In the Lower Rio Puerco area, Heshotauthla Gl/r is more common than Heshotauthla Polychrome. DATE RANGE: 1275–1450+. SLIP/SURFACE TREATMENT: exterior surfaces of jars and both surfaces of bowls are evenly slipped and polished; slip is red to orange. PAINT: glaze; bowl interiors are subglaze to glaze ranging in color from black to brown; bowl exteriors may have white mineral paint and a black glaze. TEMPER: crushed sherd-tempered sherd with mixed rock. DESIGN LAYOUT: banded elements running obliquely from rim, normally in the Heshotauthla style. DESIGN ELEMENTS: wide band around rim with pendants; parallel hatch, pendant dots; sets of parallel lines in triangular elements adjoining the base or rim lines; empty interior bowl base; designs are pendant and diagonal to rim line; bands of parallel lines; solid designs; interlocking and stacked steps; solid straight bands; interlocking or opposed zipper design; eyes. There is often no design on the exterior of bowls, but when present it usually consists of thin white lines forming geometrics and bands, often accompanied by a single glaze line. COMMENTS: in the Rio Grande, there is an early glaze ware that is very similar to Heshotauthla called Los Padillas. In many instances, they are indistinguishable from one another except for the geographic area in which they are found. Because the two types are technologically and chronologically similar, and may even originate from the same place, the Eighth Southwestern Ceramic Seminar suggested that the Los Padillas type be done away with and all early, sherd-tempered, red-slipped glaze wares be called Heshotauthla. I follow this recommendation in this study.

Kwakina Gl/poly (aka Kwakina Polychrome). In the study area, Kwakina Gl/poly was only recovered in bowl form. Although jars of this type have been reported from other regions, they are extremely rare. DATE RANGE: AD 1280–1450+. SLIP/SURFACE TREATMENT: both bowl interiors and exteriors slipped and polished; interior has a bright white to grayish-white slip, often chalky; exterior has a red to orange slip. PAINT: glaze; bowl interiors are subglaze to glaze ranging in color from black to bright grass green; bowl exteriors may have white mineral paint and a black glaze. TEMPER: crushed sherd-tempered sherd with mixed rock. DESIGN LAYOUT: banded elements running obliquely from rim, normally in the Heshotauthla style. DESIGN ELEMENTS: wide band around rim with pendants; parallel hatch, pendant dots; sets of parallel lines in triangular elements adjoining the base or rim lines; empty interior bowl base; designs are pendant and diagonal to rim line; bands of parallel lines; solid designs; interlocking and stacked steps; solid straight bands; interlocking or opposed zipper design; eyes. There is often no design on the exterior of bowls, but when present it usually consists of thin white lines forming geometrics and bands, often accompanied by a single glaze line. COMMENTS: occasionally, Kwakina Gl/poly in the study area has the exterior red slip coming up and over the rim to form a band of red slip on the interior.

Pinnawa Glaze-on-white (Gl/w). In the study area, locally produced Pinnawa Gl/w was uncommon. DATE RANGE: AD 1350–1450+. SLIP/SURFACE TREATMENT: bright white, thick, well-polished slip. PAINT: either black or bright green glaze. TEMPER: crushed sherd-tempered sherd with mixed rock. DESIGN LAYOUT: banded or single element designs. DESIGN ELEMENTS: simple parallel bands, triangles, hatching; paired stepped triangles; scrolls; stepped lines; single element designs focused on center of bowls; all exterior elements were simple unit designs. COMMENTS: Pinnawa Gl/w is similar to Kechipawan Polychrome and could be called a monochrome version of that type.

Kechipawan Polychrome. In the study area, locally produced Kechipawan Polychrome was uncommon. DATE RANGE: AD 1370–1450+. SLIP/SURFACE TREATMENT: bright white, thick, well-polished slip. PAINT: either black or bright green glaze. TEMPER: crushed sherd-tempered sherd with mixed rock. DESIGN LAYOUT: banded. DESIGN ELEMENTS: simple designs, bands and geometrics with red used as a filler; geometrics; no designs were recorded on the exterior of bowls.

Rio Grande Glaze Ware

The most common approach for dating post-1300 sites in the Rio Grande is through the use of a glaze ware rim-form seriation (figure A.1). This series, which is based primarily upon bowl rim forms, consists of six ceramic types, Glaze A–F. Within each rim form type, subtypes have been defined and named based on slip color, decoration, and/or temper. Further, Rio Grande Glaze Ware types are often divided into three temporal phases: Early (A, B), Intermediate (C, D), and Late (E, F). These divisions are based upon the observation that certain changes, other than rim form, occur over time. Glaze color, slip color, and glaze texture all change over time. In the Lower Rio Puerco area, only locally produced versions of Early and Intermediate Rio Grande Glaze Ware types were recovered. Rim sherds were assigned type names based upon slip color and rim form. Body sherds were assigned to more general categories based upon slip color, glaze color, and glaze texture. Locally produced versions of Rio Grande Glaze Ware types have a moderately coarse to fine paste. Paste color was normally deep red, but light gray and buff-gray were also noted. Pastes oxidized to a deep red or light buff in refired sherds.

Early Rio Grande Glaze Ware. Early Rio Grande Glaze Ware sherds were divided by body sherds and rim sherds. Rim sherds were then classified as Glaze A or Glaze B. Glaze A rims were further classified as Agua Fria G/r, San Clemente Polychrome, Cieneguilla Gl/y, or Cieneguilla Polychrome. Glaze B rims were further classified as Largo Gl/y, Largo Gl/r, or Largo Polychrome. If a body sherd had a lustrous glaze that held to its design line (did not run), then the sherd was assigned to a general Early Rio Grande Glaze Ware category based upon its slip and paint colors: Early Rio Grande Gl/r, Early Rio Grande Gl/y, Early Rio Grande Gl/poly (light slip interior/dark slip exterior), or Early Rio Grande other polychrome. DATE RANGE: AD 1313–1500+. SLIP/SURFACE TREATMENT: thin to thick slip on exterior of jars and interior and exterior of bowls; polish ranges from streaky to well polished; red slip may be a self-slip; slip ranges in same colors as Glaze A's described below. PAINT: thin glaze ranging from a thin matte with small streaks of vitrification to a shiny glaze; color usually intense black but may be grayish; paint is well controlled, not runny. TEMPER: usually mixed igneous rock, occasionally with sherd mixed in; may also be olivine diabase. DESIGN LAYOUT: narrow banded. DESIGN ELEMENTS: thick parallel lines, slashes, crosses, pendant triangles, lines, squiggle hatching, cross-hatching, steps, dots, ticks, checkerboards, eyes, birds, feathers, occasionally anthropomorphs.

Agua Fria Gl/r (Glaze A) is the most common pottery type recovered from Phase 2 and 3 assemblages in the study area. DATE RANGE: AD 1313–1500+. SLIP/SURFACE TREATMENT: thin to thick slip on exterior of jars and interior and exterior of bowls; polish ranges from streaky to well polished; may be a self-slip; slip ranges in color from dark red to orange-red, often the same color as the paste. PAINT: thin glaze ranging from a thin matte with small streaks of vitrification to a shiny glaze; color usually intense black but may be grayish; paint is well controlled, not runny. TEMPER: usually mixed igneous rock, occasionally with sherd mixed in; may also be olivine diabase. DESIGN LAYOUT: narrow banded. DESIGN ELEMENTS: thick parallel lines, slashes, crosses, pendant triangles, lines, squiggle hatching, cross-hatching, steps, dots, ticks, checkerboards, eyes, birds, feathers, occasionally

FIGURE A.1. Rio Grande Glaze Painted rim forms.

anthropomorphs; usually no exterior design, but multiple Xs or slashes most common when design is present.

San Clemente Polychrome (Glaze A) is the second most common pottery type recovered from Phase 2 and Phase 3 assemblages. DATE RANGE: AD 1321–1450+. SLIP/SURFACE TREATMENT: thin to thick slip on exterior of jars and interior and exterior of bowls; polish ranges from streaky to well polished; red slip may be a self-slip; interior slip normally a yellow-buff but may be a pale yellow; exterior slip dark red to orange-red, may be same color as paste. PAINT: thin glaze ranging from a thin matte with small streaks of vitrification to a shiny glaze; glaze color usually intense black to gray; glaze paint is well controlled, not runny. TEMPER: usually mixed igneous rock, occasionally with sherd mixed in; may also be olivine diabase. DESIGN LAYOUT: narrow banded. DESIGN ELEMENTS: thick parallel lines, slashes, crosses, pendant triangles, lines, squiggle hatching, cross-hatching, steps, dots, ticks, checkerboards, eyes, birds, feathers, occasionally anthropomorphs; usually no exterior design, but multiple Xs or slashes most common when design is present. COMMENTS: one slip may be applied over the other; sometimes the light slip is added as filler between painted designs, especially on jars.

Cieneguilla Gl/y and Polychrome (Glaze A) was not an uncommon type. DATE RANGE: AD 1321–1450+. SLIP/SURFACE TREATMENT: thin to thick slip on exterior of jars and interior and exterior of bowls, polish ranges from streaky to well polished; slip normally a yellow-buff but may be a pale yellow. PAINT: thin glaze ranging from a thin matte with small streaks of vitrification to a shiny glaze; glaze color ranges in color from brown to black; glaze paint is well controlled, not runny (on polychrome variety there is the addition of red matte paint used as a filler). TEMPER: usually mixed igneous rock, occasionally with sherd mixed in; may also be olivine diabase. DESIGN LAYOUT: narrow banded. DESIGN ELEMENTS: thick parallel lines; slashes and crosses near rims of jars or on exterior of bowls common; pendant triangles, lines, squiggle hatching, cross-hatching, steps, dots, ticks, checkerboards, eyes; on the exterior of bowls, elements tend to be paired slashes or crosses, or a double key figure.

Largo Gl/y, Gl/r, and Polychrome (Glaze B) were very uncommon types in the Lower Rio Puerco, but locally produced examples of all three types were recorded. DATE RANGE: AD 1410–1500+. SLIP/SURFACE TREATMENT: slipped and polished; color ranges from pale yellow to yellow-buff to red. PAINT: thin glaze ranging from a thin matte with small streaks of vitrification to a shiny glaze; glaze color ranges in color from brownish-black to black; glaze paint is well controlled, not runny (on polychrome variety there is the addition of red matte paint used as a filler on exterior designs). TEMPER: usually mixed igneous rock, occasionally with sherd mixed in; may also be olivine diabase. DESIGN LAYOUT: not a large enough sample to describe for the Lower Rio Puerco region. DESIGN ELEMENTS: lines, dots, ticks, key figures, birds, feathers; on the exterior of bowls, elements tend to be paired slashes or crosses, or a double key figure.

Intermediate Rio Grande Glaze Ware. Intermediate Rio Grande Glaze Ware sherds were divided by body sherds and rim sherds. Rim sherds were then classified as Glaze C or Glaze D. If a body sherd had a dull to lustrous glaze that was somewhat runny, then the sherd was assigned to a general Intermediate Rio Grande Glaze Ware category based upon its slip and paint colors: Intermediate Rio Grande Gl/r, Intermediate Rio Grande Gl/y, Intermediate Rio Grande Gl/poly (light slip interior/dark slip exterior), or Intermediate Rio Grande other polychrome. DATE RANGE: AD 1430–1600. SLIP/SURFACE TREATMENT: thin to thick slip on exterior of jars and interior and exterior of bowls; polish ranges from streaky to well polished; slip ranges in same colors as Glaze C and D described below. PAINT: thick glaze ranging from dull to shiny; color usually black to brownish; glaze is slightly runny, but does not completely destroy design (on some polychrome varieties there is the addition of red matte paint used as filler on exterior designs). TEMPER: usually mixed igneous rock; may also be olivine diabase. DESIGN LAYOUT: broad band. DESIGN ELEMENTS: ticks, dashes, crosses, sunbursts, butterflies, birds, sometimes key figures with red filler on exterior.

Glaze C is not a common type found in the Lower Rio Puerco ceramic assemblage and so description of the type is limited. DATE RANGE: AD 1430–1600. SLIP/SURFACE TREATMENT: thin to thick slip on exterior of jars and interior and exterior of bowls; polish ranges from streaky to well polished; slip ranges in color from pale red to light yellow-buff to yellow. PAINT: thick glaze ranging from dull to shiny; color usually black to brownish; glaze is slightly runny, but does not completely destroy design (on some polychrome varieties there is the addition of red matte paint used as filler on exterior designs). TEMPER: usually mixed igneous rock; may also be olivine diabase. DESIGN LAYOUT: broad band. DESIGN ELEMENTS: ticks, dashes, crosses, sunbursts, butterflies, birds, sometimes key figures with red filler on exterior.

Glaze D is not a common type found in the Lower Rio Puerco ceramic assemblage and so description of the type is limited. DATE RANGE: AD 1460–1550+. SLIP/SURFACE TREATMENT: thin to thick slip on exterior of jars and interior and exterior of bowls; polish normally streaky; slip ranges in color from pale red to light yellow-buff to yellow. PAINT: thick glaze ranging from dull to shiny; color usually black to brownish; glaze is slightly runny, but does not completely destroy design; there is also the addition of red matte paint used as filler on exterior and interior designs. TEMPER: usually mixed igneous rock; may also be olivine diabase. DESIGN LAYOUT: broad band. DESIGN ELEMENTS: ticks, dashes, crosses, sunbursts, butterflies, birds, sometimes key figures with red filler on exterior.

Lower Rio Puerco Wares

Although potters in the Lower Rio Puerco area produced glaze-painted pottery that shared traits with their neighbors to the west and east, they also produced Pueblo IV ceramic types unique to the area. These types include Hummingbird Red-on-buff, Pottery Mound Polychrome, and Hidden Mountain Polychrome. Locally produced types have a moderately coarse to fine paste. Hummingbird Red-on-buff often has a light-buff paste; paste color for the two glaze wares is normally deep red, but light gray and buff-gray were also noted. Pastes oxidized to a deep red or light buff in refired sherds.

Hummingbird Red-on-buff. Hummingbird Red-on-buff appears to have been produced only at Hummingbird Pueblo and only distributed in the study area. Only sherds of this type have been found, so it is difficult to describe the overall design painted onto these vessels. Jar forms are more common than bowl forms. DATE RANGE: AD 1350–1425 (?). SLIP/SURFACE TREATMENT: thick, evenly distributed slip often with excellent polish; slip normally light yellow-buff in color, but can range from light yellow to buff. On some vessels, there is a black, burnished interior. Polish on the smudged interior ranges in quality from streaky to very smooth and shiny. PAINT: mineral; red to reddish-brown. TEMPER: crushed sherd-tempered sherd with mixed rock. DESIGN LAYOUT: appears to be simple, banded designs. DESIGN ELEMENTS: simple geometrics, apparently arranged in a band.

Pottery Mound Polychrome. Production of Pottery Mound Polychrome appears to have been restricted to the village of Pottery Mound, but it was exported to Hummingbird Pueblo. Further, this type has been recovered from sites in the Rio Grande region. This type may have Glaze A, C, or D rim forms. DATE RANGE: AD 1375–1450+. SLIP/SURFACE TREATMENT: normally thick slip on exterior of jars and interior and exterior of bowls, normally well polished; red slip may be a self-slip; interior slip normally a yellow-buff but may be a pale yellow; exterior slip dark red to orange-red, may be same color as paste. PAINT: shiny black glaze that is usually well controlled, not runny; red paint on interior, may be used as filler in glaze design. TEMPER: usually mixed igneous rock, occasionally with sherd mixed in; may also be olivine diabase or crushed sherd-tempered sherd with mixed rock. DESIGN LAYOUT: overall pattern, often asymmetrical; Sikyatki design style. DESIGN ELEMENTS: stylized birds and feathers, scrolls, blocky rectilinear frets, masked figures, dragonflies, stepped clouds, crosses, stars. COMMENTS: design layout and elements are reminiscent of Sikyatki Polychrome, a Hopi Yellow Ware.

Hidden Mountain Polychrome. Production and distribution of Hidden Mountain Polychrome appears to have been mostly restricted to the village of Pottery Mound. This type may have Glaze A, C, or D rim forms (including the beveled rim). Only bowl forms of this type have been recorded. DATE RANGE: AD 1400–1450+. SLIP/SURFACE TREATMENT: normally thick slip on both interior and exterior of bowls, normally well polished; red slip is never a self-slip; interior slip normally a deep red; exterior slip normally bright white, but very pale yellow also recorded. PAINT: shiny black glaze that is usually well controlled, not runny. TEMPER: crushed sherd-tempered sherd with mixed rock. DESIGN LAYOUT: banded design on exterior of bowl; sometimes thin, simple banded design on interior. DESIGN ELEMENTS: stylized serpents, lightning, solids, stepped motifs, negative lightning, eyes.

TABLE A.1. Counts and percentages (in parentheses) of ceramics by excavation levels: Matte Painted Wares and Western Glaze Ware.

SITE	UNIT	LEV	LOC	Tularosa	Loma Fria	Socorro	St. Johns B/r & Poly	Hopi	Humm R/buff	Western Glaze
LA 416	30.75N/3.78W	1	NW	0(0)	0(0)	0(0)	0(0)	3(1)	1(0)	4(1)
LA 416	30.75N/3.78W	2	NW	0(0)	0(0)	1(0)	0(0)	7(1)	2(0)	20(2)
LA 416	30.75N/3.78W	3	NW	0(0)	0(0)	0(0)	0(0)	6(1)	0(0)	5(1)
LA 416	30.75N/3.78W	4	NW	0(0)	1(0)	0(0)	0(0)	2(0)	0(0)	2(0)
LA 416	30.75N/3.78W	5	NW	0(0)	0(0)	0(0)	0(0)	5(1)	1(0)	12(2)
LA 416	30.75N/3.78W	6	NW	1(0)	0(0)	1(0)	0(0)	3(1)	7(1)	10(2)
LA 416	30.75N/3.78W	7	NW	1(0)	0(0)	0(0)	0(0)	3(1)	1(0)	5(2)
LA 416	30.75N/3.78W	8	NW	0(0)	0(0)	0(0)	0(0)	6(2)	0(0)	4(1)
LA 416	30.75N/3.78W	9	NW	0(0)	0(0)	1(0)	0(0)	3(1)	9(2)	4(1)
LA 416	30.75N/3.78W	10	NW	1(0)	0(0)	1(0)	0(0)	15(1)	0(0)	17(2)
LA 416	30.75N/3.78W	11	NW	0(0)	0(0)	1(0)	0(0)	12(1)	0(0)	8(1)
LA 416	30.75N/3.78W	12	NW	0(0)	0(0)	1(0)	0(0)	5(1)	0(0)	3(1)
LA 416	30.75N/3.78W	13	NW	0(0)	0(0)	5(1)	1(0)	17(3)	0(0)	11(2)
LA 416	30.75N/3.78W	14	NW	0(0)	0(0)	0(0)	0(0)	4(2)	0(0)	3(1)
LA 416	30.75N/3.78W	15	NW	0(0)	1(1)	0(0)	0(0)	0(0)	0(0)	0(0)
LA 416	30.75N/3.78W	16	NW	0(0)	0(0)	0(0)	0(0)	0(0)	1(1)	0(0)
LA 416	30.75N/3.78W	17	NW	0(0)	0(0)	0(0)	0(0)	0(0)	0(0)	2(2)
LA 578	K01	1	1	0(0)	1(1)	0(0)	0(0)	0(0)	7(5)	12(8)
LA 578	K01	2	1	0(0)	0(0)	0(0)	0(0)	1(2)	1(2)	5(10)
LA 578	K01	3–4	1	0(0)	3(2)	0(0)	0(0)	0(0)	0(0)	7(5)
LA 578	M01	1	1	0(0)	1(1)	0(0)	0(0)	0(0)	4(3)	5(4)
LA 578	M01	2–3	1	0(0)	1(1)	0(0)	0(0)	0(0)	4(4)	1(1)
LA 578	M01	1–2	2	0(0)	1(2)	0(0)	0(0)	0(0)	0(0)	5(9)
LA 578	M01	1–2	3	0(0)	1(2)	0(0)	0(0)	0(0)	0(0)	5(11)
LA 578	M01	3–4	3	0(0)	0(0)	0(0)	0(0)	0(0)	8(8)	10(10)
LA 578	M01	2–6	4	0(0)	1(1)	0(0)	0(0)	0(0)	5(7)	0(0)
LA 578	M02	1	1	0(0)	1(1)	0(0)	0(0)	0(0)	0(0)	3(4)
LA 578	M02	2	1	0(0)	0(0)	0(0)	0(0)	0(0)	2(2)	5(4)
LA 578	M02	3	1	0(0)	0(0)	0(0)	0(0)	0(0)	6(8)	1(1)
LA 578	M02	4	1	0(0)	0(0)	0(0)	0(0)	0(0)	2(3)	1(1)
LA 578	M02	5	1	1(1)	3(3)	0(0)	0(0)	0(0)	6(7)	5(6)

TABLE A.1. Counts and percentages (in parentheses) of ceramics by excavation levels: Matte Painted Wares and Western Glaze Ware. *continued*

SITE	UNIT	LEV	LOC	Tularosa	Loma Fria	Socorro	St. Johns B/r & Poly	Hopi	Humm R/buff	Western Glaze
LA 578	M02	6–7	1	0(0)	9(8)	1(1)	0(0)	0(0)	0(0)	9(8)
LA 578	M02	8–9	1	1(1)	14(17)	1(1)	0(0)	0(0)	0(0)	3(4)
LA 578	M02	10–11	1	1(1)	14(16)	0(0)	3(3)	0(0)	0(0)	2(2)
LA 578	M02	1–2	2	0(0)	1(1)	0(0)	0(0)	0(0)	1(1)	4(5)
LA 578	M02	3–4	2	0(0)	0(0)	0(0)	0(0)	0(0)	0(0)	0(0)
LA 578	M02	5	2	0(0)	0(0)	0(0)	0(0)	0(0)	1(1)	0(0)
LA 578	M02	6	2	0(0)	2(3)	0(0)	0(0)	1(2)	5(9)	1(2)
LA 578	M02	7	2	0(0)	1(1)	0(0)	0(0)	0(0)	1(1)	2(3)
LA 578	M02	8–9	2	0(0)	3(9)	0(0)	0(0)	0(0)	1(3)	0(0)
LA 578	M02	10–12	2	1(2)	6(15)	0(0)	0(0)	0(0)	0(0)	2(5)
LA 578	M03	1	2	1(2)	4(9)	2(5)	1(2)	0(0)	0(0)	4(9)
LA 578	M03	2–5	2	0(0)	8(13)	1(2)	1(2)	0(0)	0(0)	0(0)
LA 578	M03	1–3	3	1(3)	4(12)	1(3)	0(0)	0(0)	0(0)	4(12)
LA 578	R02	1	1	0(0)	0(0)	0(0)	0(0)	0(0)	15(11)	19(14)
LA 578	R02	2	1	0(0)	0(0)	0(0)	2(2)	0(0)	14(16)	15(17)
LA 578	R02	4	1	0(0)	1(3)	0(0)	0(0)	0(0)	3(10)	11(37)
LA 578	R02	5	1	0(0)	1(1)	1(1)	0(0)	0(0)	2(3)	16(25)
LA 578	R02	6–7	1	0(0)	1(2)	1(2)	0(0)	0(0)	0(0)	15(27)
LA 578	R02	8–9	1	0(0)	1(1)	0(0)	0(0)	0(0)	4(3)	21(19)
LA 578	R02	10	1	0(0)	4(5)	1(1)	0(0)	0(0)	1(1)	8(10)
LA 578	R02	11–12	1	1(2)	5(8)	0(0)	2(3)	0(0)	0(0)	6(9)
LA 578	R02	13	1	1(0)	56(23)	3(1)	4(2)	0(0)	0(0)	14(6)
LA 578	R02	14	2	0(0)	25(15)	1(1)	3(2)	0(0)	0(0)	0(0)
LA 578	R02	15	2	1(1)	12(10)	0(0)	10(9)	0(0)	0(0)	0(0)
LA 578	R02	16	2	0(0)	18(17)	0(0)	3(2)	0(0)	0(0)	5(5)
LA 578	R02	17	2	2(1)	27(12)	0(0)	0(0)	0(0)	0(0)	2(1)
LA 578	R02	18	2	0(0)	17(11)	0(0)	3(1)	0(0)	0(0)	0(0)
LA 578	R02	19–21	2	0(0)	12(14)	0(0)	0(0)	0(0)	0(0)	0(0)
LA 578	R10	2–7	1	0(0)	0(0)	0(0)	0(0)	0(0)	4(3)	4(3)

TABLE A.2. Counts and percentages (in parentheses) of ceramics by excavation levels: Rio Grande and Lower Rio Puerco Glaze Wares.

SITE	UNIT	LEV	LOC	Early Gl/r	Early Gl/y	Early Gl/Poly	Early other poly	Middle RG Glaze	Pottery Mound	Hidden Mt. Poly
LA 416	30.75N/3.78W	1	NW	79(26)	22(7)	44(14)	14(5)	8(3)	19(6)	7(2)
LA 416	30.75N/3.78W	2	NW	170(18)	65(7)	136(15)	50(5)	31(3)	31(3)	18(2)
LA 416	30.75N/3.78W	3	NW	60(14)	31(7)	65(15)	8(2)	0(0)	5(1)	17(4)
LA 416	30.75N/3.78W	4	NW	62(16)	25(6)	57(15)	4(1)	16(4)	5(1)	3(1)
LA 416	30.75N/3.78W	5	NW	97(15)	48(8)	76(12)	20(3)	12(2)	18(3)	13(2)
LA 416	30.75N/3.78W	6	NW	63(12)	25(5)	33(6)	18(3)	5(1)	8(1)	4(1)
LA 416	30.75N/3.78W	7	NW	57(22)	17(6)	34(13)	12(5)	1(0)	0(0)	4(1)
LA 416	30.75N/3.78W	8	NW	93(26)	23(6)	66(18)	21(6)	4(1)	0(0)	11(3)
LA 416	30.75N/3.78W	9	NW	85(24)	22(6)	53(15)	7(2)	1(0)	1(0)	6(2)
LA 416	30.75N/3.78W	10	NW	234(22)	65(6)	98(9)	24(2)	7(1)	6(1)	7(1)
LA 416	30.75N/3.78W	11	NW	147(16)	42(5)	75(8)	7(1)	4(0)	6(1)	0(0)
LA 416	30.75N/3.78W	12	NW	99(23)	20(5)	40(9)	2(0)	1(0)	1(0)	7(2)
LA 416	30.75N/3.78W	13	NW	103(20)	27(5)	47(9)	10(2)	7(1)	4(1)	3(1)
LA 416	30.75N/3.78W	14	NW	27(12)	7(3)	15(7)	2(1)	3(1)	4(2)	0(0)
LA 416	30.75N/3.78W	15	NW	17(15)	3(3)	10(9)	2(2)	0(0)	0(0)	0(0)
LA 416	30.75N/3.78W	16	NW	18(15)	7(6)	8(7)	0(0)	0(0)	0(0)	0(0)
LA 416	30.75N/3.78W	17	NW	19(17)	3(3)	6(5)	1(1)	0(0)	1(1)	1(1)
LA 578	K01	1	1	31(22)	0(0)	9(6)	0(0)	3(2)	0(0)	0(0)
LA 578	K01	2	1	6(11)	0(0)	2(4)	1(2)	0(0)	0(0)	0(0)
LA 578	K01	3–4	1	16(12)	0(0)	7(5)	0(0)	0(0)	1(1)	0(0)
LA 578	M01	2–3	1	18(16)	3(3)	4(4)	2(2)	0(0)	0(0)	0(0)
LA 578	M01	1–2	2	9(16)	2(4)	0(0)	1(2)	0(0)	0(0)	0(0)
LA 578	M01	1–2	3	17(38)	0(0)	1(2)	0(0)	1(2)	0(0)	0(0)
LA 578	M01	3–4	3	25(26)	4(4)	0(0)	1(1)	0(0)	0(0)	0(0)
LA 578	M01	2–6	4	8(11)	5(7)	1(1)	0(0)	0(0)	0(0)	0(0)
LA 578	M02	1	1	24(35)	0(0)	4(6)	0(0)	0(0)	1(1)	1(1)
LA 578	M02	2	1	17(14)	1(1)	8(7)	0(0)	0(0)	0(0)	0(0)
LA 578	M02	3	1	11(14)	0(0)	1(1)	0(0)	0(0)	0(0)	0(0)
LA 578	M02	4	1	10(14)	1(1)	2(3)	0(0)	0(0)	0(0)	0(0)
LA 578	M02	5	1	7(8)	1(1)	0(0)	0(0)	0(0)	0(0)	0(0)
LA 578	M02	6–7	1	1(1)	2(2)	0(0)	0(0)	0(0)	0(0)	0(0)

TABLE A.2. Counts and percentages (in parentheses) of ceramics by excavation levels: Rio Grande and Lower Rio Puerco Glaze Wares. *continued*

SITE	UNIT	LEV	LOC	Early Gl/r	Early Gl/y	Early Gl/ Poly	Early other poly	Middle RG Glaze	Pottery Mound	Hidden Mt. Poly
LA 578	M02	8–9	1	0(0)	0(0)	2(2)	0(0)	0(0)	0(0)	0(0)
LA 578	M02	10–11	1	0(0)	0(0)	0(0)	0(0)	0(0)	0(0)	0(0)
LA 578	M02	1–2	2	21(25)	4(5)	8(9)	0(0)	4(5)	0(0)	0(0)
LA 578	M02	3–4	2	27(27)	4(4)	1(1)	0(0)	0(0)	0(0)	0(0)
LA 578	M02	5	2	15(22)	2(3)	0(0)	0(0)	0(0)	0(0)	0(0)
LA 578	M02	6	2	8(14)	0(0)	1(2)	0(0)	0(0)	0(0)	0(0)
LA 578	M02	7	2	10(14)	4(6)	0(0)	0(0)	0(0)	0(0)	0(0)
LA 578	M02	8–9	2	9(26)	1(3)	1(3)	0(0)	0(0)	0(0)	0(0)
LA 578	M02	10–12	2	8(20)	0(0)	0(0)	0(0)	0(0)	0(0)	0(0)
LA 578	M03	1	2	0(0)	0(0)	0(0)	0(0)	0(0)	0(0)	0(0)
LA 578	M03	2–5	2	0(0)	0(0)	0(0)	0(0)	0(0)	0(0)	0(0)
LA 578	M03	1–3	3	1(3)	0(0)	0(0)	0(0)	0(0)	0(0)	0(0)
LA 578	R02	1	1	30(22)	1(1)	3(2)	0(0)	0(0)	0(0)	0(0)
LA 578	R02	2	1	15(17)	1(1)	2(2)	1(1)	0(0)	0(0)	0(0)
LA 578	R02	4	1	0(0)	1(3)	1(3)	0(0)	0(0)	0(0)	0(0)
LA 578	R02	5	1	7(11)	1(1)	1(1)	0(0)	0(0)	0(0)	0(0)
LA 578	R02	6–7	1	4(7)	0(0)	0(0)	0(0)	0(0)	0(0)	0(0)
LA 578	R02	8–9	1	11(10)	0(0)	1(1)	1(1)	0(0)	0(0)	0(0)
LA 578	R02	10	1	19(23)	0(0)	0(0)	0(0)	0(0)	0(0)	0(0)
LA 578	R02	11–12	1	6(9)	0(0)	0(0)	0(0)	0(0)	0(0)	0(0)
LA 578	R02	13	1	0(0)	0(0)	0(0)	0(0)	0(0)	0(0)	0(0)
LA 578	R02	14	2	0(0)	0(0)	0(0)	0(0)	0(0)	0(0)	0(0)
LA 578	R02	15	2	0(0)	0(0)	0(0)	0(0)	0(0)	0(0)	0(0)
LA 578	R02	16	2	0(0)	0(0)	0(0)	0(0)	0(0)	0(0)	0(0)
LA 578	R02	17	2	0(0)	0(0)	1(0)	0(0)	0(0)	0(0)	0(0)
LA 578	R02	18	2	0(0)	0(0)	0(0)	0(0)	0(0)	0(0)	0(0)
LA 578	R02	19–21	2	0(0)	0(0)	0(0)	0(0)	0(0)	0(0)	0(0)
LA 578	R10	2–7	1	12(8)	0(0)	4(3)	0(0)	0(0)	0(0)	0(0)

TABLE A.3. Counts and percentages (in parentheses) of ceramics by excavation levels: Utility Wares.

SITE	UNIT	LEV	LOC	plain gray	smdg plain gray	indent corr gray	smear corr gray	smdg smear corr gray	mica smear corr gray	Mog Brown Ware
LA 416	30.75N/3.78W	1	NW	84(28)	14(5)	1(0)	3(1)	0(0)	0(0)	0(0)
LA 416	30.75N/3.78W	2	NW	330(36)	45(5)	2(0)	14(1)	2(0)	0(0)	1(0)
LA 416	30.75N/3.78W	3	NW	159(27)	25(6)	6(1)	36(8)	0(0)	1(0)	0(0)
LA 416	30.75N/3.78W	4	NW	80(21)	6(1)	0(0)	109(28)	9(2)	7(2)	0(0)
LA 416	30.75N/3.78W	5	NW	176(28)	10(2)	0(0)	123(20)	12(2)	0(0)	1(0)
LA 416	30.75N/3.78W	6	NW	114(22)	13(2)	0(0)	202(38)	17(3)	1(0)	0(0)
LA 416	30.75N/3.78W	7	NW	59(22)	3(1)	0(0)	63(24)	2(1)	1(0)	0(0)
LA 416	30.75N/3.78W	8	NW	75(21)	4(1)	0(0)	56(15)	0(0)	0(0)	0(0)
LA 416	30.75N/3.78W	9	NW	60(17)	1(0)	0(0)	89(25)	11(3)	5(1)	0(0)
LA 416	30.75N/3.78W	10	NW	208(20)	1(0)	0(0)	345(33)	15(1)	4(0)	9(1)
LA 416	30.75N/3.78W	11	NW	532(59)	6(1)	0(0)	55(6)	1(0)	0(0)	3(0)
LA 416	30.75N/3.78W	12	NW	107(25)	0(0)	0(0)	131(30)	9(2)	0(0)	3(1)
LA 416	30.75N/3.78W	13	NW	180(36)	28(6)	2(0)	52(10)	4(1)	1(0)	0(0)
LA 416	30.75N/3.78W	14	NW	108(49)	18(8)	1(0)	30(13)	0(0)	0(0)	0(0)
LA 416	30.75N/3.78W	15	NW	20(17)	6(5)	0(0)	44(38)	13(11)	0(0)	0(0)
LA 416	30.75N/3.78W	16	NW	63(52)	4(3)	1(1)	19(16)	0(0)	0(0)	0(0)
LA 416	30.75N/3.78W	17	NW	58(51)	0(0)	3(3)	17(15)	0(0)	2(2)	0(0)
LA 578	K01	1	1	14(10)	0(0)	9(6)	40(28)	2(1)	14(10)	0(0)
LA 578	K01	2	1	4(8)	0(0)	3(6)	14(27)	5(10)	10(19)	0(0)
LA 578	K01	3–4	1	5(4)	5(4)	12(9)	42(32)	7(5)	28(21)	0(0)
LA 578	M01	1	1	34(29)	16(14)	1(1)	10(8)	1(1)	8(7)	0(0)
LA 578	M01	2–3	1	50(45)	11(10)	3(3)	5(4)	0(0)	8(7)	0(0)
LA 578	M01	1–2	2	26(48)	2(4)	0(0)	3(5)	0(0)	6(11)	0(0)
LA 578	M01	1–2	3	17(38)	0(0)	0(0)	3(7)	0(0)	0(0)	0(0)
LA 578	M01	3–4	3	34(35)	1(1)	1(1)	10(10)	0(0)	3(3)	0(0)
LA 578	M01	2–6	4	31(41)	7(9)	4(5)	5(7)	0(0)	8(11)	0(0)
LA 578	M02	1	1	16(23)	2(3)	3(4)	7(10)	0(0)	4(6)	3(4)
LA 578	M02	2	1	63(52)	1(1)	0(0)	17(14)	0(0)	7(6)	0(0)
LA 578	M02	3	1	40(51)	1(1)	1(1)	8(10)	2(3)	5(6)	2(3)
LA 578	M02	4	1	22(31)	5(7)	2(3)	14(19)	3(4)	8(11)	2(3)

TABLE A.3. Counts and percentages (in parentheses) of ceramics by excavation levels: Utility Wares. *continued*

SITE	UNIT	LEV	LOC	plain gray	smdg plain gray	indent corr gray	smear corr gray	smdg smear corr gray	mica smear corr gray	Mog Brown Ware
LA 578	M02	5	1	28(31)	10(11)	2(2)	13(15)	0(0)	11(12)	2(2)
LA 578	M02	6–7	1	28(27)	1(1)	16(15)	31(29)	0(0)	8(7)	1(1)
LA 578	M02	8–9	1	10(12)	2(2)	25(30)	20(24)	0(0)	4(5)	1(1)
LA 578	M02	10–11	1	15(17)	0(0)	32(37)	18(21)	0(0)	1(1)	1(1)
LA 578	M02	1–2	2	28(33)	1(1)	1(1)	9(11)	2(2)	1(1)	0(0)
LA 578	M02	3–4	2	25(25)	3(3)	4(4)	25(25)	1(1)	6(6)	2(2)
LA 578	M02	5	2	31(46)	0(0)	1(1)	7(10)	3(4)	7(10)	1(1)
LA 578	M02	6	2	19(33)	0(0)	0(0)	7(12)	0(0)	12(21)	1(2)
LA 578	M02	7	2	19(27)	0(0)	10(14)	15(22)	0(0)	7(10)	0(0)
LA 578	M02	8–9	2	0(0)	0(0)	9(26)	4(12)	0(0)	6(18)	0(0)
LA 578	M02	10–12	2	6(15)	0(0)	8(20)	8(20)	0(0)	0(0)	1(2)
LA 578	M03	1	2	15(34)	0(0)	11(26)	4(9)	0(0)	0(0)	1(2)
LA 578	M03	2–5	2	16(26)	1(2)	15(25)	3(5)	3(5)	4(7)	9(15)
LA 578	R02	1	1	25(18)	0(0)	6(4)	15(11)	0(0)	23(17)	0(0)
LA 578	R02	2	1	11(12)	0(0)	7(8)	15(17)	0(0)	4(4)	1(1)
LA 578	R02	4	1	3(10)	0(0)	4(13)	4(13)	0(0)	2(7)	0(0)
LA 578	R02	5	1	6(9)	0(0)	13(20)	10(15)	0(0)	7(11)	0(0)
LA 578	R02	6–7	1	8(14)	0(0)	9(16)	8(14)	0(0)	10(18)	0(0)
LA 578	R02	8–9	1	13(11)	0(0)	15(13)	12(11)	0(0)	32(28)	2(2)
LA 578	R02	10	1	5(6)	0(0)	25(30)	0(0)	0(0)	19(23)	0(0)
LA 578	R02	11–12	1	2(3)	0(0)	10(16)	22(34)	0(0)	10(16)	0(0)
LA 578	R02	13	1	9(4)	0(0)	67(28)	30(12)	0(0)	54(22)	2(1)
LA 578	R02	14	2	20(12)	2(1)	84(51)	13(8)	0(0)	7(4)	9(5)
LA 578	R02	15	2	11(9)	0(0)	55(47)	16(14)	0(0)	5(4)	6(5)
LA 578	R02	16	2	16(15)	0(0)	47(44)	6(6)	0(0)	4(4)	8(7)
LA 578	R02	17	2	15(6)	1(0)	146(64)	5(2)	0(0)	29(12)	1(0)
LA 578	R02	18	2	29(19)	0(0)	81(53)	17(11)	0(0)	4(3)	2(1)
LA 578	R02	19–21	2	22(27)	0(0)	41(50)	2(2)	0(0)	1(1)	4(5)
LA 578	R10	2–7	1	4(3)	0(0)	4(3)	58(39)	2(1)	57(38)	0(0)

APPENDIX B

Seriation of Ceramic Types from the Lower Rio Puerco District

This section presents a seriation using ceramic types (described in appendix A) collected from the well-stratified trash middens and trash-filled rooms described in chapter 3. The resulting chronology suggests that excavation levels from Hummingbird Pueblo and Pottery Mound can be divided into three consecutive phases ranging in time from approximately AD 1275 to 1425+. Excavation levels divided by site and these three phases provide the basic divisions of analysis for the research in this volume.

The Lower Rio Puerco archaeological district does not have a single well-developed chronology for decorated ceramic assemblages. Instead, it is at the boundary of two different *archaeological* traditions of decorated ceramic analysis—the Western Pueblo region and the Rio Grande region. In general, archaeologists who work in the Western Pueblo region focus primarily on slip color, design layout, and design elements when recording pottery (e.g., Carlson 1970; Hays-Gilpin and van Hartesveldt 1998; Woodbury and Woodbury 1966). In the Rio Grande region, archaeologists tend to focus more on temper type, surface treatment, and, with the introduction of glaze technology, rim form (e.g., Habicht-Mauche 1993; Shepard 1942; Warren 1979). The most common approach for dating post-1300 sites in the Rio Grande region is through the use of a glaze ware rim-form seriation developed by Alfred Kidder and Anna Shepard (1936) and then expanded by Mera (1935).

While both archaeological approaches to ceramic typology are useful for the region in which they were developed, neither approach is without problems, nor was one the obvious approach for this research. As a result, various attributes were recorded for each sherd in this study (see code sheet at the end of this appendix) and both approaches, as well as various combinations, were explored with the statistical methods described below. For the purposes of creating a time-sensitive seriation, the best approach (presented here) was the one followed by Western Pueblo archaeologists. A seriation based on either the Rio Grande rim-form typology or a modified rim-form typology that I developed to include unusual forms simply did not seriate. In other words, rim-form types did not cluster into groups that corresponded with stratified trash levels.

Statistical Methods

In archaeological research, seriation is most commonly the ordering of observations relative to time (Duff 1996). In this analysis, the observations are counts of decorated and undecorated ceramic types from stratified trash deposits. Three different analytical techniques are combined to build this seriation: correspondence analysis (CA), k-means cluster analysis, and mean ceramic dating.

Correspondence analysis is a multivariate scaling procedure similar to both principal components analysis and multidimensional scaling. Its strengths lie in its ability to use counts (contingency tables data) and to display cases and variables in the same spatial dimensions. This latter strength helps to simultaneously evaluate the relative contribution of variables and cases. For a more detailed description of this technique, and its application in archaeological seriation, see Baxter (1994), Bolviken and colleagues (1982), Duff (1996), Ihm (1987), and Laxton and Restorick (1989).

Although CA provides the seriation, the combination of k-means cluster analysis with mean ceramic dating allows for the grouping of excavation levels into chronological periods as well as assigning tentative calendar dates to these periods. K-means cluster analysis is a nonhierarchical clustering technique used for grouping cases (Baxter 1994; Kintigh and Ammerman 1982). Its advantage over other clustering methods is that as a nonhierarchical technique it minimizes intracluster variation while maximizing intercluster variation. Further, comparison of the actual data with randomized data provides a means to help determine whether the actual data cluster in a meaningful sense or as could have simply happened by chance (Kintigh 2002).

For historic pottery assemblages, a mean ceramic date is calculated by multiplying the total frequency of a ceramic type within an assemblage with its *median* manufacture date, summing this product for all ceramic types, and then dividing this sum by the total number of sherds (South 1978). To calculate such a date obviously requires having a median manufacture date for each ceramic type. As such, the technique is more problematic with prehistoric ceramic collections. Although it has been applied successfully to ceramic assemblages in the Kayenta area (Christenson 1994), these assemblages were associated with multiple tree-ring dates. Andrew Gomolak (1980) has argued that the frequencies of prehistoric ceramic types he used when calculating mean ceramic dates were skewed. The data are not available from the Lower Rio Puerco area to assess an actual *median* date for ceramic types. In the following analysis, I use the *midpoint* of the commonly agreed upon temporal range for the better-dated ceramic types in my assemblage (table B.1). This approach provides a guideline for dating Hummingbird Pueblo and Pottery Mound that can be refined as better absolute dates become available.

TABLE B.1. List of ceramic types used in seriation.

Type	Date Range	Midpoint
Tularosa Black-on-white	1200–1275	1237.5
Loma Fria Black-on-white	1200–1275	1237.5
Socorro Black-on-white	1200–1400	1300.0
St. Johns Black-on-red and Polychrome	1175–1300	1237.5
Western Pueblo glaze ware	1275–1450	1362.5
Early Rio Grande Glaze-on-red	1313–1500	1406.5
Early Rio Grande Glaze-on-yellow	1321–1450	1385.5
Early Rio Grande Glaze-on-polychrome	1321–1450	1385.5
Early Rio Grande other glaze polychrome	1350–1450	1400.0
Middle Rio Grande Glaze Ware	1430–1550	1490.0
Pottery Mound Polychrome	not used in mean ceramic date calculation	
Hidden Mountain Polychrome	not used in mean ceramic date calculation	
Hopi Yellow Ware	not used in mean ceramic date calculation	
Hummingbird Buff Ware	not used in mean ceramic date calculation	
Indented corrugated gray ware	not used in mean ceramic date calculation	
Smeared corrugated gray ware	not used in mean ceramic date calculation	
Smudged smeared corrugated gray ware	not used in mean ceramic date calculation	
Micaceous smeared corrugated gray ware	not used in mean ceramic date calculation	
Plain gray ware	not used in mean ceramic date calculation	
Smudged plain gray ware	not used in mean ceramic date calculation	
Mogollon Brown Ware	not used in mean ceramic date calculation	

NOTE: Rio Grande Glaze Ware, Hopi Yellow Ware, and Mogollon Brown Ware are all established ceramic wares in the archaeological literature. Hummingbird Buff Ware is a new ware defined in this research. Locally produced utility wares have a gray paste and are therefore referred to as gray wares in this research. However, these gray wares are not part of any established ware defined for other regions of the Southwest. Western Pueblo glaze ware is not an established ware but for the purposes of this research combines Acoma Glaze Ware and Zuni Glaze Ware.

The Analysis

I relied on Statistica, XLSTAT, and Tools for Quantitative Archaeology (Kintigh 1994) software packages for computations. To reduce the chance of error due to small sample size, each case (excavation level) used in the analysis was required to have at least 20 sherds identifiable to type. Twenty was chosen as a cutoff to guarantee that no one sherd would ever

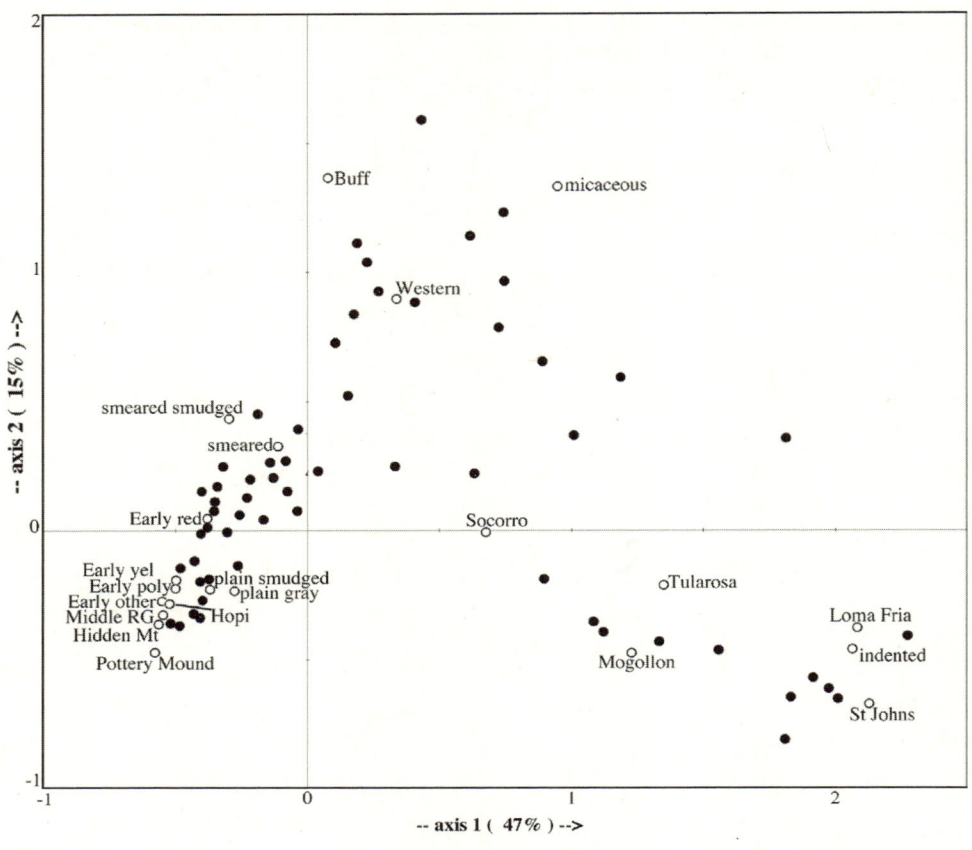

FIGURE B.1. Correspondence analysis results showing relative contribution of ceramic types on excavation levels from the Lower Rio Puerco area.

represent more than 5 percent of a level's assemblage. Adjoining levels with too few sherds were combined to meet this cutoff. Several analyses were conducted on different combinations of ceramic types (i.e., only decorated wares or only undecorated wares). Because all these analyses provided similar results, the following analysis includes all decorated and undecorated types with occurrences of more than 10 sherds within the total ceramic assemblage. As such, this analysis provides a means to examine the temporal relationship between the most common decorated and undecorated pottery types recovered from the Lower Rio Puerco area.

Correspondence analysis was performed on ceramic type counts from 60 excavation levels (17 from Pottery Mound and 43 from Hummingbird Pueblo). A plot of the first two CA axes (figure B.1; table B.2) shows the relative contributions of these ceramic types in the Lower Rio Puerco assemblage. Axis 1 accounts for 47 percent of the variance and can be interpreted as time. Axis 1 places the thirteenth-century ceramic types to the right, with later types to the

TABLE B.2. Factor loadings, eigenvalues, and percent variance for first five factors from CA of ceramic type assemblage.

Type	Factor 1	Factor 2	Factor 3	Factor 4	Factor 5
Tularosa	1.35	-0.21	-0.32	0.21	0.24
Loma Fria	2.08	-0.38	-0.14	-0.04	-0.20
Socorro	0.68	0	0.16	0.11	0.06
St. Johns	2.13	-0.68	-0.42	0.61	0.74
Western	0.34	0.90	0.56	-0.08	0.74
Early Gl/r	-0.38	0.04	-0.01	-0.06	0.08
Early Gl/y	-0.50	-0.22	-0.11	-0.18	0.06
Early Gl/poly	-0.50	-0.21	-0.12	-0.31	0.05
Early other	-0.54	-0.28	-0.09	-0.57	0.18
Middle Glaze	-0.55	-0.32	0.02	-0.65	0.12
PM Poly	-0.57	-0.48	0.17	-0.76	0.06
Hid. Mt. Poly	-0.57	-0.36	-0.15	-0.66	0.16
Hopi	-0.53	-0.28	-0.07	-0.05	-0.05
Hum. Buff	0.08	1.37	0.95	0.46	1.01
Plain gray	-0.27	-0.23	0.29	0.22	-0.11
Smudged gray	-0.37	-0.22	0.47	-0.24	-0.28
Indented gray	2.07	-0.46	-0.05	-0.10	0.14
Smeared gray	-0.12	0.33	-0.56	0.15	0
Smear smdge.	-0.30	0.44	-0.86	0.21	-0.20
Micaceous	0.95	1.33	0.38	-0.33	-0.64
Brown Ware	1.23	-0.48	-0.15	0.78	0.09
Eigen values	0.56	0.18	0.12	0.06	0.06
% variance	47	15	10	5	5
cumulative %	47	62	72	77	82

left. Axis 2 accounts for 15 percent of the variance and can be interpreted as a combination of temporal and possibly functional differences.

The *k*-means cluster analysis groups together excavation levels containing similar standardized percents of the same ceramic types used in the CA. These data were standardized using z-scores so as to provide more weight to the decorated ceramic types, which have smaller sample sizes than the undecorated types but better temporal control. The *k*-means program used in this analysis provides a method to evaluate the clustering apparent in the actual data by comparing it with clustering observed in randomized data (Kintigh 1994). The cluster solution at which the greatest difference between the average Sum of the Squared Distances (SSD) for the random data and original data occurs is considered to be the "best" solution (Kintigh 1994; Kintigh and Ammerman 1982). Using the standardized percentages discussed above, 25 random data runs were generated. By comparing the average SSE for the

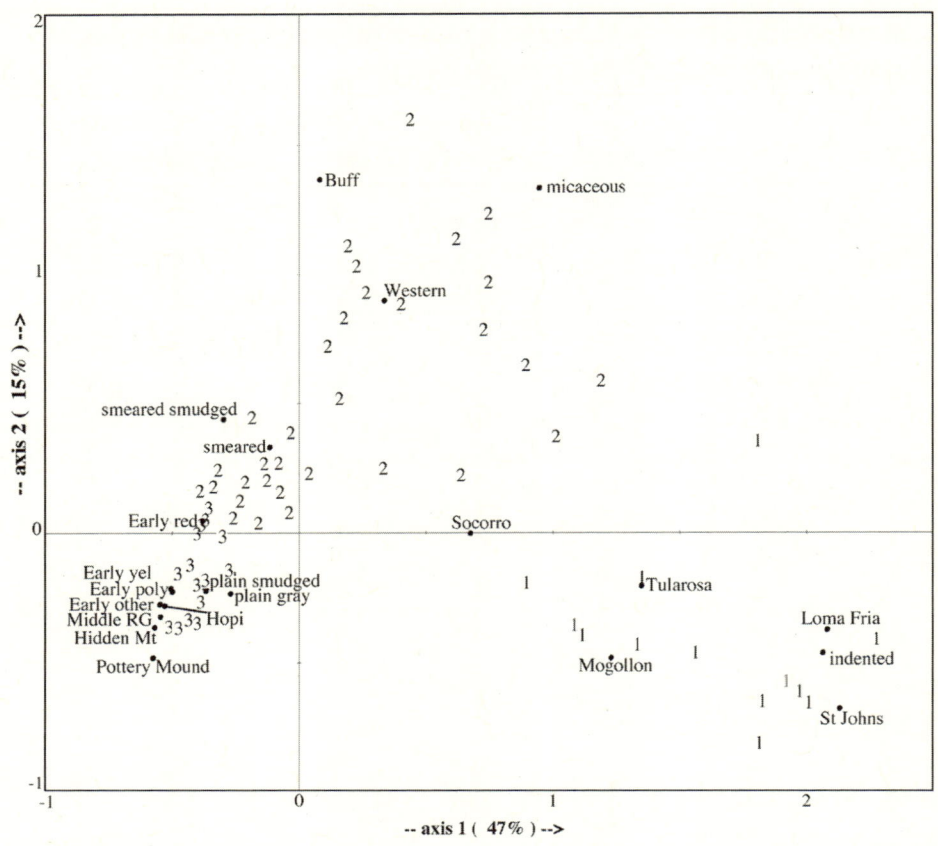

FIGURE B.2. Correspondence analysis results plotted by *k*-means three-cluster solution.

random runs with the SSE for the original run, the *k*-means three-cluster solution was determined to be optimal (tables B.3 and B.4).

A plot of the first two CA axes with excavation levels plotted by their *k*-means three-cluster solution (figure B.2) shows that these clusters can be interpreted as separating the ceramic assemblage based on temporally significant types. Mean ceramic dates (table B.3) and stratigraphic position (table B.5) strengthen this interpretation. Cluster 1 contains levels composed mostly of black-on-white pottery types, St. Johns types, and indented corrugated gray ware. Levels assigned to this cluster are always the lowest levels stratigraphically (table B.5). Cluster 2 contains levels composed mostly of Western Pueblo glaze ware, Early Rio Grande Glaze-on-red, and Hummingbird Buff Ware. This cluster is represented almost exclusively by excavation levels from Hummingbird Pueblo (LA 578). Cluster 3 contains levels composed mostly of Early Rio Grande Glaze-on-yellow and Glaze-on-polychrome, Middle Rio Grande Glaze Ware, Pottery Mound Polychrome, Hidden Mountain Polychrome, and Hopi Yellow Ware. This cluster, with one exception, contains levels only from Pottery Mound (LA 416).

TABLE B.3. Mean and standard deviation for *k*-means three-cluster solution as well as mean ceramic date (MCD) for each cluster.

Ceramic Type	Cluster 1 MCD = AD 1286	Cluster 2 MCD = AD 1387	Cluster 3 MCD = AD 1417
Tularosa B/w	1.08±1.11	0.09±0.39	0±0
Loma Fria B/w	14.15±3.69	1.75±2.46	0.07±0.26
Socorro B/w	1.08±1.55	0.16±0.45	0.13±0.52
St. Johns B/r & Polychrome	1.92±2.43	0.16±0.63	0±0
Western Pueblo glaze ware	1.78±5.54	0.12±0.49	1.33±0.82
Early Rio Grande Gl/r	3.38±3.91	3.47±4.04	0.33±0.72
Early Rio Grande Gl/y	0.13±0.34	7.81±8.92	1.60±1.12
Early Rio Grande Gl/poly	0±0	16.25±8.60	19.47±4.93
Early Rio Grande other poly	0±0	1.81±2.04	5.87±1.30
Middle Rio Grande Glaze	0.54±0.55	2.56±2.51	11.67±3.73
Pottery Mound Polychrome	0±0	0.41±0.71	2.60±1.92
Hidden Mountain Polychrome	0±0	0.12±0.49	1.73±1.53
Hopi Yellow Ware	0±0	0.09±0.30	1.60±1.64
Hummingbird Buff Ware	0±0	0.06±0.25	1.60±1.12
Indented corrugated gray ware	17.00±8.90	25.31±16.90	29.67±11.58
Smeared corrugated gray ware	2.00±0.21	2.41±3.81	2.73±2.71
Smudged smeared corrugated gray ware	38.46±13.84	7.16±7.94	0.20±0.56
Mica smeared corrugated gray ware	11.54±7.17	16.59±10.04	17.73±11.52
Plain gray ware	0.38±1.39	1.31±2.78	1.13±1.13
Smudged plain gray ware	4.85±6.16	11.69±8.52	0.27±0.59
Mogollon Brown Ware	3.69±4.03	0.66±1.12	0.13±0.35

Stratigraphy and sherd density were used to examine whether a cultural hiatus existed between any of the three defined phases (table B.5). If a hiatus had occurred, then natural layers of culturally sterile deposits may have formed between levels classified to different phases. Excavation notes and stratigraphic profiles occasionally describe thin (<1 cm) lenses of sand occurring throughout the deposits; however, no sterile layers occurred between deposits classified to different phases.

Depositional and postdepositional processes may cause a tapering off of artifact densities toward the beginning and end of an occupational sequence. If a hiatus existed between phases, the difference between ceramic densities from two levels classified to different phases may be expected to be higher than differences between levels from the same phase. The only

TABLE B.4. Excavation levels (Site/Unit/Level/Locus) presented by *k*-means three-cluster solution.

Cluster 1	Cluster 2	Cluster 3
LA 578/M02/8–9/1	LA 416/30.75N:3.78W/15/NW	LA 416/30.75N:3.78W/1/NW
LA 578/M02/10–11/1	LA 416/30.75N:3.78W/16/NW	LA 416/30.75N:3.78W/2/NW
LA 578/M02/10/2	LA 416/30.75N:3.78W/17/NW	LA 416/30.75N:3.78W/3/NW
LA 578/M03/1/2	LA 578/K01/1/1	LA 416/30.75N:3.78W/4/NW
LA 578/M03/2/2	LA 578/K01/2/1	LA 416/30.75N:3.78W/5/NW
LA 578/M03/1/3	LA 578/K01/3–4/1	LA 416/30.75N:3.78W/6/NW
LA 578/R02/13/1	LA 578/M01/1/1	LA 416/30.75N:3.78W/7/NW
LA 578/R02/14/2	LA 578/M01/2/1	LA 416/30.75N:3.78W/8/NW
LA 578/R02/15/2	LA 578/M01/1/2	LA 416/30.75N:3.78W/9/NW
LA 578/R02/16/2	LA 578/M01/1/3	LA 416/30.75N:3.78W/10/NW
LA 578/R02/17/2	LA 578/M01/3/3	LA 416/30.75N:3.78W/11/NW
LA 578/R02/18/2	LA 578/M01/2/4	LA 416/30.75N:3.78W/12/NW
LA 578/R02/19–21/2	LA 578/M02/1/1	LA 416/30.75N:3.78W/13/NW
	LA 578/M02/2/1	LA 416/30.75N:3.78W/14/NW
	LA 578/M02/3/1	LA 578/M02/1/1–2
	LA 578/M02/4/1	
	LA 578/M02/5/1	
	LA 578/M02/6–7/1	
	LA 578/M02/3/2	
	LA 578/M02/5/2	
	LA 578/M02/6/2	
	LA 578/M02/7/2	
	LA 578/M02/8/2	
	LA 578/R02/1/1	
	LA 578/R02/2/1	
	LA 578/R02/4/1	
	LA 578/R02/5/1	
	LA 578/R02/6–7/1	
	LA 578/R02/8–9/1	
	LA 578/R02/10/1	
	LA 578/R02/11–12/1	
	LA 578/R10/2–7/1	

instance where this occurs is in the Pottery Mound deposits, where the difference in densities between Levels 14 and 15 is the highest in the unit. Although this may reflect a cultural hiatus between Phases 2 and 3 at Pottery Mound, I am more inclined to believe that it reflects Level 15's positioning near sterile deposits, where artifact densities tend to be lighter. The three deepest levels at Pottery Mound—Levels 15, 16, and 17—all had relatively light artifact densities, possibly due to mixing with sterile soils.

TABLE B.5. Selected excavation units used to examine the relationship between *k*-means cluster assignment, stratigraphic placement, and sherd density.

Cluster	Site	Unit	Level	Locus	Sherds/ Cubic Meter
2	LA 578	R02	1	1	685
2	LA 578	R02	2	1	440
2	LA 578	R02	4	1	150
2	LA 578	R02	5	1	325
2	LA 578	R02	6–7	1	140
2	LA 578	R02	8–9	1	280
2	LA 578	R02	10	1	320
2	LA 578	R02	11–12	1	410
1	LA 578	R02	13	1	600
1	LA 578	R02	14	2	800
1	LA 578	R02	15	2	550
1	LA 578	R02	16	2	543
1	LA 578	R02	17	2	228
1	LA 578	R02	18	2	150
1	LA 578	R02	19–21	2	130
3	LA 578	M02	1–2	2	425
2	LA 578	M02	3–4	2	490
2	LA 578	M02	5	2	680
2	LA 578	M02	6	2	570
2	LA 578	M02	7	2	690
2	LA 578	M02	8–9	2	170
1	LA 578	M02	10–12	2	133
3	LA 416	30.75N/3.78W	1	NW Quad	242
3	LA 416	30.75N/3.78W	2	NW Quad	740
3	LA 416	30.75N/3.78W	3	NW Quad	339
3	LA 416	30.75N/3.78W	4	NW Quad	310
3	LA 416	30.75N/3.78W	5	NW Quad	499
3	LA 416	30.75N/3.78W	6	NW Quad	420
3	LA 416	30.75N/3.78W	7	NW Quad	210
3	LA 416	30.75N/3.78W	8	NW Quad	290
3	LA 416	30.75N/3.78W	9	NW Quad	286
3	LA 416	30.75N/3.78W	10	NW Quad	846
3	LA 416	30.75N/3.78W	11	NW Quad	847
3	LA 416	30.75N/3.78W	12	NW Quad	432
3	LA 416	30.75N/3.78W	13	NW Quad	377
3	LA 416	30.75N/3.78W	14	NW Quad	292
2	LA 416	30.75N/3.78W	15	NW Quad	186
2	LA 416	30.75N/3.78W	16	NW Quad	194
2	LA 416	30.75N/3.78W	17	NW Quad	180

Discussion and Conclusion

The above analyses divide excavation levels from Hummingbird Pueblo and Pottery Mound into three time phases. Excavation levels were combined using these three temporal phases, along with spatial considerations, as a guideline. These combined levels provide the basic divisions for analysis in the research presented in this volume (see table B.4).

Phase 1, with a mean ceramic date of AD 1286, is dominated by black-on-white ceramic types and represents the late Pueblo III and early Pueblo IV occupation at Hummingbird Pueblo. It also represents the introduction of Western Pueblo glaze ware into the Lower Rio Puerco area, as well as the transition to local glaze paint production. Since the earliest Western Pueblo glaze-painted pottery is dated at AD 1275 (Eckert 2003), it is doubtful that Phase 1 dates any earlier than this. The earliest glaze-painted pottery in the Rio Grande region has been dated to AD 1313 (Cordell 1975); glaze paint technology likely did not reach the Lower Rio Puerco area much earlier. As such, AD 1286 may more appropriately be considered a *begin* date for Phase 1, rather than a *mean* date. The mean ceramic date as calculated for Phase 1 is biased toward an early date due to the substantial amount of locally produced white ware recovered. Excavation levels assigned to Phase 1 are only represented at Hummingbird Pueblo, and at least some of these levels may be associated with the stone-robbed roomblock underneath M01 (which dates to Phase 2) described earlier in the appendix. However, the radiocarbon dates clustering around AD 1300 and recovered from the two adobe portions of Hummingbird Pueblo suggest that these roomblocks were established during Phase 1 as well.

Phase 2, with a mean ceramic date of AD 1387, is the best-represented phase in number of excavation levels from Hummingbird Pueblo. This phase also appears to mark the initial occupation of Pottery Mound. Phase 2 may be associated with the early component of Pottery Mound discussed above, as well as the 1381v tree-ring date recovered from trash-fill. Phase 3, with a mean ceramic date of AD 1417, is mostly represented by excavation levels from Pottery Mound and corresponds with the remaining tree-ring dates from that site (1411v, 1418v, 1427v). Hummingbird Pueblo is represented by only one excavation level from Phase 3, which may reflect the tail end of this site's occupation. As all of the stratified trash from the mound beneath the masonry roomblock at Hummingbird Pueblo dates to either Phase 1 or 2, this portion of the site was likely the last to be occupied.

Finally, the issues of contemporaneity and sample size need to be addressed. First, there is no Phase 1 sample from Pottery Mound or the region immediately around it available. In the following analyses, I discuss this phase in the southern portion of the study area based upon observations noted by other researchers. Second, Phase 2 is not well represented at Pottery Mound. Similarly, Phase 3 is not well represented at Hummingbird Pueblo. I do not know if this is due to sampling strategy or occupation differences between the two villages. Although there is probably some temporal overlap between Phases 2 and 3, there is no way to evaluate how much. In the analyses presented in this volume, I address these issues of contemporaneity and sample size where appropriate and attempt to control for them where possible. With these concerns kept in mind, the chronology created above allows for the comparison of material culture trends between Hummingbird Pueblo and Pottery Mound, as well as examination of changes in material culture through time within each village.

Code Sheet for Ceramic Decorative and Technological Attributes

This section presents the code sheet for the ceramic decorative and technological attributes recorded on sherds in this study. The complete data set is available from the author.

SITE Site number (416 = Pottery Mound, 578 = Hummingbird Pueblo)
UNIT Unit number (NOTE: for Pottery Mound, Unit NW refers to trash unit 30.75N/3.78W)
LEVEL Level number
LOCUS Locus number (NOTE: for Pottery Mound, Locus NW refers to NW quad of unit)
SPEC Specimen number assigned to each artifacts bag in the Hummingbird Pueblo assemblage
LOT Sequential number assigned to each sherd
SIZE Size of sherds measured in 2 sq cm increments
DEC/UND Record decorated or undecorated (utility) ware
    0. Indeterminate
    1. Undecorated
    2. Decorated
TYPE Ceramic ware and type. Note that codes for sherds that can only be identified at the ware level end in 00 (i.e., 2100 = Cibola Gray Ware) and that many type names allowable are informal types. When in doubt, only the ware code is entered.

01 Cibola White Ware
0100 Untyped Cibola White Ware
0101 Untyped, unpainted
0102 Untyped, painted
0110 La Plata B/w
0111 White Mound B/w
0112 Kiatuthlanna B/w
0113 Red Mesa B/w
0114 Gallup B/w
0115 Chaco B/w
0116 Chaco/McElmo B/w
0117 Escavada B/w
0118 Puerco B/w
0119 Corrugated Reserve B/w
0120 Reserve B/w
0121 Tularosa B/w
0122 Pinedale B/w
0123 Klagetoh B/w

05 Rio Puerco of the East White Ware
0500 Untyped Rio Puerco White Ware
0501 Untyped Basketmaker III–Pueblo I
0502 Untyped Pueblo II–Pueblo III
0505 Loma Fria B/w

06 Rio Grande Carbon Painted White Wares
0600 Untyped Rio Grande Carbon Painted White Ware
0601 Untyped Basketmaker III–Pueblo I
0602 Untyped Pueblo II–Pueblo III
0603 Untyped Pueblo III
0604 Untyped Pueblo IV
0611 Casa Salazar B/w
0612 Vallecitos B/w
0616 Santa Fe B/w
0620 Galisteo B/w

07 Rio Grande Mineral Painted White Wares
0700 Untyped Rio Grande Mineral Painted White Ware
0701 Untyped Basketmaker III–Pueblo I
0702 Untyped Pueblo II–Pueblo III
0703 Untyped Pueblo III
0704 Untyped Pueblo IV
0711 Kwahe'e B/w
0720 Socorro B/w
0721 Chupadero B/w
0750 Jemez B/w

08 Biscuit and Biscuitoid Ware
0800 Untyped Biscuit Ware
0803 Untyped Pueblo III
0804 Untyped Pueblo IV
0811 Wiyo B/w
0815 Biscuit A
0816 Biscuit B

09 Untyped White Ware
0900 Untyped White Ware
0920 Pueblo II White Ware
0921 Pueblo II White Ware, mineral paint
0922 Pueblo II White Ware, organic paint
0930 Pueblo III White Ware
0931 Pueblo III White Ware, mineral paint
0932 Pueblo III White Ware, organic paint
0940 Pueblo IV White Ware
0941 Pueblo IV White Ware, mineral paint
0942 Pueblo IV White Ware, organic paint
0990 Untyped White Ware, mineral paint
0995 Untyped White Ware, organic paint
0999 White Ware, no paint

10 White Mountain Red Ware
1000 Untyped White Mountain Red Ware
1001 Untyped Polychrome
1002 Untyped, unpainted
1011 Puerco B/r
1012 Wingate B/r
1013 Wingate Polychrome, Houck variety (red-slipped band)
1014 Wingate Polychrome, Querino variety (red paint, cream slip)
1015 Wingate B/r Corrugated (B/r interior, corrugated exterior)
1016 St. Johns B/r
1017 St. Johns Polychrome
1018 Springerville Polychrome

20 Western Glaze Ware
2000 Untyped Western Glaze Ware
2001 Untyped Western Glaze Ware, polychrome
2002 Untyped Western Glaze Ware, unpainted
2011 Heshotauthla B/r
2012 Heshotauthla Polychrome
2013 Kwakina Polychrome
2014 Pinedale B/r
2015 Pinedale Polychrome
2016 Pinnawa Gl/w
2017 Pinnawa R/w
2018 Kechipawan Polychrome

25 Rio Grande Glaze Ware (RGG)
2500 Untyped Rio Grande Glaze Ware
2501 Untyped Rio Grande Glaze Ware, polychrome
2502 Untyped Rio Grande Glaze Ware, unpainted

Rim Sherds
2510 Glaze A
2511 Glaze A Agua Fria Gl/r
2512 Glaze A San Clemente Polychrome
2513 Glaze A Arenal Polychrome
   (Heshotauthla RGG variety)
2514 Glaze A Cieneguilla Gl/y
2515 Glaze A Cieneguilla Polychrome
2520 Glaze B
2521 Glaze B Largo Gl/y
2522 Glaze B Largo Gl/r
2523 Glaze B Largo Polychrome
2524 Glaze B Medio Polychrome
2530 Glaze C
2531 Glaze C Espinosa Polychrome
2540 Glaze D
2541 Glaze D San Lazaro Polychrome
2550 Glaze E
2560 Glaze F

Body Sherds
2570 Early Rio Grande Gl/r
2571 Early Rio Grande Gl/y
2572 Early Rio Grande Glaze
   light interior/dark exterior
2573 Early Rio Grande Glaze other polychrome
2575 Intermediate Rio Grande Gl/r
2576 Intermediate Rio Grande Gl/y
2577 Intermediate Rio Grande Glaze
   light interior/dark exterior
2578 Intermediate Rio Grande Glaze other polychrome
2580 Late Rio Grande Gl/r
2581 Late Rio Grande Gl/y
2582 Late Rio Grande Glaze
   light interior/dark exterior
2583 Late Rio Grande Glaze other polychrome

2590 Lower Rio Puerco Glaze Ware
2591 Rim Pottery Mound Polychrome
2592 Rim Hidden Mountain Polychrome
2593 Body Pottery Mound Polychrome
2594 Body Hidden Mountain Polychrome

30 Buff Wares
3000 Untyped Zuni Buff Ware
3002 Zuni Buff Ware, unpainted
3005 Matsaki Brown-on-buff
3006 Matsaki Polychrome
3020 Untyped Lower Rio Puerco Buff Ware
3021 Lower Rio Puerco Buff Ware, unpainted
3022 Lower Rio Puerco Buff Ware,
   unpainted and smudged
3025 Hummingbird Red-on-buff
3026 Hummingbird Red-on-buff, smudged

35 Yellow Wares
3500 Untyped Hopi Yellow Ware
3502 Hopi Yellow Ware, unpainted
3505 Jeddito Brown-on-yellow
3506 Sityatki Polychrome

50–69 General Gray Wares
5001 Plain Gray Ware
5002 Plain Gray Ware, micaceous
5003 Plain Gray Ware, smudged
5005 Plain Corrugated
5006 Plain Corrugated, smudged
5007 Indented Corrugated
5008 Indented Corrugated, smudged
5009 Smeared Corrugated
5010 Smeared Corrugated, smudged
5015 Neckbanded Corrugated
5016 Neckbanded Corrugated, smudged
5017 Clapboard Corrugated
5018 Clapboard Corrugated, smudged
5020 Zoned Corrugated
5021 Zoned Corrugated, smudged
5022 Patterned Corrugated
5023 Patterned Corrugated, smudged
5024 Incised Corrugated
5025 Incised Corrugated, smudged
6900 Untyped Gray Ware

70 Mogollon Brown Ware
7000 Untyped Mogollon Brown Ware
7001 Plain Mogollon Brown Ware
7002 Smudged Mogollon Brown Ware
7003 Corrugated Smudged Mogollon Brown Ware
7004 Corrugated Mogollon Brown Ware, not smudged
7011 Woodruff Brown (same as Forestdale)
7012 Woodruff Smudged (same as Forestdale)
7013 Alma Plain
7014 Reserve Indented Corrugated, smudged
7015 Woodruff Red (Woodruff Brown with red slip)
7018 McDonald Corrugated
7900 Untyped Brown Ware

80 General Black Ware
8000 Untyped Black Ware
8001 Plain Black Ware

90 Untyped and Unidentifiable Wares
9100 Unidentified by analyzer, but potentially identifiable
9200 Untyped Ware (unique, or potentially new, type)
9999 Unidentifiable Ware (due to size, damage, etc.)

TREAT/I Interior Surface Treatment
  0. Indeterminate: cannot tell due to burning, size, or uncertainty of treatment
  1. Rough: temper protrudes, no effort at modification
  2. Scraped: scraping marks, scratches, drag lines where temper protrudes
  3. Smoothed: smooth but not shiny; can have a few wiping marks, pits, or burnishing marks (smooth or shiny streaks); temper for the most part does not protrude but may be visible
  4. Polished: reflects some light
  5. Smudged: black, shiny, usually well polished; must penetrate core
  6. Slipped: fine layer of clay on the surface, usually contrasts with paste
  7. Fugitive red
  15. Other: note in comments
  95. Surface missing: surface spalled, eroded, or abraded away; also used for items with no interior surface (i.e., figurines)

TREAT/E Exterior Surface Treatment
  0. Indeterminate: cannot tell due to burning, size, or uncertainty of treatment
  1. Rough: temper protrudes, no effort at modification
  2. Scraped: scraping marks, scratches, drag lines where temper protrudes
  3. Smoothed: smooth but not shiny; can have a few wiping marks, pits, or burnishing marks (smooth or shiny streaks); temper for the most part does not protrude but may be visible
  4. Polished: reflects some light
  5. Smudged: black, shiny, usually well polished; must penetrate core

6. Slipped: fine layer of clay on the surface, usually contrasts with paste
7. Fugitive red
15. Other: note in comments
40. Clapboard corrugated wide (> 10 mm)
41. Clapboard corrugated narrow (< 10 mm)
42. Indented corrugated
43. Zoned corrugated
44. Obliterated corrugated
45. Incised corrugated
46. Scored corrugated
47. Tooled (engraved) corrugated
48. Punctate corrugated
49. Plain corrugated
50. Neckbanded wide (> 10 mm)
51. Neckbanded narrow (< 10 mm)
52. Indented neck corrugated
53. Zoned neck corrugated
60. Indeterminate corrugated
80. Appliqué
81. Basket impressed
95. Surface missing: surface spalled, eroded, or abraded away; also used for items with no interior surface (i.e., figurines)

POL/I Polishing Interior: reflects at least some light (has luster), may be poor or streaky to fine and shiny
1. Not polished
2. Streaky, or striations visible
3. Low luster
10. High luster
95. Surface missing or indeterminate

POL/E Polishing Exterior: same codes as Polishing Interior (above)

SLIP/I Slipped Interior: has a layer of fine clay on the surface; slip is usually of contrasting color to paste—may be thin and watery or thick and visible in cross section; most will also be polished
1. Self-slip
2. Thin slip: temper visible
3. Thick slip: not temper visible
4. Crackled slip: thin
5. Crackled slip: thick
6. Fugitive red slip
10. Not slipped
95. Surface missing or indeterminate

SLIP/E Slipped Exterior: same codes as Slipped Interior (above)
IA Indentation Alignment: indented corrugated sherds only
- 0. Indeterminate
- 1. Aligned
- 2. Not aligned
- 10. Not indented

#CORR Number of corrugations per 3 sq cm; corrugated sherds > 3 sq cm only

SOOT Sooting: recognized as gritty black deposit or carbon residue
- 0. Indeterminate
- 1. Present on exterior only
- 2. Present on interior only
- 3. Present on both surfaces
- 4. Present on edge or edges only
- 10. None

FORM Form or Vessel Shape
- 0. Indeterminate
- 1. Bowl
- 2. Jar
- 3. Seed jar
- 4. Ladle
- 5. Scoop
- 6. Figurine/Effigy vessel
- 7. Pitcher
- 8. Worked sherd
- 15. Other: note in comments

PART Part of Vessel Represented
- 0. Indeterminate
- 1. Rim
- 2. Neck
- 3. Body
- 4. Handle
- 5. Neck and body
- 6. Handle and body
- 7. Complete
- 15. Other: note in comments; use for figurines where part is same as form

RIM FORM Rim forms of the Lower Rio Puerco area (figure B.3). These rim forms do NOT necessarily correspond to the Rio Grande rim-form typology (see figure A.1) but were developed for the study area to test whether rim forms observed in the study area (1) seriated and (2) were similar to Rio Grande forms.

FIGURE B.3. Rim forms on pottery recovered from Hummingbird Pueblo and Pottery Mound in the Lower Rio Puerco area.

RIM DIA Rim Diameter
%RIM Percentage of Rim Present
MOD Modification: indicates use or changes after firing
- 0. Indeterminate
- 1. One ground edge
- 2. Two or more ground edges
- 3. Flaked edge or edges
- 4. Drill (repair) hole
- 5. Abraded
- 6. Use wear
- 15. Other: note in comments
- 99. None

PT Paint Type
- 0. Indeterminate
- 1. Organic: blurry edges; often has watery appearance; usually flat back; soaks into clay body; no surface relief
- 2. Mineral: usually dense; may be crackled or blistered; hard edges; often sits on surface; often a brown or reddish brown or warm black
- 3. Mineral red
- 4. Mineral/organic: often brown but soaked into clay body and somewhat blurry at edges; parts may sit on surface or be crackled
- 5. Kaolin: white clay paint
- 6. Matte polychrome
- 7. Glaze polychrome
- 8. Glaze
- 99. Absent

RATIO Ratio of Black-to-white or Black-to-red
- 0. Indeterminate (burned, etc.)
- 1. Low (much more white/red than black)
- 2. Medium (fairly even)
- 3. High (much more black than white/red)
- 99. Not a black-on-white or black-on-red sherd or no visible paint

MOTIF# Motif: specific elements visible on sherd, see list below; Motif1, Motif2, and Motif3 used to record up to three elements; additional ones noted in comments
- 1. Rim design—solid
- 2. Rim design—ticking
- 3. Rim design—checkerboard
- 4. Rim design—dot, dash
- 8. White filler
- 9. Red filler
- 10. Thin parallel lines

11. Thick parallel lines
12. Squiggle lines
13. Thin curved lines
14. Thick curved lines
15. Single line (may occur with other element)
20. Single, solid triangle
21. Attached triangles
22. Indeterminate triangle
23. Opposed solid triangles
24. Indeterminate solid triangle
25. Indeterminate open triangle
26. Opposed, mirrored, solid triangles
27. Offset and opposed triangles
28. Attached, opposed, and oblique triangles
29. Attached triangles, hatched filled
30. Rectilinear element—solid fill
31. Rectilinear element—hatched fill
32. Interlocking rectilinear scroll—hatched fill
33. Interlocking rectilinear scroll—solid fill
34. Interlocking rectilinear scroll—opposed hatched and solid fill
35. Opposed rectilinear elements—hatched fill
36. Opposed rectilinear elements—solid fill
37. Opposed rectilinear elements—opposed hatched and solid fill
40. Circular scroll—solid fill
41. Circular scroll—hatched fill
42. Interlocking circular scroll—hatched fill
43. Interlocking circular scroll—solid fill
44. Interlocking circular scroll—opposed hatched and solid fill
45. Circular scroll—opposed hatched and solid fill
50. Single stepped element—solid fill
51. Single stepped element—hatched fill
52. Opposed stepped elements—solid fill
53. Opposed stepped elements—hatched fill
54. Opposed stepped elements—opposed solid and hatched fill
55. Banded stepped elements—solid fill
60. Open circle
61. Open circle with dot
62. Solid circle
63. Negative circle
64. Negative circle with dot
65. Concentric circles
70. Open square

71. Open square with dot
72. Solid square
73. Negative square
74. Negative square with dot
80. Open diamond
81. Open diamond with dot
82. Solid diamond
83. Negative diamond
84. Negative diamond with dot
90. Dots
91. Pendant dots or ticks
92. Ticked flag
93. Zigzag
94. Parallel zigzags
95. X
96. Barbs
97. Cross
98. Fret
99. Slashes
100. Concentric sunburst
101. Nested chevrons
102. Checkerboard
103. Diamond checkerboard
104. Crosshatched diamonds
105. Squiggle hatch fill
106. Grid, or open checkerboard
107. "Key" design
108. Dragonfly
109. Step motif (Hesh)
110. Scallops
120. Humanoid figure
121. Face/Mask
122. Hand
123. Bird
124. Feather
125. Mammal: note in comments
126. Arrow
127. Bull's eye
128. "Eye"
129. Stepped cloud
130. Snake
131. Spiral

150. Indeterminate element
151. Indeterminate solid element
152. Indeterminate hatched element
153. Indeterminate opposed element
154. Indeterminate interlocking element

COUNT Number of sherds in provenience that are identical in all attributes

COMMENTS

TEMPER Temper Type: determined through analysis with binocular microscope
- 0. Untempered
- 1. Mixed igneous rock
- 2. Intermediate igneous rock
- 3. Tuff/Pumice/Ash
- 10. Quartz sand
- 11. Arkosic sand
- 20. Metamorphic rock
- 30. Crushed sherd
- 31. Crushed sherd with mixed rock
- 32. Crushed sherd with tuff/pumice/ash
- 33. Crushed sherd with sand
- 99. Indeterminate

APPENDIX C

Description of Petrographic Temper Types

This section presents a description of the methods used in the petrographic portion of this study, the petrographic temper types defined in this study for the first time, references to previously described temper types recognized in this study, and an interpretation of production source. Methods used in this study began during the course of attribute analysis, where pottery sherds from each site were sorted into separate categories based upon type. These pottery types were further divided into separate categories based upon recognizable differences in paste and temper type as observed under a binocular microscope. Ceramic types were sorted based upon color and texture of paste matrix, as well as differences in the type, range, and relative proportion of mineralogical and lithic inclusions. On average, two sherds per site from each temper group within each major ceramic type were selected for petrographic analysis, resulting in 178 thin sections (100 from Hummingbird Pueblo, 78 from Pottery Mound).

Although the petrographic samples were prepared by three different people for this study (Elizabeth Garrett made the samples from Pottery Mound as part of her own research, while Paul Boni and Bruce Tanner made the samples from Hummingbird Pueblo specifically for this study), the method of sample preparation for petrographic thin sections is fairly standard. An approximately 5 mm thick slice was removed from the edge of a sherd using a diamond-edged circular saw. Because pottery samples are often too brittle to grind, each pottery slice was infused with an epoxy and allowed to solidify. The cut edge of each sample was then ground flat, mounted on a standard petrographic slide, and ground on lapidary wheels of decreasing coarseness. Final grinding was done by hand until a uniform thickness of 0.03 mm was achieved. Each sample was polished to remove any surface scratches and was then ready for petrographic analysis.

Using a standard petrographic microscope, each slide was examined for general characteristics and then a point count sampling was performed. General characteristics recorded included paste matrix color and texture as well as sorting of nonplastic inclusions. For the point count sampling, a 0.5 mm micrometer grid overlay was placed over each slide. One hundred intersection points on the grid were then analyzed. Information recorded for each point included whether or not the point sampled the paste matrix, a void, or a nonplastic inclusion. The following information was recorded for all nonplastic inclusions: mineral or lithic identification, size, and angularity. A summary of point counts of each petrographic thin section is available upon request from the author.

Data from the point count sampling were compared to determine the range and proportion of mineralogically distinct temper types represented in the study area. The specific mineral and lithic inclusions were compared with both the known distribution of geological resources, as well as a collection of petrographic slides representing a subset of these geological sources, in the study area to determine if such materials were locally available. Seemingly exotic inclusion types were then compared to written descriptions of temper types, as well as petrographic slides sampled from other regions when available, in an effort to identify a possible source area. Eighteen temper types were identified in this study; descriptions of these types are presented below.

Type 0: Untempered

A total of 3 percent (n = 5) of the petrographic samples examined in this study was classified as Type 0: Untempered (temper type through binocular microscope: untempered). Untempered sherds were divided into subtypes based upon the color and texture of the paste matrix. Subtype 0a has a silty to sandy paste matrix that ranges from red to light brown in color. Subtype 0b has a silty paste matrix that is tan to yellow in color. Subtype 0c has a sandy paste matrix with stray pieces of olivine diabase and ranges in color from red to light brown. In hand samples, the body of untempered sherds appears as a fine-grained, homogenous matrix ranging in color from cold gray to deep red. The production source of untempered sherds as a group cannot be determined; however, I have speculated in this volume that some untempered vessels were produced at Pottery Mound, possibly by immigrants from the Hopi Mesas. This speculation is based upon two observations: (1) many of the untempered sherds have the same colored and textured paste matrix as locally produced sherds, and (2) some of these untempered sherds with the same colored and textured paste matrix have a stray piece of olivine diabase, which has been sourced to the nearby Hidden Mountain.

Types I–X: Igneous Rocks

A total of 7 percent (n = 12) of the petrographic samples examined in this study was classified as Type I: Olivine Diabase (temper type through binocular microscope: intermediate igneous rock). Olivine diabase was originally described by Shepard (1942) as "basalt with ophitic texture" or "ophitic basalt" in thin section and "crystalline basalt" in hand section; this same type was called "Zia basalt" by Warren (1976). In this study, olivine diabase is holocrystalline, being mostly composed of calcic plagioclase (bytownite) with crystals of augite, olivine, and magnetite throughout, and with rare pieces of hornblende. The plagioclase crystals often intersect with the crystals of augite and olivine. Some olivine shows evidence, in the form of a bright red rind, of partially altering to oxyhornblende. Occasionally, some of the plagioclase shows evidence of altering to sericite. Paste matrix is a homogenous dark brown-red in thin section with stray pieces of biotite, augite, hornblende, and pieces of Hidden Mountain igneous rocks (described below). Under a binocular microscope, olivine diabase appears as black-and-white to purple-gray pieces of angular, igneous rock in a red to deep-red paste. In hand section, individual fragments of olivine diabase could be difficult to distinguish from augite monzonite (described below). In this study, augite monzonite tended to look more black and white (salt-and-pepper) overall and occurred in a yellowish to tan paste matrix. Olivine diabase from this study has been sourced to Hidden Mountain, located in the study area. It should be noted that, petrographically, distinguishing between a piece of olivine diabase from Hidden Mountain and a piece from the Zia area is difficult without further criteria. I assumed that all olivine diabase tempered sherds in this study were from the Lower Rio Puerco area based upon the following observations: (1) sherds tempered with olivine diabase have the same colored and textured paste matrix as locally produced sherds tempered with Hidden Mountain igneous rocks; (2) olivine diabase from the Zia area is not described as having hornblende present and is described as having only rare pieces of olivine; and (3) olivine diabase from the Zia area most commonly occurs in Late Rio Grande Glaze Ware, which is not present in the ceramic assemblages examined in this study.

A total of 2 percent (n = 3) of the petrographic samples examined in this study was classified as Type II: Hornblende Latite (temper type through binocular microscope: intermediate igneous rock). This type has been adequately described and discussed by Shepard (1936, 1942) as one of several types of intermediate volcanic rock and by Warren (1976) and Habicht-Mauche (1993) as hornblende latite. It has been sourced to the Espinosa volcanics that outcrop in various places throughout the Galisteo basin and Tonque valley.

A total of 0.6 percent (n = 1) of the petrographic samples examined in this study was classified as Type III: Augite Monzonite (temper type through binocular microscope: intermediate igneous rock). This type has been adequately described and discussed as a variety of andesite by Shepard (1936, 1942), as augite latite or San Marcos latite by Warren (1976), and as augite monzonite by Habicht-Mauche (1993). This temper type has been sourced to the Espinosa volcanics that outcrop in the Galisteo basin and is specifically associated with the site of San Marcos.

A total of 33 percent (n = 59) of the petrographic samples examined in this study was classified as Type IV: Hidden Mountain Igneous Rock (temper type through binocular microscope: mixed igneous rock). This temper type has not been described in detail before but may have been described, in part, as various types of basalts (including ophitic basalt, vitrophyric basalt, intergranular basalt, vesicular basalt, scoria, olivine basalt, and Zia basalt) by Shepard (1942) and Warren (1976). This temper type is actually a mix of igneous rocks with similar mineralogical and chemical composition, but different textures. Minerals present include abundant calcic plagioclase (bytownite), augite, magnetite, oxyhornblende, and rare pieces of olivine and hornblende. Textures range from holocrystalline to crystalline to vitrophyric. Some pieces are clearly vesicular. Olivine or hornblende phenocrysts usually show evidence, in the form of a bright red rind, of partially altering to oxyhornblende. Sometimes, much of the plagioclase shows evidence of altering to sericite. Condition of rocks ranges from angular, fresh pieces with little to no altering of minerals to highly weathered pieces. Paste matrix is a homogenous dark brown-red in thin section with stray pieces of biotite, augite, and hornblende. Under a binocular microscope, Hidden Mountain igneous rock appears as pieces of angular to subrounded pieces of rock, mostly black in color, but ranging from black to purple-gray. In hand section, paste matrix in glaze-painted sherds tempered with this material is normally red-orange, red-brown, or deep red, occasionally buff; in white wares and utility wares, paste matrix is gray to dark gray-brown, but upon refiring it changes to the same suite of reds as the glaze-painted sherds. This suite of igneous rocks has been sourced to Hidden Mountain in the Lower Rio Puerco and possibly other unnamed volcanic outcrops in the study area. In general, igneous rock texture is related to cooling temperature, and so a variety of textures may be present in any single igneous rock formation. The diversity of rock textures seen in sherds produced in the study area may be the result of collecting tempering material from different locations around an outcrop, how the tempering material was collected (fresh pieces of rock versus weathered pieces), and whether or not residual clays from these outcrops were being used to make pottery.

A total of 0.6 percent (n = 1) of the petrographic samples examined in this study was classified as Type V: Ash (temper type through binocular microscope: tuff/pumice/ash). This type has been adequately described as ash by Habicht-Mauche (1993). It has been sourced generally to the Pajarito Plateau and Española Valley.

A total of 0.6 percent (n = 1) of the petrographic samples examined in this study was classified as Type VI: Weathered Pumice (temper type through binocular microscope: tuff/pumice/ash). This type may be the same as the welded tuff described for the Alfred Herrera Site in the Cochiti area (Warren 1976). In the study area, this type appears as pieces of rounded to subrounded igneous rock composed of nothing more than a fine-grained groundmass, often with a micaceous appearance. Occasionally, the structure of the pumice is still apparent. Paste matrix is buff colored, with many pieces of glass as well as stray pieces of plagioclase (sanadine), muscovite, and biotite. This class of temper has been sourced generally to the Jemez Mountains and Pajarito Plateau, but this particular subtype may be specifically from the Cochiti area.

A total of 0.6 percent (n = 1) of the petrographic samples examined in this study was classified as Type VII: Weathered Tuff (temper type through binocular microscope: tuff/pumice/ash). This type has been adequately described and discussed by Shepard (1942) as devitrified tuff. This temper type has been sourced to the Cochiti district but, previous to this study, had only been recognized in Late Rio Grande Glaze Ware.

A total of 0.6 percent (n = 1) of the petrographic samples examined in this study was classified as Type VIII: Tonque Ash (temper type through binocular microscope: intermediate igneous rock). This type has been adequately described and discussed as Hornblende Latite by Warren (1976) and as a Tonque Ash by Habicht-Mauche (1993). This temper type has been sourced to the Espinosa volcanics that outcrop in the Galisteo and Tonque valleys but is most characteristic of the glaze-painted pottery recovered from Tonque Pueblo.

A total of 0.6 percent (n = 1) of the petrographic samples examined in this study was classified as Type IX: Pumice (temper type through binocular microscope: tuff/pumice/ash). This type has been adequately described and discussed as pumice by Habicht-Mauche (1993). This general class of temper has been sourced to Arroyo Hondo Pueblo near Santa Fe.

A total of 0.6 percent (n = 1) of the petrographic samples examined in this study was classified as Type X: Rhyolite (temper type through binocular microscope: intermediate igneous rock). This type has been adequately described and discussed as rhyolite by both Warren (1976) and Habicht-Mauche (1993). This temper has been sourced to the Jemez Mountains and Pajarito Plateau.

Types XI–XII: Metamorphic Rocks

A total of 2 percent (n = 4) of the petrographic samples examined in this study was classified as Type XI: Quartz-Mica Schist (temper type through binocular microscope: metamorphic rock). This type has been described, in part, as micaceous clay by Warren (1980). This temper type actually reflects the use of a residual clay with the following inclusions: fine to medium inclusions of subangular quartz, platy muscovite, biotite, chlorite, some opaques, and very coarse pieces of quartz-mica schist. Paste matrix is a homogenous brown, with a somewhat silty texture. Under a binocular microscope, residual quartz-mica schist appears as a brown micaceous paste with stray pieces of quartz and dark red-brown rock. The paste matrix refires to a dark red-brown. This residual clay has been sourced to the Sandia Mountains east of Albuquerque. Source was determined partially through Warren's (1980) description, but more through comparison of Lower Rio Puerco petrographic samples to the few petrographic samples from Tijeras made by Elizabeth Garrett.

A total of 2 percent (n = 4) of the petrographic samples examined in this study was classified as Type XII: Gneiss (temper type through binocular microscope: metamorphic rock). This temper actually reflects the use of a residual clay with the following inclusions: fine to medium inclusions of subangular quartz, platy muscovite, biotite, some opaques, rare hornblende, and very coarse pieces of hornblende gneiss. Paste matrix is a homogenous brown, with a somewhat silty texture. Under a binocular microscope, residual hornblende gneiss appears as a brown micaceous paste with stray pieces of banded rock. The paste matrix refires a dark red-brown. The petrographic samples of this temper type from this study did not satisfactorily match any of the comparative petrographic samples available, and so this temper type has not been adequately sourced. It most likely comes from the Central Rio Grande region. Chemical and mineral similarity to Temper Type XI (described above) suggests it may come from a slightly different outcrop of metamorphic rock in the Sandia Mountains. However, hornblende gneiss is a characteristic temper type from San Cristobal (Capone 1995) during the Protohistoric era, is common in the culinary ware from Arroyo Hondo (Habicht-Mauche 1993), and has also been described for the glaze ware from the Abó Pass area (Shepard 1942). Samples from this study tempered with hornblende gneiss may also fall into the range of variability from any of these regions as well.

Type XIII: Sedimentary Rocks

A total of 0.6 percent (n = 1) of the petrographic samples examined in this study was classified as Type XIII: Lithic Sand (temper type through binocular microscope: lithic sand). Lithic sand is sand composed of well-rounded rock fragments. In this study, rocks with different mineralogical and chemical compositions were present including basalt, intermediate igneous rock, granite, gneiss, and sandstone. Minerals present include quartz, bytownite, k-feldspar, muscovite, calcite, opaques, hornblende, and rare pieces of oxyhornblende. Condition of rock fragments is usually rounded to well rounded with a fair degree of weathering. Paste matrix is a sandy, light brown in thin section. Under a binocular microscope, lithic sand appears as rounded pieces of rock, mostly dark in color, but ranging from black to purple-gray to buff. In hand section, paste matrix is purple gray. This temper type has not been adequately sourced. The use of sand temper is not uncommon in numerous regions of the Pueblo Southwest throughout the Pueblo periods.

Types XIV–XVII: Sherd Tempers

A total of 12 percent (n = 21) of the petrographic samples examined in this study was classified as Type XIV: Sherd-Tempered Sherd and Igneous Rock (temper type through binocular microscope: crushed sherd with mixed rock). This temper type was divided into subtypes based upon the type of igneous rock identified in thin section as occurring with the sherd-tempered sherd. Subtype XIVa has sherd-tempered sherd with vitrophyric basalt; this subtype has a homogenous red-brown paste in thin section. In hand section, paste matrix in glaze-painted sherds tempered with this material is normally red-orange, red-brown, or deep red, occasionally buff; in white wares and utility wares, paste matrix is gray to dark gray-brown, but upon refiring it changes to the same suite of reds as the glaze-painted sherds. This subtype is assumed to be local to the Lower Rio Puerco area based on the similarity of its paste with other local wares. Subtype XIVb has sherd-tempered sherd with olivine diabase; this type also occurs in a homogenous red-brown paste in thin section. In hand section, this paste matrix is the same as Subtype XIVa. This subtype is also assumed to be local to the study area. Subtype XIVc has sherd-tempered sherd and feldspathic porphyry; this temper subtype occurs in a mottled paste in thin section that appears to be a mix of clays and is assumed to be local based on its occurrence in some Lower Rio Puerco Red-on-buff ware and Loma Fria B/w. In hand section, paste matrix is a gritty gray. Subtype XIVd has sherd-tempered sherd and Hornblende latite; the paste matrix in thin section is a homogenous dark brown and is assumed to come from the Alameda area (northern part of the Albuquerque district) based upon similarity of temper and paste to petrographic slides in the Anna Shepard collection. In hand section, paste matrix is a very dark gray. Subtype XIVe has sherd-tempered sherd and brown vitrophyric basalt; the paste matrix is yellow-gray in thin section. This subtype has been nominally identified as coming from the Acoma region based upon the pottery types it occurs in as well as descriptions provided by Dr. Dittert of Arizona State University. In hand section, paste matrix is light gray to white and very dense. Subtype XIVf has sherd-tempered sherd and Hidden Mountain igneous rock; this subtype has a homogenous red-brown paste in thin section and is assumed to be local to the

Lower Rio Puerco area based on the similarity of its paste with other local wares as well as its sourcing of rock types to the Hidden Mountain. Subtype XIVg has sherd-tempered sherd and granite; this subtype occurs in a tan-brown matrix in thin section and a dark gray matrix in hand section. The source of this subtype is not known.

A total of 4 percent (n = 7) of the petrographic samples examined in this study was classified as Type XV: Sherd and Schist (temper type through binocular microscope: crushed sherd with mixed rock). This temper type was subdivided into subtypes based upon the type of schist rock identified in thin section as occurring with the sherd-tempered sherd. Subtype XVa has sherd with quartz-mica schist; this subtype may be considered a sherd-tempered version of Type XI (described above), as its paste matrix, mineral inclusions, and texture are the same. This subtype is assumed to come from the Sandia Mountains east of Albuquerque. Subtype XVb has sherd and semischist; this temper occurs in a homogenous tan matrix in thin section, which appears as a medium gray paste in hand section. The sherd temper occurs in a semischist residual clay. The source of this subtype has not been determined.

A total of 19 percent (n = 34) of petrographic samples examined in this study was classified as Type XVI: Sherd, Igneous Rock, and Quartz-Mica Schist (temper type through binocular microscope: crushed sherd with mixed rock). This temper type includes a mix of sherd (normally sherd tempered), Hidden Mountain igneous rock (described above), and quartz-mica schist. Inclusions are normally poorly sorted and are angular to well rounded. Mineral inclusions include quartz, plagioclase, muscovite, biotite, and the occasional augite. Rare pieces of quartzite and diabase were also noted. Paste matrix in thin section is normally a homogenous red to red-brown while in hand section it behaves the same way as subtype XIVa described above. Temper type XVI is assumed to be local to the Lower Rio Puerco area based upon its abundance in the study area, the similarity of its paste matrix to other local types, and the presence of Hidden Mountain igneous rocks. This temper type was divided into subtypes based upon the presence or absence of an unidentified blue mineral: Subtype XVIa has sherd, igneous rocks, and quartz-mica schist without the blue mineral; while subtype XVIb has sherd, igneous rocks, and quartz-mica schist with the blue mineral.

A total of 12 percent (n = 21) of petrographic samples examined in this study was classified as Type XVII: sherd-tempered sherd (temper type through binocular microscope: crushed sherd or crushed sherd with sand). This type was divided into three subtypes: Type XVIIa has only sherd-tempered sherd; Type XVIIb has sherd-tempered sherd with sandstone in paste matrix; and Type XVIIc has sherd-tempered sherd with some igneous rock-tempered sherds. The paste matrix in thin section for most sherds tempered with Type XVII was yellow-brown to brown-gray, while in hand section paste matrix was normally a light gray to cold gray. Angular to rounded inclusions tended to be fairly well sorted. Other inclusions included quartz, muscovite, opaques, and the occasional piece of quartzite. Based upon the ceramic types and technology of sherds tempered with Type XVII, sherds with this temper are assumed to have been produced in the Western Pueblo region.

APPENDIX D

Code Sheet and Summary Tables for Faunal Analysis

This section presents the code sheet for the faunal analysis performed by Tiffany Clark (a graduate student at Arizona State University at the time of the analysis) as well as a summary of her findings (see tables D.1–D.5 beginning on page 170). The complete data set is available upon request from the author.

    Site Site Number (416 = Pottery Mound, 578 = Hummingbird Pueblo)
    Unit Unit Number (NOTE: For Pottery Mound, Unit NW refers to trash unit 30.75N/3.78W)
    Lev Level Number
    Locus Locus Number (NOTE: for Pottery Mound, Unit NW refers to NW quad of unit)
    Species Species or Size Class
        000 Unidentified Remains (prehistoric)
        001 Unidentified Remains (unsorted by size class)
        002 Small Mammal: Rabbit/Rodent-Sized
        003 Small Mammal: Rodent-Sized
        004 Small Mammal: Rabbit-Sized
        005 Small–Medium Mammal
        006 Medium Mammal (Carnivore-Sized)
        007 Medium–Large Mammal
        008 Large Mammal (Ungulate-Sized)
        009 Unidentified Small Animal
        010 Indeterminate Class

Common Name	Scientific Name
Artiodactyls	**Order Artiodactyla**
011 Indeterminate Artiodactyl	Indeterminate Artiodactyla
012 Elk	*Cervus elaphus*
013 Deer	*Odocoileus* sp.
014 Mule Deer	*Odocoileus hemionus*
015 White-Tailed Deer	*Odocoileus americana*
016 Pronghorn	*Antilocapra americana*
017 Bison	*Bison bison*
018 Bison/Domestic Cattle	*Bison bison/Bos taurus*
019 Bighorn/Domestic Sheep	*Ovis* sp.
020 Bighorn Sheep	*Ovis canadensis*
Lagomorphs	**Order Lagomorpha**
031 Indeterminate Rabbit	Indeterminate Lagomorpha
032 Cottontail	*Sylvilagus* sp.
033 Eastern Cottontail	*Sylvilagus floridanus*
034 Nuttall's Cottontail	*Sylvilagus nuttallii*
035 Desert Cottontail	*Sylvilagus audubonii*
036 Jackrabbit	*Lepus* sp.
037 Black-Tailed Jackrabbit	*Lepus californicus*
038 Antelope Jackrabbit	*Lepus alleni*
Rodents	**Order Rodentia**
041 Indeterminate Rodents	Indeterminate Rodentia
042 Ground Squirrel	*Ammospermophilus/Spermophilus* sp.
043 Harris's Antelope Squirrel	*Ammospermophilus harrisii*
044 Rock Squirrel	*Spermophilus variegatus*
045 Round-Tailed G. Squirrel	*Spermophilus tereticaudus*
046 Pocket Gopher	*Thomomys* sp.
047 Botta's Pocket Gopher	*Thomomys bottae*
048 Pocket Mouse	*Perognathus* sp.
049 Kangaroo Rat	*Dipodomys* sp.
050 Ord's Kangaroo Rat	*Dipodomys ordii*
051 Banner-Tailed Kangaroo Rat	*Dipodomys spectabilis*
052 Merriam's Kangaroo Rat	*Dipodomys merriami*
053 Desert Kangaroo Rat	*Dipodomys deserti*
054 Beaver	*Castor canadensis*
055 So. Grasshopper Mouse	*Onychomys torridus*
056 Western Harvest Mouse	*Reithrodontomys megalotis*
057 White-Footed Mouse	*Peromyscus* sp.
058 Abert's Squirrel	*Sciurus aberti*
059 Cotton Rat	*Sigmodon* sp.
060 Hispid Cotton Rat	*Sigmodon hispidus*

061	Arizona Cotton Rat	*Sigmodon arizonae*
062	Wood Rat	*Neotoma* sp.
063	White-Throated Wood Rat	*Neotoma albigula*
064	Desert Wood Rat	*Neotoma lepida*
065	Muskrat	*Ondatra zibethicus*
066	Deer Mouse	*Peromyscus maniculatus*
067	No. Grasshopper Mouse	*Onychomys leucogaster*
068	Piñon Mouse	*Peromyscus truei*
069	Porcupine	*Erethizon dorsatum*
070	Chipmunk	*Eutamias* sp.
071	Cliff Chipmunk	*Eutamias dorsalis*
072	Colorado Chipmunk	*Eutamias quadrivittatus*
073	Prairie Dog	*Cynomys* sp.
074	Gunnison's Prairie Dog	*Cynomys gunnisoni*
075	Indeterminate Sciurid	*Sciurus* sp.

Carnivores — **Order Carnivora**

100	Indeterminate Carnivore	Indeterminate Carnivora
101	Indeterminate Small Carnivore	Indeterminate Small Carnivora
102	Indeterminate Large Carnivore	Indeterminate Large Carnivora
103	Indeterminate Canid	Indeterminate Canidae
105	Coyote/Dog	*Canis* sp.
106	Domestic Dog	*Canis familiaris*
107	Coyote	*Canis latrans*
108	Gray Wolf	*Canis lupus*
109	Red Fox	*Vulpes vulpes*
110	Kit Fox	*Vulpes macrotis*
111	Gray Fox	*Urocyon cinereoargenteus*
112	Grizzly Bear	*Ursus arctos*
113	Black Bear	*Ursus americanus*
114	Raccoon	*Procyon lotor*
115	Coati	*Nasua nasua*
116	Ringtail	*Bassariscus astutus*
117	Long-Tailed Weasel	*Mustela frenata*
118	Black-Footed Ferret	*Mustela nigripes*
119	Badger	*Taxidea taxus*
120	Western Spotted Skunk	*Spilogale gracilis*
121	Striped Skunk	*Mephitis mephitis*
122	Hooded Skunk	*Mephitis macroura*
123	Hog-Nosed Skunk	*Conepatus mesoleucus*
124	River Otter	*Lutra canadensis*
125	Jaguar	*Panthera onca*

126	Ocelot	*Leopardus pardalis*
127	Mountain Lion	*Puma concolor*
128	Bobcat	*Lynx rufus*

FISHES
CLASS OSTEICHTHYES

200	Indeterminate Fishes	Indeterminate Osteichthyes

Minnows — **Family Cyprinidae**

201	Indeterminate Minnow	Indeterminate Cyprinidae
202	Chub	*Gila* sp.
203	Bonytail Chub	*Gila elegans*
204	Humpback Chub	*Gila cypha*
205	Roundtail Chub	*Gila robusta*
206	Gila Chub	*Gila intermedia*
207	Spikedace	*Meda fulgida*
208	Woundfin	*Plagopterus argentissimus*
209	Colorado Squawfish	*Ptychocheilus lucius*
210	Longfin Dace	*Agosia chrysogaster*
211	Speckled Dace	*Rhinichthys osculus*

Suckers — **Family Catostomidae**

216	Indeterminate Suckers	Indeterminate Catostomidae
217	Razorback Sucker	*Xyrauchen texanus*
218	Gila Coarse-Scaled Sucker	*Catostomus insignis*
219	Flannelmouth Sucker	*Catostomus latipinnis*
220	Sucker	*Catostomus* sp.
221	Gila Mountain Sucker	*Catostomus clarkii*

AMPHIBIANS
CLASS AMPHIBIA

300	Indeterminate Amphibians	Indeterminate Amphibia
301	Indeterminate Frogs and Toads	Indeterminate Salientia
302	Spadefoot Toad	*Scaphiopus* sp.
303	Indeterminate Toads	Indeterminate Bufonidae
304	Toads	*Bufo* sp.
305	Colorado River Toad	*Bufo alvarius*
306	Great Plains Toad	*Bufo cognatus*
307	Indeterminate Frog	Indeterminate Ranidae
308	Leopard Frog	*Rana pipiens*

REPTILES
CLASS REPTILIA

400	Indeterminate Reptiles	Indeterminate Reptilia

Turtles — **Order Testudines**

401	Turtles	Indeterminate Testudines
402	Yellow Mud Turtle	*Kinosternon flavescens*

403	Sonoran Mud Turtle	*Kinosternon sonoriense*
404	Western Box Turtle	*Terrapene ornata*
405	Desert Tortoise	*Gopherus agassizii*
406	Painted Turtle	*Chrysemys picta*

Lizards and Snakes — **Order Squamata**

410	Indeterminate Lizards and Snakes	Indeterminate Squamata
411	Indeterminate Lizards	Indeterminate Sauria
412	Indeterminate Iguanids	Indeterminate Iguanidae
413	Desert Iguana	*Dipsosaurus dorsalis*
414	Chuckwalla	*Sauromalus ater*
415	Collared Lizard	*Crotaphytus collaris*
416	Side-Blotched Lizard	*Uta stansburiana*
417	Horned Lizard	*Phrynosoma* sp.
418	Indeterminate Teiids	Indeterminate Teiidae
419	Whiptail	*Cnemidophorus* sp.
420	Western Whiptail	*Cnemidophorus tigris*
421	Venomous Lizards	Helodermatidae
422	Gila Monster	*Heloderma suspectum*
423	Indeterminate Snakes	Indeterminate Serpentes
424	Colubrids	Colubridae
425	Gopher Snake	*Pituophis catenifer*
426	Pit Vipers	Viperidae
427	Rattlesnakes	*Crotalus* sp.
428	Garter Snake	*Thamnophis sirtalis*

BIRDS — **CLASS AVES**

500	Indeterminate Birds	Indeterminate Aves
501	Indeterminate Small Bird	Indeterminate Small Aves
502	Indeterminate Medium Bird	Indeterminate Medium Aves
503	Indeterminate Large Bird	Indeterminate Large Aves
504	Indeterminate Very Large Bird	Indeterminate Very Large Aves

Grebes — **Order Podicipediformes**
Grebes — **Family Podicipedidae**

506	Grebe	*Grebe* sp.
507	Least Grebe	*Tachybaptus dominicus*
508	Pied-Billed Grebe	*Podilymbus podiceps*
509	Horned Grebe	*Podiceps auritus*
510	Red-Necked Grebe	*Podiceps grisegena*
511	Eared Grebe	*Podiceps nigricollis*
512	Western Grebe	*Aechmophorus occidentalis*
513	Clark's Grebe	*Aechmophorus clarkii*

Pelicans and Their Allies — Order Pelecaniformes
    Pelicans — Family Pelecanidae
        516 White Pelican — *Pelecanus erythrorhynchos*
        517 Brown Pelican — *Pelecanus occidentalis*
Herons and Bitterns — Order Ciconiiformes
    Herons — Family Ardeidae
        518 Great Blue Heron — *Ardea herodias*
Swans, Geese, Ducks, and Allies — Order Anseriformes
Swans, Geese, and Ducks — Family Anatidae
        519 Canada Goose — *Branta canadensis*
        520 Snow Goose — *Chen caerulescens*
        521 Duck — *Anas* sp.
        522 Mallard Duck — *Anas platyrhynchos*
Vultures, Hawks, and Falcons — Order Falconiformes
        524 Hawks, Falcons — Indeterminate Falconiformes
American Vultures — Family Cathartidae
        525 Turkey Vulture — *Cathartes aura*
        526 Black Vulture — *Coragyps atratus*
        527 California Condor — *Gymnogyps californianus*
Eagles and Hawks — Family Accipitridae
        529 Eagles, Hawks — Indeterminate Accipitridae
        530 Osprey — *Pandion haliaetus*
        531 Black-Shouldered Kite — *Elanus caeruleus*
        532 Mississippi Kite — *Ictinia mississippiensis*
        533 Bald Eagle — *Haliaeetus leucocephalus*
        534 Northern Harrier (Marsh Hawk) — *Circus cyaneus*
        535 Hawk — *Accipiter* sp.
        536 Sharp-Shinned Hawk — *Accipiter striatus*
        537 Cooper's Hawk — *Accipiter cooperii*
        538 Northern Goshawk — *Accipiter gentilis*
        539 Common Black-Hawk — *Buteogallus anthracinus*
        540 Harris's Hawk — *Parabuteo unicinctus*
        541 Hawk — *Buteo* sp.
        542 Red-Shouldered Hawk — *Buteo lineatus*
        543 Broad-Winged Hawk — *Buteo platypterus*
        544 Swainson's Hawk — *Buteo swainsoni*
        545 Zone-Tailed Hawk — *Buteo albonotatus*
        546 Red-Tailed Hawk — *Buteo jamaicensis*
        547 Ferruginous Hawk — *Buteo regalis*
        548 Rough-Legged Hawk — *Buteo lagopus*
        549 Golden Eagle — *Aquila chrysaetos*

Caracaras and Falcons — **Family Falconidae**
- 551 Falcon — Indeterminate Falconidae
- 552 Crested Caracara — *Polyborus plancus*
- 553 American Kestrel — *Falco sparverius*
- 554 Merlin — *Falco columbarius*
- 555 Peregrine Falcon — *Falco peregrinus*
- 556 Prairie Falcon — *Falco mexicanus*

Cranes, Rails, and Allies — **Order Gruiformes**
Cranes — **Family Gruidae**
- 557 Whooping Cranes — *Grus americana*
- 558 Sandhill Crane — *Grus canadensis*
- 559 Crane — *Grus* sp.

Gallinaceous Birds — **Order Galliformes**
Grouse, Quails, and Allies — **Family Phasianidae**
- 560 Quail — *Callipepla* sp.
- 561 Scaled Quail — *Callipepla squamata*
- 562 Gambel's Quail — *Callipepla gambelii*

Turkeys — **Subfamily Meleagridinae**
- 565 Turkey — *Meleagris gallopavo*

Shorebirds, Gulls, and Allies — **Order Charadriiformes**
Plovers — **Family Charadriidae**
- 568 Killdeer — *Charadrius vociferus*

Pigeons and Doves — **Order Columbiformes**
Pigeons and Doves — **Family Columbidae**
- 563 Dove, Pigeon — Indeterminate Columbidae
- 564 White-Winged Dove — *Zenaida asiatica*
- 566 Mourning Dove — *Zenaida macroura*
- 567 Inca Dove — *Columbina inca*

Parrots, Macaws, and Allies — **Order Psittaciformes**
Lories, Parrots, and Macaws — **Family Psittacidae**
- 570 Macaw — Indeterminate Psittacidae
- 571 Military Macaw — *Ara militaris*
- 572 Scarlet Macaw — *Ara macao*
- 573 Thick-Billed Parrot — *Rhynchopsitta pachyrhyncha*

Cuckoos, Roadrunners, and Anis — **Order Cuculiformes**
Cuckoos, Roadrunners, and Anis — **Family Cuculidae**
- 575 Roadrunner — *Geococcyx californianus*

Owls — **Order Strigiformes**
Barn Owls — **Family Tytonidae**
- 580 Barn Owl — *Tyto alba*

Typical Owls			**Family Strigidae**
	581	Great Horned Owl	*Bubo virginianus*
	582	Elf Owl	*Micrathene whitneyi*
	583	Burrowing Owl	*Athene cunicularia*
	589	Screech Owl	*Megascops asio*
Woodpeckers			**Order Piciformes**
Woodpeckers			**Family Picidae**
	584	Woodpecker	Indeterminate Picidae
	585	Gila Woodpecker	*Melanerpes uropygialis*
	586	Northern Flicker	*Colaptes auratus*
Perching Birds			**Order Passeriformes**
	587	Perching Birds	Indeterminate Passeriformes
Jays, Magpies, and Crows			**Family Corvidae**
	591	Jays, Crows	Indeterminate Corvidae
	592	Steller's Jay	*Cyanocitta stelleri*
	593	Scrub Jay	*Aphelocoma coerulescens*
	594	Common Raven	*Corvus corax*
Wrens			**Family Troglodytidae**
	593	Cactus Wren	*Campylorhynchus brunneicapillu*
Mockingbirds and Thrashers			**Family Mimidae**
	596	Northern Mockingbird	*Mimus polyglottos*
	597	Thrashers	*Toxostoma* sp.
Blackbirds and Orioles			**Family Fringillidae**
	600	Meadowlarks, Blackbirds	Indeterminate Fringillidae
	602	Western Meadowlark	*Sturnella neglecta*
	603	Red-Winged Blackbird	*Agelaius phoeniceus*
	604	Great-Tailed Grackle	*Quiscalus mexicanus*
	605	Common Grackle	*Quiscalus quiscula*
	606	Hooded Oriole	*Icterus cucullatus*
DOMESTIC HISTORIC ANIMALS			
	700	Dog	*Canis familiaris*
	701	Domestic Cat	*Felis domestica*
	702	Horse/Burro	*Equus* sp.
	703	Horse	*Equus caballus*
	704	Burro	*Equus asinus*
	705	Pig	*Sus scrofa*
	706	Cow	*Bos taurus*
	707	Sheep/Goat	*Ovis/Capra* sp.
	708	Sheep/Pig	*Ovis aries/Sus scrofa*
	709	Sheep	*Ovis aries*
	710	Goat	*Capra hircus*

711	Historic Indeterminate Artiodactyla	Indeterminate Artiodactyla
712	Very Large Mammal	Unidentified Very Large Mammal
713	Indeterminate Bird	Indeterminate Aves
714	Duck	*Anas* sp.
715	Turkey	*Meleagris gallopavo*
716	Chicken	*Gallus gallus*
717	Indeterminate Bird (Eggshell)	Indeterminate Bird (probably chicken)

INTRODUCED HISTORIC ANIMALS IN ARIZONA

801	Virginia Opossum	*Didelphis virginiana*
802	Black Rat	*Rattus rattus*
803	Norway Rat	*Rattus norvegicus*
804	House Mouse	*Mus musculus*
805	Collared Peccary	*Tayassu tajacu*
806	Bullfrog	*Rana catesbeiana*
807	Pacific Pond Turtle	*Actinemys marmorata*
808	Spiny Softshell Turtle	*Apalone spinifera*
809	European Starling	*Sturnus vulgaris*

MISCELLANEOUS

900	Pleistocene Tortoise	*Gopherus* sp.

Element	**Element**
001	Basiooccipital
002	Occipital
003	Sphenoid
004	Pterygoid
005	Vomer
006	Palatine
007	Interpariental
008	Parietal
009	Frontal
010	Temporal
011	Occipital condyle
012	Frontal/Parietal
013	Temporal/Occipital
014	Temporal/Parietal
015	Temporal/Frontal
016	Bulla
017	Squamous
018	Supraorbital
019	Petrous

020 Zygomatic arch
021 Malar
022 Lacrimal
023 Nasal
024 Premaxilla with teeth
025 Premaxilla without teeth
026 Maxilla with teeth
027 Maxilla without teeth
028 Maxilla-Premaxilla with teeth
029 Maxilla-Premaxilla without teeth
030 Nearly complete skull with teeth
031 Nearly complete mandible without teeth
032 Rear half of skull (minus maxilla-premaxilla)
033 Nearly complete mandible with teeth
034 Nearly complete mandible without teeth
035 Mandibular symphysis with anterior teeth
036 Mandibular symphysis without anterior teeth
037 Mandibular body with molars-premolars
038 Mandibular body without molars-premolars
039 Mandibular body and symphysis with teeth
040 Mandibular body and symphysis without teeth
041 Mandibular ventral border only
042 Mandibular angle and/or ascending ramus only
043 Unidentified skull fragment
044 Hyoid
045 Horn core
046 Antler fragment
047 Antler (shed)
048 Antler with frontal
049 Antler/Horn core
052 Atlas
053 Axis
054 Cervical vertebrae
055 Thoracic vertebrae
056 Lumbar vertebrae
057 Sacrum
058 Caudal vertebrae
059 Unfused verebral pad
060 Unfused verebral spinous process cap
061 Unidentified vertebrae fragment
063 Rib
064 Unfused proximal rib epiphysis

065 Coastal cartilage
066 Unidentified rib/vertebrae process fragment
067 Sternebra
068 Manubrium
069 Sternum
070 Scapula
071 Clavicle
072 Coracoid
073 Humerus
074 Radius
075 Ulna
076 Radius/Ulna fused
077 Radial carpal (scaphoid)
078 Indeterminate carpal (lunate or semilunate)
079 Ulnar carpal (cuneiform)
080 Accessory carpal (pisiform)
081 First carpal (trapezium)
082 Second carpal (trapezoid)
083 Third carpal (capitate or magnum)
084 Fourth carpal (unciform)
085 Radial-Intermediate carpal
086 Second-Third carpal
088 Metacarpal I
089 Metacarpal II
090 Metacarpal III
091 Metacarpal IV
092 Metacarpal V
093 Metacarpal II–III (ungulates)
094 Metacarpal indeterminate
095 Proximal sesamoid (f)
096 Distal sesamoid (f)
097 Sesamoid (f)
098 First phalanx (f)
099 Second phalanx (f)
100 Third phalanx (f)
101 First or second phalanx (f)
102 Complete pelvis with sacrum
103 Complete pelvis without sacrum
104 Innominate
116 Femur
117 Patella
118 Tibia

119 Fibula
121 Lateral malleolus
122 Astragalus (talus or tibial-tarsus)
123 Calcaneous (fibular tarsal)
124 Central tarsal (navicular)
125 First tarsal
126 Second tarsal
127 Third tarsal
128 Fourth tarsal (cuboid)
129 Central-Fourth tarsal (navicular-cuboid)
130 First-Second tarsal
131 Second-Third tarsal
133 Metatarsal I
134 Metatarsal II
135 Metatarsal III
136 Metatarsal IV
137 Metatarsal V
138 Metatarsal III–IV (ungulates)
139 Metatarsal indeterminate
140 Proximal sesamoid (r)
141 Distal sesamoid (r)
142 Sesamoid (r)
143 First phalanx (r)
144 Second phalanx (r)
145 Third phalanx (r)
146 First or second phalanx (r)
147 Metapodial I
148 Metapodial II–V
149 Metapodial III–IV
150 Metapodial indeterminate
151 Proximal sesamoid (f/r)
152 Distal sesamoid (f/r)
153 Sesamoid (f/r)
154 First phalanx (f/r)
155 Second phalanx (f/r)
156 Third phalanx (f/r)
157 First or second phalanx
158 Second or third phalanx
159 Lateral second phalanx
160 Laterial third phalanx
161 Laterial first or second phalanx
162 Tarsal/Carpal

163 Ossified tendon
164 Reduced metapodial (dew claw)
166 Tooth
167 Enamel fragment
168 Molar
169 Premolar
170 Molar/Premolar
171 Canine
172 Incisor
173 Lower P1
174 Lower P2
175 Lower P3
176 Lower P4
177 Lower M1
178 Lower M2
179 Lower M3
180 Upper Pl
181 Upper P2
182 Upper P3
183 Upper P4
184 Upper M1
185 Upper M2
186 Upper M3
198 Unidentified long bone fragment
199 Unidentified fragment

Fish Elements

200 Unidentified fish vertebrae
201 Caudal vertebrae
202 Trunk vertebrae
203 Dentary
204 Secondary pectoral girdle
205 Scale
206 Palatine
207 Opercle
208 Quadrate
209 Urohyal
210 Articular
211 Post-Temporal
212 Maxillary
213 Phryngeal arch (5th gill)
214 First vertebrae

215 Modified second vertebrae
216 Skull roof
217 Subopercolum
218 Preoperculum
219 Hypomandible
220 Cleithrum
221 Radials

Amphibian Elements
300 Tibio-Fibula
301 Episternum/Omisternum
302 Urostyle
303 Radio-Ulna

Reptile Elements
400 Snake vertebrae
401 Turtle carapace
402 Turtle plastron
403 Lizard skull fragment

Bird Elements
500 Ungual phalange (terminal phalanx)
501 Coccygeal vertebrae
502 Pygostyle
503 Quadrate
504 Scapholuna
505 "Beak"
506 Pollex
507 Second or third phalange
508 Windpipe
509 Furcula
510 Coracoid
511 Tibiotarsus
512 Tarsometatarsus
513 Carpometacarpus
514 Phalange I–Digit II
515 Phalange II–Digit II
516 Digit III
517 Synsacrum
518 Jugal
519 Basal Phalange–Digit I
520 Eggshell

Side Side or Symmetry
- 01 Left
- 02 Right
- 04 Indeterminate
- 05 Not applicable

Cond Condition
- 01 Complete
- 02 Complete except for unfused epiphysis (es)
- 03 Nearly complete (slightly broken or damaged)
- 04 More than n% complete
- 05 n% to n% complete
- 07 Less than n% complete
- 08 Indeterminate
- 09 Not applicable

Frag Origin of Fragmentation
- 01 Largely pre- or slightly postdepositional
- 02 Partly predepositional and partly recent damage
- 03 Largely recent damage
- 06 Indeterminate
- 07 Not applicable

Prox Proximal-Distal (excludes teeth, vertebrae, skull, and mandible)
- 01 Complete
- 02 Proximal epiphysis only
- 03 Proximal end
- 04 Proximal shaft minus proximal epiphysis (unfused)
- 05 Proximal shaft fragment
- 06 Proximal end and shaft (broken)
- 07 Shaft (both ends broken)
- 08 Distal epiphysis only
- 09 Distal end
- 10 Distal shaft minus distal epiphysis
- 11 Distal shaft fragment
- 12 Distal end and shaft fragment (broken)

Innominates only
- 14 Complete innominate
- 15 Ilium, ischium, pubis present in portions—no acetabulum
- 16 Ilium, ischium, pubis, acetabulum present in portions
- 17 Pubis

- 18 Ilium
- 19 Ischium
- 20 Ischium with acetabulum
- 21 Ischium without acetabulum
- 22 Ilium with acetabulum
- 23 Ilium without acetabulum
- 24 Pubis without acetabulum
- 25 Acetabulum area only
- 26 Ischium and pubis present in portions with acetabulum
- 27 Ilium and pubis present in portions with acetabulum
- 28 Ilium and Ischium present in portions with acetabulum
- 88 Indeterminate
- 99 Not applicable

Dor Dorsal-Ventral (only for vertebrae)
- 01 Complete (both ventral and dorsal parts present)
- 02 Vertebral body only
- 03 Vertebral arch with nearly complete processes
- 04 Spinous process
- 05 Spinous process (dorsal)
- 06 Spinous process (midsection)
- 07 Spinous process (unfused cap or summit)
- 08 Spinous process (ventral)
- 09 Vertebral body and part of arch
- 10 Vertebral arch fragment only
- 11 Vertebral pad
- 12 Vertebral articular surface
- 13 Spinous process with part of vertebral body
- 14 Vertebral body with ventral process
- 15 Vertebral body and arch with no processes
- 88 Indeterminate vertebral fragment
- 99 Not applicable

Fusion Fusion
- 01 Fused
- 02 Fusing
- 03 Unfused
- 88 Indeterminate
- 99 Not applicable

Burn Burning
- 01 Calcined
- 02 Charred
- 03 Partially charred
- 04 Cooking brown
- 06 Unburned
- 88 Indeterminate

Gnaw Gnawing
- 01 Rodent gnawed
- 02 Carnivore gnawed
- 03 Gnawed
- 04 Possible gnawing
- 05 Ungnawed
- 88 Indeterminate
- 99 Not applicable

Butch Butchering Marks
- 01 V-shaped grooves
- 02 U-shaped grooves
- 03 Parallel striations
- 04 Present
- 05 Possibly present
- 06 Absent
- 88 Indeterminate
- 99 Not applicable

Act# Actual Number of Fragments: actual bone count (including old and recent breaks)

Min# Minimum Number of Fragments: minimum bone count (after refitting or estimating minimum count after potential refitting)

Weight Weight (in grams)

TABLE D.1. Summary of major taxa from Phase 1 Hummingbird Pueblo*

Scientific Name	Common Name	NISP	% NISP	MNI	%MNI
IDENTIFIED REMAINS		950	72	39	100
Class Mammalia	**Mammals**	941	71	38	97
Order Artiodactyla	Artiodactyls	36	3	2	5
Indeterminate Artiodactyla	Indeterminate Artiodactyls	32	2	n/a	n/a
Odocoileus sp.	Deer	1	0	1	3
Antilocapra americana	Pronghorn Antelope	3	0	1	3
Order Lagomorpha	Rabbits	805	61	34	87
Indeterminate Lagomorph	Indeterminate Rabbits	44	3	n/a	n/a
Sylvilagus sp.	Cottontail	320	24	20	51
Lepus sp.	Jackrabbit	441	33	14	36
Order Rodentia	Rodents	93	7	n/a	n/a
Order Carnivora	Carnivores	7	0	2	5
Indeterminate Carnivora	Indeterminate Carnivores	5	0	n/a	n/a
Mustela frenata	Long-Tailed Weasel	1	0	1	3
Lynx rufus	Bobcat	1	0	1	3
Class Aves	**Birds**	9	1	1	3
Other Aves	Wild Birds	2	0	n/a	n/a
Subfamily Meleagridinae	Turkeys	7	0	1	3
UNIDENTIFIED REMAINS		368	28	n/a	n/a
Class Mammalia	**Mammals**	322	24	n/a	n/a
	small mammals	271	21	n/a	n/a
	medium mammals	25	2	n/a	n/a
	large mammals	36	3	n/a	n/a
Class Aves	**Birds**	38	3	n/a	n/a
Indeterminate Class	**Unidentifiable Bone**	8	1	n/a	n/a
TOTAL FAUNAL REMAINS		1318	100	39	100

* For detailed summary of bird species see chapter 7.

TABLE D.2. Summary of major taxa from Phase 2 Hummingbird Pueblo*

Scientific Name	Common Name	NISP	% NISP	MNI	%MNI
IDENTIFIED REMAINS		**1652**	**70**	**58**	**100**
Class Mammalia	**Mammals**	**1534**	**65**	**55**	**95**
Order Artiodactyla	Artiodactyls	47	2	2	4
Indeterminate Artiodactyla	Indeterminate Artiodactyls	42	2	n/a	n/a
Odocoileus sp.	Deer	2	0	1	2
Antilocapra americana	Pronghorn Antelope	3	0	1	2
Order Lagomorpha	Rabbits	1309	56	50	86
Indeterminate Lagomorph	Indeterminate Rabbits	22	1	n/a	n/a
Sylvilagus sp.	Cottontail	832	35	37	64
Lepus sp.	Jackrabbit	455	19	13	22
Order Rodentia	Rodents	170	7	n/a	n/a
Order Carnivora	Carnivores	8	0	3	5
Indeterminate Carnivora	Indeterminate Carnivores	5	0	n/a	n/a
Canis sp.	Coyote/Dog	9	0	1	2
Lynx rufus	Bobcat	5	0	1	2
Urocyon cinereoargenteus	Gray Fox	1	0	1	2
Class Reptilia	**Reptiles**	**1**	**0**	**n/a**	**n/a**
Class Aves	**Birds**	**117**	**5**	**3**	**5**
Subfamily Meleagridinae	Turkeys	92	4	3	n/a
Other Aves	Wild Birds	25	1	n/a	n/a
UNIDENTIFIED REMAINS		**695**	**30**	**n/a**	**n/a**
Class Mammalia	Mammals	591	25	n/a	n/a
	small mammals	459	19	n/a	n/a
	medium mammals	80	3	n/a	n/a
	large mammals	52	2	n/a	n/a
Class Aves	**Birds**	**94**	**4**	**n/a**	**n/a**
Indeterminate Class	**Unidentifiable Bone**	**10**	**0**	**n/a**	**n/a**
TOTAL FAUNAL REMAINS		**2347**	**100**	**58**	**100**

* For detailed summary of bird species see chapter 7.

TABLE D.3. Summary of major taxa from Phase 3 Hummingbird Pueblo*					
Scientific Name	Common Name	NISP	% NISP	MNI	%MNI
IDENTIFIED REMAINS		**12**	**50**	**3**	**100**
Class Mammalia	**Mammals**	**12**	**50**	**3**	**100**
Order Artiodactyla	Artiodactyls	7	29	1	33
Indeterminate Artiodactyla	Indeterminate Artiodactyls	6	25	n/a	n/a
Antilocapra americana	Pronghorn Antelope	1	4	1	
Order Lagomorpha	Rabbits	4	17	2	66
Sylvilagus sp.	Cottontail	2	8	1	33
Lepus sp.	Jackrabbit	2	8	1	33
Order Rodentia	Rodents	1	4	n/a	n/a
UNIDENTIFIED REMAINS		**12**	**50**	**n/a**	**n/a**
Class Mammalia	**Mammals**	**11**	**46**	**n/a**	**n/a**
	small mammals	4	17	n/a	n/a
	large mammals	7	29	n/a	n/a
Indeterminate Class	**Unidentifiable Bone**	1	0	n/a	n/a
TOTAL FAUNAL REMAINS		**24**	**100**	**3**	**100**

* For detailed summary of bird species see chapter 7.

TABLE D.4. Summary of major taxa from Phase 2 Pottery Mound*

Scientific Name	Common Name	NISP	% NISP	MNI	%MNI
IDENTIFIED REMAINS		65	79	6	100
Class Mammalia	**Mammals**	61	74	5	83
Order Artiodactyla	Artiodactyls	6	7	n/a	n/a
Indeterminate Artiodactyla	Indeterminate Artiodactyls	6	7	n/a	n/a
Order Lagomorpha	Rabbits	52	63	4	67
Sylvilagus sp.	Cottontail	3	4	1	17
Lepus sp.	Jackrabbit	49	60	3	50
Order Rodentia	Rodents	1	1	n/a	n/a
Order Carnivora	Carnivores	2	2	1	17
Canis sp.	Coyote/Dog	2	2	1	17
Class Aves	**Birds**	4	5	1	17
Subfamily Meleagridinae	Turkeys	4	5	1	17
UNIDENTIFIED REMAINS		17	21	n/a	n/a
Class Mammalia	**Mammals**	13	16	n/a	n/a
	small mammals	7	8	n/a	n/a
	medium mammals	3	4	n/a	n/a
	large mammals	3	4	n/a	n/a
Class Aves	**Birds**	4	5	n/a	n/a
TOTAL FAUNAL REMAINS		82	100	6	100

* For detailed summary of bird species see chapter 7.

TABLE D.5. Summary of major taxa from Phase 3 Pottery Mound*

Scientific Name	Common Name	NISP	% NISP	MNI	%MNI
IDENTIFIED REMAINS		5449	64	141	100
Class Mammalia	**Mammals**	4879	57	124	88
Order Artiodactyla	Artiodactyls	195	2	4	3
Indeterminate Artiodactyla	Indeterminate Artiodactyls	166	2	n/a	n/a
Odocoileus sp.	Deer	4	0	2	1
Antilocapra americana	Pronghorn Antelope	25	0	2	1
Order Lagomorpha	Rabbits	4423	52	116	82
Indeterminate Lagomorph	Indeterminate Rabbits	64	1	n/a	n/a
Sylvilagus sp.	Cottontail	1394	16	48	34
Lepus sp.	Jackrabbit	2965	35	64	45
Order Rodentia	Rodents	360	4	n/a	n/a
Order Carnivora	Carnivores	261	3	4	3
Indeterminate Carnivora	Indeterminate Carnivores	253	3	n/a	n/a
Canis sp.	Coyote/Dog	5	0	1	1
Canis lupus	Gray Wolf	1	0	1	1
Vulpes macrotis	Kit Fox	1	0	1	1
Lynx rufus	Bobcat	1	0	1	1
Class Osteichthyes	**Fish**	39	0	n/a	n/a
Class Reptilia	**Reptiles**	5	0	n/a	n/a
Class Aves	**Birds**	526	6	17	12
Subfamily Meleagridinae	Turkeys	417	5	17	12
Other Aves	Wild Birds	109	1	n/a	n/a
UNIDENTIFIED REMAINS		3090	36	n/a	n/a
Class Mammalia	**Mammals**	2192	26	n/a	n/a
	small mammals	1630	19	n/a	n/a
	medium mammals	346	4	n/a	n/a
	large mammals	216	2	n/a	n/a
Class Aves	**Birds**	840	10	n/a	n/a
Indeterminate Class	**Unidentifiable Bone**	58	1	n/a	n/a
TOTAL FAUNAL REMAINS		8539	100	141	100

* For detailed summary of bird species see chapter 7.

References

Adams, E. C. 1991. *The Origin and Development of the Pueblo Katsina Cult*. University of Arizona Press, Tucson.

———. 1994. The Katsina Cult: A Western Pueblo Perspective. In *Kachinas in the Pueblo World*, edited by P. Schaafsma, pp. 35–45. University of New Mexico Press, Albuquerque.

———, and A. I. Duff (editors). 2004. *The Protohistoric Pueblo World, AD 1275–1600*. University of Arizona Press, Tucson.

———, V. M. LaMotta, and K. Dongoske. 2004. Hopi Settlement Clusters Past and Present. In *The Protohistoric Pueblo World, AD 1275–1600*, edited by E. C. Adams and A. I. Duff, pp. 128–36. University of Arizona Press, Tucson.

Adler, M. A. 1989. Ritual Facilities and Social Integration in Nonranked Societies. In *The Architecture of Social Integration in Prehistoric Pueblos*, edited by W. D. Lipe and M. Hegmon, pp. 35–52. Occasional Papers No. 1. Crow Canyon Archaeological Center, Cortez, Colorado.

———. 1996. "The Great Period": The Pueblo World during the Pueblo III Period, AD 1150–1350. In *The Prehistoric Pueblo World, AD 1150–1350*, edited by M. Adler, pp. 1–10. University of Arizona Press, Tucson.

———. 2002. Architecture and Ancestral Pueblo Migration: Recent Research at Chaves-Hummingbird Pueblo, LA 578. Paper presented at the Pecos Conference, New Mexico.

———. 2003. Architecture and Ancestral Pueblo Migration: Recent Research at Chaves-Hummingbird Pueblo, LA 578. Poster presented at the 68th Annual Meeting of the Society for American Archaeology, Milwaukee, Wisconsin.

Ahlstrom, R. V. N., C. R. Van West, and J. S. Dean. 1995. Environmental and Chronological Factors in the Mesa Verde–Northern Rio Grande Migration. *Journal of Anthropological Archaeology* 14(2):125–42.

Altschul, J. H. 1987. Social Districts of Teotihuacan. In *Teotihuacan: Nuevos datos, nuevas síntesis, nuevos problemas*, edited by E. McClung de Tapia and E. Rattray, pp. 191–217. Instituto de Investigaciones Antropológicas, Universidad Nacional Autónoma de México, Mexico City.

Anderson, F. G. 1951. The Kachina Cult of the Pueblo Indians. Unpublished PhD dissertation, Department of Anthropology, University of New Mexico, Albuquerque.

Anthony, D. W. 1990. Migration in Archaeology: The Baby and the Bathwater. *American Anthropologist* 92:895–914.

Arnold, D. E. 1989. Patterns of Learning, Residence and Descent among Potters in Ticul, Yucatan, Mexico. In *Archaeological Approaches to Cultural Identity*, edited by S. J. Shennan, pp. 174–84. Routledge, London.

Bandelier, A. F. 1892. *Final Report of Investigations among the Indians of the Southwestern United States, Carried on Mainly in the Years from 1880 to 1885, Part II*. Papers of the Archaeological Institution of America, American Series 4. Archaeological Institute of America, Cambridge, Massachusetts.

Barrett, J. C. 2001. Agency, the Duality of Structure, and the Problem of the Archaeological Record. In *Archaeological Theory Today*, edited by I. Hodder, pp. 141–64. Blackwell, Malden, Massachusetts.

Barth, F. 1969. Introduction. In *Ethnic Groups and Boundaries*, edited by F. Barth, pp. 9–38. Little, Brown, Boston.

Baxter, M. J. 1994. *Exploratory Multivariate Analysis in Archaeology*. Edinburgh University Press, Edinburgh.

Beal, J. D. 1987. Foundation of the Rio Grande Classic: The Lower Chama River, AD 1300–1500. Southwest Archaeological Consultants, Inc. Manuscript prepared for the Office of Cultural Affairs, Historic Preservation Division, Santa Fe, New Mexico.

Bernardini, W. 1998. Conflict, Migration, and the Social Environment: Interpreting Architectural Change in Early and Late Pueblo IV Aggregations. In *Migration and Reorganization: The Pueblo IV Period in the American Southwest*, edited by K. A. Spielmann, pp. 91–114. Anthropological Research Papers No. 51. Arizona State University, Tempe.

———. 2002. The Gathering of the Clans: Understanding Migration into the Hopi Area, AD 1275–1400. Paper presented at the 67th Annual Meeting of the Society for American Archaeology, Denver, Colorado.

———, and G. Brown. 2004. The Formation of Settlement Clusters on Anderson Mesa. In *The Protohistoric Pueblo World, AD 1275–1600*, edited by E. C. Adams and A. I. Duff, pp. 108–18. University of Arizona Press, Tucson.

Bice, R. A., and W. A. Sundt. 1972. *Prieta Vista, A Small Pueblo III Ruin in North Central New Mexico*. Albuquerque Archaeological Society, Albuquerque, New Mexico.

Biella, J. V. 1979. Changing Residential Patterns among the Anasazi, AD 750–1525. In *Adaptive Change in the Northern Rio Grande Valley: Archaeological Investigations in Cochiti Resevoir, New Mexico*, edited by J. V. Biella and R. C. Chapman. Office of Contract Archeology, Department of Anthropology, University of New Mexico, Albuquerque.

Bolviken, E., E. Helskog, K. Helskog, I. Marie Holm-Olsen, L. Solheim, and R. Bertelsen. 1982. Correspondence Analysis: An Alternative to Principle Components. *World Archaeology* 14:14–60.

Bourdieu, P. 1977. *Outline of a Theory of Practice*. Cambridge University Press, London.

———. 1980. *Le sens pratique*. Translated by R. Nice. Les Editions de Minuit, Paris.

———. 1984. *Distinction: A Social Critique of the Judgment of Taste*. Harvard University Press, Cambridge, Massachusetts.

Bradley, R. J. 1999. Shell Exchange within the Southwest: The Casas Grandes Interaction Sphere. In *The Casas Grandes World*, edited by C. F. Schaafsma and C. L. Riley, pp. 213–28. University of Utah Press, Salt Lake City.

———. 2000. Networks of Shell Ornament Exchange: A Critical Assessment of Prestige Economies in the North American Southwest. In *The Archaeology of Regional Interaction: Religion, Warfare, and Exchange across the American Southwest and Beyond*, edited by M. Hegmon, pp. 167–88. University Press of Colorado, Boulder.

Brandt, E. A. 1994. Egalitarianism, Hierarchy and Centralization in the Pueblos. In *The Ancient Southwest Community: Models and Methods for the Study of Prehistoric Social Organization*, edited by W. H. Wills and R. D. Leonard, pp. 9–24. University of New Mexico Press, Albuquerque.

Brody, J. J. 1964. Design Analysis of the Rio Grande Glaze Pottery of Pottery Mound, New Mexico. Unpublished MA thesis, Department of Art History, University of New Mexico, Albuquerque.

———. 1977. *Mimbres Painted Pottery*. University of New Mexico Press, Albuquerque.

Brown, L. A., and R. L. Sanders. 1981. Toward a Development Paradigm of Migration with Particular Reference to Third World Settings. In *Migration Decision Making: Multidisciplinary Approaches to Microlevel Studies in Developed and Developing Countries*, edited by G. F. DeLong and R. W. Gardner, pp. 149–85. Pergamon Press, New York.

Brugge, D. M. 1969. Pueblo Factionalism and External Relations. *Ethnohistory* 16(2):191–200.

Bunzel, R. L. 1992. *Zuni Ceremonialism*. University of New Mexico Press, Albuquerque. Originally published 1932, Smithsonian Institution, Washington, DC.

Cadwallader, M. 1992. *Migration and Residential Mobility, Macro and Micro Approaches*. University of Wisconsin Press, Madison.

Cameron, C. M. 1995. Migration and the Movement of Southwestern Peoples. In *Special Issue: Migration and the Movement of Southwestern Peoples*, edited by C. M. Cameron. *Journal of Anthropological Archaeology* 14(2):104–24.

Capone, P. 1995. Mission Pueblo Ceramic Analyses: Implications for Protohistoric Interaction Networks and Cultural Dynamics. Unpublished PhD dissertation, Department of Anthropology, Harvard University, Cambridge, Massachusetts.

Carlson, R. L. 1970. *White Mountain Redware: A Pottery Tradition of East-Central Arizona and Western New Mexico*. Anthropological Papers No. 19. University of Arizona Press, Tucson.

———. 1982. The Mimbres Kachina Cult. In *Mogollon Archaeology: Proceedings of the 1980 Mogollon Conference*, edited by P. H. Beckett and K. Silverbird, pp. 147–67. Acoma Books, Ramona, California.

Chada, B. R. 1993. *An Archaeological Survey of 36 Homesites, Main Water Lines, Service Lines, and a Housing Development near Canoncito, Bernalillo, and Valencia Counties, New Mexico*. Archaeology Department Report Number NNAD 93–168, Navajo Nation.

Christenson, A. L. 1994. A Test of Mean Ceramic Dating Using Well-Dated Kayenta Anasazi Sites. *Kiva* 59(3):297–317.

Colton, H. S. 1943. The Principle of Analogous Pottery Types. *American Anthropologist* 45(2):316–20.

———. 1953. *Potsherds: An Introduction to the Study of Prehistoric Southwestern Ceramics and Their Use in Historic Reconstruction*. Museum of Northern Arizona Bulletin 25. Northern Arizona Society of Science and Art, Flagstaff.

——— (editor). 1955. *Pottery Types of the Southwest No. 3A and 3B*. Museum of Northern Arizona Ceramic Series No. 3. Northern Arizona Society of Science and Art, Flagstaff.

——— (editor). 1956. *Pottery Types of the Southwest No. 3C*. Museum of Northern Arizona Ceramic Series No. 3. Northern Arizona Society of Science and Art, Flagstaff.

———, and L. L. Hargrave. 1937. *Handbook of Arizona Pottery Wares*. Museum of Northern Arizona Bulletin 11. Northern Arizona Society of Science and Art, Flagstaff.

Conkey, M. W., and C. A. Hastorf (editors). 1990. *The Uses of Style in Archaeology*. Cambridge University Press, Cambridge.

Connelly, J. C. 1979. Hopi Social Organization. In *Southwest*, edited by A. Ortiz, pp. 539–43. Handbook of North American Indians, Vol. 9, W. C. Sturtevant, general editor. Smithsonian Institution, Washington, DC.

Cordell, L. S. 1975. *The 1974 Excavation of Tijeras Pueblo*. Archaeology Report No. 5, USDA Forest Service, Southwestern Region, Albuquerque, New Mexico.

———. 1979. *A Cultural Resources Overview of the Middle Rio Grande Valley, New Mexico*. USDA Forest Service and USDI Bureau of Land Management, Albuquerque and Santa Fe, New Mexico.

———. 1980. The Setting. In *Tijeras Canyon, Analyses of the Past*, edited by L. S. Cordell, pp. 1–12. Maxwell Museum of Anthropology and University of New Mexico Press, Albuquerque.

———. 1995. Tracing Migration Pathways from the Receiving End. In *Special Issue: Migration and the Movement of Southwestern Peoples*, edited by C. M. Cameron. *Journal of Anthropological Archaeology* 14(2):203–11.

———. 1997. *Archaeology of the Southwest*. 2nd ed. Academic Press, New York.

———. 1998. *Before Pecos: Settlement Aggregation at Rowe, New Mexico*. Anthropological Papers No. 6. Maxwell Museum of Anthropology, University of New Mexico, Albuquerque.

Costin, C. L. 1998. Introduction: Craft and Social Identity. In *Craft and Social Identity*, edited by C. L. Costin and R. P. Wright, pp. 3–18. Archeological Papers No. 8. American Anthropological Association, Arlington, Virginia.

Crawford, G. W., and D. G. Smith. 1996. Migration in Prehistory: Princess Point and the Northern Iroquoian Case. *American Antiquity* 61(4):782–90.

Creamer, W. 1993. *The Architecture of Arroyo Hondo Pueblo, New Mexico*. School of American Research Press, Santa Fe, New Mexico.

Creel, D., and C. McKusick. 1994. Prehistoric Macaws and Parrots in the Mimbres Area, New Mexico. *American Antiquity* 59(3):510–24.

Crotty, H. K. 1987. Masks Portrayed in Pueblo IV Kiva Murals: New Evidence for the Origins of Pueblo Ceremonialism. Manuscript on file at the Maxwell Museum of Anthropology, University of New Mexico, Albuquerque.

———. 1990. Protohistoric Anasazi Kiva Murals: Variation in Imagery as a Reflection of Differing Social Contexts. Manuscript on file at the Maxwell Museum of Anthropology, University of New Mexico, Albuquerque.

———. 1995. Anasazi Mural Art of the Pueblo IV Period, AD 1300–1600: Influences, Selective Adaptation, and Cultural Diversity in the Prehistoric Southwest. Unpublished PhD dissertation, Department of Art History, University of California, Los Angeles.

Crown, P. L. 1994. *Ceramics and Ideology: Salado Polychrome Pottery*. University of New Mexico Press, Albuquerque.

——— (editor). 2000. *Women and Men in the Prehispanic Southwest: Labor, Power, and Prestige*. School of American Research Press, Santa Fe, New Mexico.

———, J. D. Orcutt, and T. A. Kohler. 1996. Pueblo Cultures in Transition: The Northern Rio Grande. In *The Prehistoric Pueblo World, AD 1150–1350*, edited by M. Adler, pp. 145–69. University of Arizona Press, Tucson.

———, and W. H. Wills. 1995. Origins of Southwestern Ceramic Containers: Women's Time Allocation and Economic Intensification. *Journal of Anthropological Research* 51(2):173–86.

Crown-Robertson, P. L. 1978. Migration Theory in Archaeology. Manuscript on file, Arizona State Museum, University of Arizona, Tucson.

Dean, J. S., R. C. Euler, G. J. Gumerman, F. Plog, R. H. Hevly, and T. N. V. Karlstrom. 1985. Human Behavior, Demography, and Paleoenvironment on the Colorado Plateaus. *American Antiquity* 50(3):537–54.

———, and J. C. Ravesloot. 1993. The Chronology of Cultural Interaction in the Gran Chichimeca. In *Culture and Contact: Charles C. DiPeso's Gran Chichimeca*, edited by A. I. Woosley and J. C. Ravesloot, pp. 83–104. Amerind Foundation New World Studies Series No. 2. University of New Mexico Press, Albuquerque.

———, and W. J. Robinson. 1979. *Computer Cartography and the Reconstruction of Dendroclimatic Variability in the American Southwest, AD 680 to 1970*. Anthropological Research Papers No. 15. Arizona State University, Tempe.

DeBoer, W. R. 1990. Interaction, Imitation, and Communication as Expressed in Style: The Ucayali Experience. In *Uses of Style in Archaeology*, edited by M. W. Conkey and C. A. Hastorf, pp. 82–104. Cambridge University Press, Cambridge.

———, and J. A. Moore. 1982. The Measurement and Meaning of Stylistic Diversity. *Nawpa Pachu* 20:147–62.

Deetz, J. 1965. *The Dynamics of Stylistic Change in Arikara Ceramics*. Illinois Studies in Anthropology No 4. University of Illinois Press, Urbana.

———. 1996. *In Small Things Forgotten, The Archaeology of Early American Life*. Doubleday, New York.

Dietler, M., and I. Herbich. 1998. *Habitus*, Techniques, Style: An Integrated Approach to the Social Understanding of Material Culture and Boundaries. In *The Archaeology of Social Boundaries*, edited by M. Stark, pp. 232–64. Smithsonian Institution Press, Washington, DC.

DiPeso, C. C., J. B. Rinaldo, and G. J. Fenner. 1974. *Casas Grandes: A Fallen Trading Center of the Gran Chichimeca*. Vol. 6: *Ceramics*. Amerind Foundation and Northland Press, Dragoon and Flagstaff, Arizona.

Dobres, M. A., and J. E. Robb (editors). 2000. *Agency in Archaeology*. Routledge, London.

Donnan, C. B. 1971. Ancient Peruvian Potters' Marks and Their Interpretation through Ethnographic Analogy. *American Antiquity* 36(4):460–66.

Douglas, J. E. 1992. Distant Sources, Local Contexts: Interpreting Nonlocal Ceramics at Paquimé (Casas Grandes) Chihuahua. *Journal of Anthropological Research* 48:1–24.

Douglas, M. 1982. *Natural Symbols: Explorations in Cosmology*. Pantheon Books, New York.

Dozier, E. P. 1966. *Hano: A Tewa Community in Arizona*. Holt, Rinehart and Winston, New York.

———. 1970. *The Pueblo Indians of North America*. Holt, Rinehart and Winston, New York.

Duff, A. I. 1998. The Process of Migration in the Late Prehistoric Southwest. In *Migration and Reorganization: The Pueblo IV Period in the American Southwest*, edited by K. A. Spielmann, pp. 31–52. Anthropological Research Papers No. 51. Arizona State University, Tempe.

———. 2000. Scale, Interaction, and Regional Analysis in Late Pueblo Prehistory. In *The Archaeology of Regional Interaction: Religion, Warfare, and Exchange across the American Southwest and Beyond. Proceedings of the 1996 Southwest Symposium*, edited by M. Hegmon, pp. 71–98. University of Colorado Press, Boulder.

Duff, A. I. L. 1996. Ceramic Micro-Seriation: Types of Attributes? *American Antiquity* 61(1):89–101.

———. 2002. *Western Pueblo Identities: Regional Interaction, Migration, and Transformation*. University of Arizona Press, Tucson.

Durand, S. R., and W. B. Hurst. 1991. A Refinement of Anasazi Cultural Chronology in the Middle Rio Puerco Valley Using Multidimensional Scaling. In *Anasazi Puebloan Adaptation in Response to Climatic Stress: Prehistory of the Middle Rio Puerco Valley*, pp. 233–55. USDI Bureau of Land Management, Albuquerque, New Mexico.

Dutton, B. P. 1963. *Sun Father's Way*. University of New Mexico Press, Albuquerque.

Eck, D. C. 1981. *Laguna Junior High: An Archaeological Survey of Approximately 90 Acres near Laguna, New Mexico*. Office of Contract Archeology, University of New Mexico, Albuquerque.

Eckert, S. L. 1999. Report on the 1998 Excavations at Hummingbird Pueblo, New Mexico. Paper presented at the 64th Annual Meeting of the Society for American Archaeology, Chicago.

———. 2001. Pueblo IV Identity and Community Formation along the Lower Rio Puerco Drainage. Paper presented at the 66th Annual Meeting of the Society for American Archaeology, New Orleans, Louisiana.

———. 2003. Social Boundaries, Immigration and Ritual Systems: A Case Study from the American Southwest. Unpublished PhD dissertation, Department of Anthropology, Arizona State University, Tempe.

———. 2006a. Black-on-White to Glaze-on-Red: Migration, Ritual and Exchange in the Middle Rio Grande. In *The Social Life of Pots: Glaze Wares and Cultural Transformation in the Late Precontact Southwest*, edited by J. A. Habicht-Mauche, S. L. Eckert, and D. Huntley, pp.163–78. University of Arizona Press, Tucson.

———. 2006b. The Production and Distribution of Glaze-Painted Pottery in the Pueblo Southwest: A Synthesis. In *The Social Life of Pots: Glaze Wares and Cultural Transformation in the Late Precontact Southwest*, edited by J. A. Habicht-Mauche, S. L. Eckert, and D. Huntley, pp. 34–59. University of Arizona Press, Tucson.

———. 2007. Petrographic Report on 14 Chupadero Black-on-White Pottery Sherds Recovered from the Salinas and Sierra Blanca Regions of New Mexico. Report submitted to Tiffany Clark, Desert Archaeology, Tempe, Arizona.

———, and L. S. Cordell. 2004. Pueblo IV Community Formation in the Central Rio Grande Valley (Albuquerque, Cochiti, and Lower Rio Puerco Districts). In *The Protohistoric Pueblo World, AD 1275–1600*, edited by E. C. Adams and A. I. Duff, pp. 35–42. University of Arizona Press, Tucson.

Edelman, S. A. 1979. San Ildefonso Pueblo. In *Southwest*, edited by A. Ortiz, pp. 308–16. Handbook of North American Indians, Vol. 9, W. C. Sturtevant, general editor. Smithsonian Institution, Washington, DC.

Eggan, F. 1950. *Social Organization of the Western Pueblos*. University of Chicago Press, Chicago.

Eidenbach, P. L. (editor). 1982. *Inventory Survey of the Lower Hidden Mountain Floodpool, Lower Rio Puerco Drainage, Central New Mexico*. Human Systems Research, Inc., Tularosa, New Mexico.

———, and B. Gossett. 1982. Project Background. In *Inventory Survey of the Lower Hidden Mountain Floodpool, Lower Rio Puerco Drainage, Central New Mexico*, edited by P. L. Eidenbach, pp. 3–17. Human Systems Research, Inc., Tularosa, New Mexico.

Eighth Southwestern Ceramic Seminar. 1966. Rio Grande Glazes. Museum of New Mexico, Santa Fe, September 23–24.

Emslie, S. D. 1981. Prehistoric Agricultural Ecosystems: Avifauna from Pottery Mound, New Mexico. *American Antiquity* 46(4):853–61.

———, and L. L. Hargrave. 1978. *An Ethnobiological Study of the Avifauna from Pottery Mound, New Mexico*. Paper presented at the 43rd Annual Meeting of the Society for American Archaeology, Tucson, Arizona.

Ezzo J. A. 1991. Dietary Change at Grasshopper Pueblo, Arizona: The Evidence from Bone Chemistry Analysis. Unpublished PhD dissertation, Department of Anthropology, University of Wisconsin, Madison.

———, and T. Douglas Price. 2002. Migration, Regional Reorganization, and Spatial Composition at Grasshopper Pueblo, Arizona. *Journal of Archaeological Science* 29(5):499–520.

Fenenga, F. 1956. Excavations at Site LA 2567. In *Pipeline Archaeology, Reports of Salvage Operations in the Southwest on El Paso Natural Gas Company Projects, 1950–1953*, edited by F. Wendorf, N. Fox, and O. L. Lewis, pp. 233–41. Laboratory of Anthropology, Santa Fe, New Mexico, and Museum of Northern Arizona, Flagstaff.

———, and T. S. Cummings. 1956. LA 2569: Cerros Mojinos, A Late Pueblo II–Early Pueblo III Village on the Rio Puerco near Los Lunas, New Mexico. In *Pipeline Archaeology, Reports of Salvage Operations in the Southwest on El Paso Natural Gas Company Projects, 1950–1953*, edited by F. Wendorf, N. Fox, and O. L. Lewis, pp. 242–55. Laboratory of Anthropology, Santa Fe, New Mexico, and Museum of Northern Arizona, Flagstaff.

Fenton, W. N. 1957. *Factionalism at Taos Pueblo, New Mexico*. Smithsonian Institution, Bureau of American Ethnology Bulletin 164, pp. 301–44. Government Printing Office, Washington, DC.

Ferg, A. 1982. 14th Century Kachina Depictions on Ceramics. In *Collected Papers in Honor of John H. Runyon*, edited by G. X. Fitzgerald, pp. 13–29. Papers of the Archaeological Society of New Mexico No. 7. Archaeological Society of New Mexico, Albuquerque.

Ferguson, T. J. 1989. Comment on Social Integration and Anasazi Architecture. In *The Architecture of Social Integration in Prehistoric Pueblos*, edited by W. D. Lipe and M. Hegmon, pp. 169–74. Occasional Papers No. 1. Crow Canyon Archaeological Center, Cortez, Colorado.

Fewkes, J. W. 1973. *Prehistoric Hopi Pottery Designs*. Dover Press, New York.

Fitzsimmons, J. P. 1959. The Structure and Geomorphology of West-Central New Mexico. In *Guidebook of West-Central New Mexico*, pp. 112–16. 10th Field Conference, New Mexico Geological Society, Socorro.

Fowler, B. 1997. *Pierre Bourdieu and Cultural Theory: Critical Investigations*. Sage Publications, Thousand Oaks, California.

Fox, R. 1967. *The Keresan Bridge: A Problem in Pueblo Ethnology*. Humanities Press, New York.

Friedrich, M. H. 1970. Design Structure and Social Interaction: Archaeological Implications of an Ethnographic Analysis. *American Antiquity* 35(3):332–43.

Gerow, P. A. 1998. *The Hawk–Rio Puerco Project: Excavations at Seven Sites in the Middle Rio Puerco Valley, New Mexico*. Office of Contract Archeology, University of New Mexico, Albuquerque.

———. 2001. *Investigations at LA 3549 and LA 3552: Two Early Pueblo Sites along I-40 near Laguna, New Mexico*. Office of Contract Archeology, University of New Mexico, Albuquerque.

Giddens, A. 1984. *The Constitution of Society: Outline of the Theory of Structuration*. University of California Press, Berkeley and Los Angeles.

Gnabasik, V. 1981. *Faunal Utilization by the Pueblo Indians*. Unpublished MA thesis, Department of Anthropology, Eastern New Mexico University, Portales.

Goffman, E. 1974. *Frame Analysis: An Essay on the Organization of Experience*. Harper and Row, New York.

Gomolak, A. R. 1980. Another Cheap Shot at Normative Thought. *Pottery Southwest* 7(3):5–8.

Gosselain, O. P. 1992. Technology and Style: Potters and Pottery among the Bafia of Cameroon. *Man* 27(4):559–86.

Gossett, C. 1982. Lithic Material Types of the Lower Rio Puerco. In *Inventory Survey of the Lower Hidden Mountain Floodpool, Lower Rio Puerco Drainage, Central New Mexico*, edited by P. L. Eidenbach, pp. 213–17. Human Systems Research, Inc., Tularosa, New Mexico.

Graves, M. W. 1994. Community Boundaries in the Late Prehistoric Puebloan Society: Kalinga Ethnoarchaeology as a Model for the Southwestern Production and Exchange of Pottery. In *The Ancient Southwestern Community: Models and Methods for the Study of Prehistoric Social Organization*, edited by W. H. Wills and R. D. Leonard, pp. 149–69. University of New Mexico Press, Albuquerque.

Graves, W. M. 1996. Social Power and Prestige Enhancement among the Protohistoric Salinas Pueblos, Rio Grande Valley, New Mexico. Unpublished MA thesis, Department of Anthropology, Arizona State University, Tempe.

———, and S. L. Eckert. 1998. Decorated Ceramic Distributions and Ideological Developments in the Rio Grande Valley, New Mexico. In *Migration and Reorganization: The Pueblo IV Period in the American Southwest*, edited by K. Spielmann, pp. 263–84. Anthropological Research Papers No. 51. Arizona State University, Tempe.

———, and K. A. Spielmann. 2000. Leadership, Long-Distance Exchange, and Feasting in the Protohistoric Rio Grande. In *Alternative Leadership Strategies in the Prehispanic Southwest*, edited by B. J. Mills, pp. 45–59. University of Arizona Press, Tucson.

Greenberg, L. 1975. Art as a Structural System: A Study of Hopi Pottery Designs. *Studies in the Anthropology of Visual Communication* 2(1):35–50.

Habicht-Mauche, J. 1993. *The Pottery from Arroyo Hondo Pueblo, New Mexico: Tribalization and Trade in the Northern Rio Grande*. School of American Research Press, Santa Fe, New Mexico.

Habicht-Mauche, J. A. 2006. The Social History of Southwestern Glaze Wares. In *The Social Life of Pots: Glaze Wares and Cultural Transformation in the Late Precontact Southwest*, edited by J. A. Habicht-Mauche, S. L. Eckert, and D. Huntley, pp. 3–16. University of Arizona Press, Tucson.

———, and K. Nelson. 2006. Lead, Paint, and Pots: Rio Grande Intercommunity Dynamics from a Glaze Ware Perspective. In *The Social Life of Pots: Glaze Wares and Cultural Transformation in the Late Precontact Southwest*, edited by J. A. Habicht-Mauche, S. L. Eckert, and D. Huntley, pp. 197–215. University of Arizona Press, Tucson.

Hardin, M. A. 1980. Models of Decoration. In *The Many Dimensions of Pottery: Ceramics in Archaeology and Anthropology*, edited by S. E. van der Leeuw and A. C. Pritchard, pp. 575–607. Universiteit van Amsterdam, Amsterdam.

———. 1984. Models of Decoration. In *The Many Dimensions of Pottery: Ceramics in Archaeology and Anthropology*, edited by A. C. Pritchard and S. E. van der Leeuw, pp. 573–614. University of Amesterdam Press, Netherlands.

Harris, A. H. 1976. Faunal Remains from LA 70. In *Archaeological Excavations at Pueblo del Encierro, LA 70; Cochiti Dam Salvage Project, Cochiti, New Mexico: Final Report 1964–1965 Field Seasons*, edited by D. H. Snow, pp. H1–H60. Laboratory of Anthropology Notes No. 98. Museum of New Mexico, Santa Fe.

Hastorf, C. 1990. One Path to the Heights: Negotiating Political Inequality in the Sausa of Peru. In *The Evolution of Political Systems: Sociopolitics in Small-Scale Sedentary Societies*, edited by S. Upham, pp. 147–77. Cambridge University Press, Cambridge.

Haury, E. W. 1958. Evidence at Point of Pines for a Prehistoric Migration from Northern Arizona. In *Migrations in New World Culture History*, edited by R. H. Thompson, pp. 1–6. Social Science Bulletin No. 27. University of Arizona Press, Tucson.

Hawley, F. 1937. Pueblo Social Organization as a Lead to Pueblo History. *American Anthropologist* 39(3):504–22.

———. 1950. Big Kivas, Little Kivas, and Moiety Houses in Historical Reconstruction. *Southwest Journal of Anthropology* 6:286–302.

Hayashida, F. 1999. Style, Technology and State Production: Inka Pottery Manufacture in the Leche Valley. *American Antiquity* 10(4):337–52.

Hayes, A. C., J. N. Young, and A. H. Warren. 1981. *Excavation of Mound 7: Gran Quivira National Monument, New Mexico*. Publications in Archeology 16. USDI National Park Service, Washington, DC.

Hays-Gilpin, K. 1996. Anasazi Iconography: Medium and Motif. In *Interpreting Southwestern Diversity: Underlying Principles and Overarching Patterns*, edited by P. R. Fish and J. J. Reid, pp. 55–67. Anthropological Research Papers No. 48. Arizona State University, Tempe.

———, and J. H. Hill. 1999. The Flower World in Material Culture: An Iconographic Complex in the Southwest and Mesoamerica. *Journal of Anthropological Research* 55(1):1–37.

Hays-Gilpin, K. A., and E. van Hartesveldt. 1998. *Prehistoric Ceramics of the Puerco Valley: The 1995 Chambers-Sanders Trust Lands Ceramic Conference*. Ceramic Series No.7. Museum of Northern Arizona, Flagstaff.

Hegmon, M. 1989. Social Integration and Architecture. In *The Architecture of Social Integration in Prehistoric Pueblos*, edited by W. D. Lipe and M. Hegmon, pp. 5–14. Occasional Papers No. 1. Crow Canyon Archaeological Center, Cortez, Colorado.

———. 1995. *The Social Dynamics of Pottery Style in the Early Puebloan Southwest*. Occasional Papers No. 5. Crow Canyon Archaeological Center, Cortez, Colorado.

———. 1998. Technology, Style, and Social Practices: Archaeological Approaches. In *The Archaeology of Social Boundaries*, edited by M. Stark, pp. 264–80. Smithsonian Institution Press, Washington, DC.

Helms, M. 1979. *Ancient Panama: Chiefs in Search of Power*. University of Texas Press, Austin.

Herhahn, C. 1995. An Exploration of Technology Transfer in the Fourteenth-Century Río Grande Valley, New Mexico: A Compositional Analysis of Glaze Paints. Unpublished MA thesis, Department of Anthropology, Arizona State University, Tempe.

———. 2006. Rio Grande Glaze Paint Composition and Cultural Transmission: Insights to Social Interaction in the Fourteenth to Seventeenth Centuries. In *The Social Life of Pots: Glaze Wares and Cultural Transformation in the Late Precontact Southwest*, edited by J. A. Habicht-Mauche, S. L. Eckert, and D. Huntley, pp. 179–96. University of Arizona Press, Tucson.

Hibben, F. C. 1955. Excavations at Pottery Mound, New Mexico. *American Antiquity* 21(2):179–80.

———. 1966. A Possible Pyramidal Structure and Other Mexican Influences at Pottery Mound, New Mexico. *American Antiquity* 31(4):522–29.

———. 1975. *Kiva Art of the Anasazi at Pottery Mound*. KC Publications, Las Vegas, Nevada.

———. 1993. Pottery Mound Burials. Unpublished report. Manuscript (acc. #93.28.8) on file at the Maxwell Museum of Anthropology, University of New Mexico, Albuquerque.

Hill, J. N. 1970. *Broken K Pueblo: Prehistoric Social Organization in the American Southwest*. Anthropological Papers No. 18. University of Arizona Press, Tucson.

———, and R. K. Evans. 1972. A Model for Classification and Typology. In *Models in Archaeology*, edited by D. L. Clarke, pp. 231–73. Methuen, London.

Hitchcock, R. K., and L. E. Bartram Jr. 1998. Social Boundaries, Technical Systems, and the Use of Space and Technology in the Kalahari. In *The Archaeology of Social Boundaries*, edited by M. T. Stark, pp. 12–59. Smithsonian Institution Press, Washington, DC.

Hodder, I. 1977. The Distribution of Material Culture in the Baringo District, Western Kenya. *Man* 12(1):239–69.

———. 1979a. Social and Economic Stress and Material Culture Patterning. *American Antiquity* 44(4):446–54.

———. 1979b. Pottery Distributions: Service and Tribal Areas. In *Pottery and the Archaeologist*, edited by M. Millett, pp. 7–23. Occasional Publication No. 4. Institute of Archaeology, London.

———. 1982. *Symbols in Action: Ethnoarchaeological Studies of Material Culture*. Cambridge University Press, Cambridge.

———. 1990. Style as Historical Quality. In *The Uses of Style in Archaeology*, edited by M. Conkey and C. Hastorf, pp. 44–51. Cambridge University Press, New York.

Huntley, D. A. 2006. From Recipe to Identity: Exploring Fourteenth Century Zuni Social Dynamics through Ceramic Compositional Analysis. In *The Social Life of Pots: Glaze Wares and Cultural Transformation in the Late Precontact Southwest*, edited by J. A. Habicht-Mauche, S. L. Eckert, and D. Huntley, pp.105–23. University of Arizona Press, Tucson.

Ihm, P. 1987. Seriation and Application of Correspondence Analysis to the Ordering of Type Frequency Tables. In *P.A.C.T. 16, Data Processing and Mathematics Applied to Archaeology*, edited by F. Djindjian and H. Ducasse, pp. 363–77. Council of Europe, Ravello.

Irwin-Williams, C. 1967. Picosa: The Elementary Southwestern Culture. *American Antiquity* 32(4):441–57.

———. 1973. The Oshara Tradition: Origins of Anasazi Culture. *Contributions in Anthropology* 1(4):48–54. Eastern New Mexico University, Portales.

Johnson, G. A. 1982. Organizational Structure and Scalar Stress. In *Theory and Explanation in Archaeology: The Southhampton Conference*, edited by C. Renfrew, M. J. Rowlands, and B. A. Segraves, pp. 389–421. Academic Press, New York.

Jones, D. L. 1995. Identifying Production Groups within a Single Community: Rio Grande Glaze-Decorated Ceramics at Quarai Pueblo. Unpublished MA thesis, Department of Anthropology, Arizona State University, Tempe.

Jones, S. 1997. *The Archaeology of Ethnicity*. Routledge, London.

Judge, W. J. 1973. *The Paleoindian Occupation of the Central Rio Grande Valley, New Mexico*. University of New Mexico Press, Albuquerque.

Kelley, V. C. 1977. *Geology of the Albuquerque Basin, New Mexico*. Memoir 33. New Mexico Bureau of Mines and Mineral Resources, Socorro, New Mexico.

Kenagy, S. G. 1977. Zuni Pottery Aesthetic, 1880–1930: A Social, Cultural, and Psychological Study of Indigenous Aesthetic Preference. Unpublished MA thesis, California State University, Long Beach.

———. 1986. Ritual Pueblo Ceramics. Unpublished PhD dissertation, Department of Art and Art History, University of New Mexico, Albuquerque.

Kidder, A. V. 1958. *Pecos, New Mexico: Archaeological Notes*. Papers of the Robert S. Peabody Foundation for Archaeology Vol. 5. The Foundation, Phillips Academy, Andover, Massachusetts.

———, and A. O. Shepard. 1936. The Glaze-Paint, Culinary, and Other Wares. In *The Pottery of Pecos*, Vol. 2. Papers of the Southwestern Expedition No. 7. Published for Phillips Academy by Yale University Press, New Haven, Connecticut.

Kimmel, A. M. 1981. Factionalism in Hopi and Taos Pueblos. *Chesopiean* 19(3/4):45–64.

Kintigh, K. W. 1985. *Settlement, Subsistence, and Society in Late Zuni Prehistory*. Anthropological Papers No. 44. University of Arizona Press, Tucson.

———. 1996. The Cibola Region in the Post-Chacoan Era. In *The Prehistoric Pueblo World, AD 1150–1350*, edited by M. A. Adler, pp. 131–44. University of Arizona Press, Tucson.

———. 1998. Political Organization of the Protohistoric Cities of Cibola. Paper presented at The Transition from Prehistory to History in the Southwest Conference, Albuquerque, New Mexico.

———. 2002. Tools for Quantitative Archaeology: Programs for Quantitative Analysis in Archaeology. Available from author at School of Human Evolution and Social Change, Arizona State University, Tempe.

———, and A. Ammerman. 1982. Heuristic Approaches to Spatial Analysis in Archaeology. *American Antiquity* 47(1):41–63.

Kroeber, A. 1917. *Zuñi Kin and Clan*. Anthropological Papers of the American Museum of Natural History, Vol. 18, Pt. 2, pp. 39–204. The Trustees, New York.

Ladd, E. J. 1963. Zuni Ethno-Ornithology. Unpublished MA thesis, Department of Anthropology, University of New Mexico, Albuquerque.

———. 1979. Zuni Social and Political Organization. In *Southwest*, edited by A. Ortiz, pp. 482–91. Handbook of North American Indians, Vol. 9, W. C. Sturtevant, general editor. Smithsonian Institution, Washington, DC.

Lang, R. W. 1993. Additional Report: Analysis and Seriation of Stratigraphic Ceramic Samples from Arroyo Hondo Pueblo. In *The Pottery from Arroyo Hondo Pueblo, New Mexico: Tribalization and Trade in the Northern Rio Grande*, by J. Habicht-Mauche, pp. 166–81. School of American Research Press, Santa Fe, New Mexico.

Lange, C. H. 1958. The Keresan Component of Southwestern Pueblo Culture. *Southwestern Journal of Anthropology* 14:34–50.

———. 1979. Cochiti Pueblo. In *Southwest*, edited by A. Ortiz, pp. 366–78. Handbook of North American Indians, Vol. 9, W. C. Sturtevant, general editor. Smithsonian Institution, Washington, DC.

Laxton, R. R., and J. Restorick. 1989. Seriation, Similarity, and Consistency. In *Computer Applications and Quantitative Methods in Archaeology*, edited by S. Rahtz and J. Richards, pp. 214–25. BAR International Series 548. British Archaeological Reports, Oxford.

LeBlanc, S. A. 1999. *Prehistoric Warfare in the American Southwest*. University of Utah Press, Salt Lake City.

Lekson, S. H. 1989. Kivas? In *The Architecture of Social Integration in Prehistoric Pueblos*, edited by W. D. Lipe and M. Hegmon, pp. 161–68. Occasional Papers No. 1. Crow Canyon Archaeological Center, Cortez, Colorado.

———. 1995. Introduction. In *Special Issue: Migration and the Movement of Southwestern Peoples*, edited by C. M. Cameron. *Journal of Anthropological Archaeology* 14(2):99–103.

———, M. Bletzer, and A. C. MacWilliams. 2004. Pueblo IV in the Chihuahuan Desert. In *The Protohistoric Pueblo World, AD 1275–1600*, edited by E. C. Adams and A. I. Duff, pp. 53–61. University of Arizona Press, Tucson.

Levy, J. E. 1992. *Orayvi Revisited: Social Stratification in an "Egalitarian" Society*. School of American Research, Santa Fe, New Mexico.

Lightfoot, K. G., A. Martinez, and A. M. Schiff. 1998. Daily Practice and Material Culture in Pluralistic Social Settings: An Archaeological Study of Culture Change and Persistence from Fort Ross, California. *American Antiquity* 63(2):199–222.

Lindsay, A. J. 1987. Anasazi Population Movements to Southeastern Arizona. *American Archaeology* 6(3):190–98.

Lipe, W. D. 1989. Social Scale of Mesa Verde Anasazi Kivas. In *The Architecture of Social Integration in Prehistoric Pueblos*, edited by W. D. Lipe and M. Hegmon, pp. 53–72. Occasional Papers No. 1. Crow Canyon Archaeological Center, Cortez, Colorado.

———. 1995. The Depopulation of the Northern San Juan: Conditions in the Turbulent 1200s. In *Special Issue: Migration and the Movement of Southwestern Peoples*, edited by C. M. Cameron. *Journal of Anthropological Archaeology* 14(2):143–69.

Longacre, W. A. 1970. *Archaeology as Anthropology: A Case Study*. Anthropological Papers No. 17. University of Arizona Press, Tucson.

———. 1991. Sources of Ceramic Variability among the Kalinga of Northern Luzon. In *Ceramic Ethnoarchaeology*, edited by W. A. Longacre, pp. 95–111. University of Arizona Press, Tucson.

Love, D. W., J. W. Hawley, and J. D. Young. 1982. Preliminary Report on the Geomorphic History of the Lower Rio Puerco in Relation to Archaeological Sites and Cultural Resources of the Lower Hidden Mountain Dam Site. In *Inventory Survey of the Lower Hidden Mountain Floodpool, Lower Rio Puerco Drainage, Central New Mexico*, edited by P. L. Eidenbach, pp. 21–65. Human Systems Research, Inc., Tularosa, New Mexico.

Luhrs, D. L. 1937. The Identification and Distribution of the Ceramic Types in the Rio Puerco Area, Central New Mexico. Unpublished MA thesis, Department of Anthropology, University of New Mexico, Albuquerque.

MacEachern, S. 1998. Scale, Style, and Cultural Variation: Technological Traditions in the Northern Mandara Mountains. In *The Archaeology of Social Boundaries*, edited by M. T. Stark, pp. 107–31. Smithsonian Institution Press, Washington, DC.

Marshall, M. P., and H. J. Walt. 1984. *Rio Abajo: Prehistory and History of a Rio Grande Province*. New Mexico Historic Preservation Program, Santa Fe.

McGuire, R. H. 1986. Economies and Modes of Production in the Prehistoric Southwestern Periphery. In *Ripples in the Chichimec Sea*, edited by F. J. Mathien and R. H. McGuire, pp. 243–69. Southern Illinois University Press, Carbondale.

———. 1992. *A Marxist Archaeology*. Academic Press, San Diego, California.

McKusick, C. R. 1981. *The Faunal Remains of Las Humanas*. Publications in Archeology 17. USDI National Park Service, Washington, DC.

———. 1982. *Avifauna from Grasshopper Pueblo*. Anthropological Papers No. 40. University of Arizona Press, Tucson.

Mera, H. P. 1935. *Ceramic Clues to the Prehistory of North Central New Mexico*. Technical Series Bulletin No. 8. Archaeological Survey/Laboratory of Anthropology. Edwards Brothers, Ann Arbor, Michigan.

Mills, B. (editor). 1993. *Across the Colorado Plateau, Anthropological Studies for the Transwestern Pipeline Expansion Project*. Vol. 16: *Interpretation of Ceramic Artifacts*. Office of Contract Archeology and Maxwell Museum of Anthropology, University of New Mexico, Albuquerque.

Minnis, P. E. 1988. Four Examples of Specialized Production at Casas Grandes, Northwestern Chihuahua. *Kiva* 53(2):181–93.

———, M. E. Whalen, J. H. Kelley, and J. D. Stewart. 1993. Prehistoric Macaw Breeding in the North American Southwest. *American Antiquity* 58(3):270–76.

Morris, E. 1938. Mummy Cave. *Natural History* 42:127–38.

Moulard, B. 1984. *Within the Underworld Sky: Mimbres Ceramics in Context*. Twelve Trees Press, Pasadena, California.

Munson, M. K. 2000. Sex, Gender, and Status: Human Images from the Classic Mimbres. *American Antiquity* 65(1):127–43.

Naranjo, T. 1995. Thoughts on Migration by Santa Clara Pueblo. In *Special Issue: Migration and the Movement of Southwestern Peoples*, edited by C. M. Cameron. *Journal of Anthropological Archaeology* 14(2):247–50.

Nequatewa, E. 1994. *Truth of a Hopi: Stories Relating to the Origin, Myths, and Clan Histories of the Hopi*. Northland Publishing, Flagstaff, Arizona. Originally published 1936.

Neuberger, E. 1977. Internal Migration: A Comparative Systemic Overview. In *Internal Migration: A Comparative Perspective*, edited by A. A. Brown and E. Neuberger, pp. 463–79. Academic Press, New York.

Neusius, S. 1985. Faunal Resource Use: Perspectives from the Ethnographic Record. In *Dolores Archaeological Program: Studies in Environmental Archaeology*, compiled by K. Petersen, V. Clay, M. Matthews, and S. Neusius, pp. 101–15. Bureau of Reclamation, Engineering and Research Center, Denver, Colorado.

Ofstadt, H. 1981. Identity and Minority: Value Conflicts of Identity. In *Strangers in the World*, edited by L. Eitinger and D. Schwarz, pp. 42–69. Hans Huber Publishers, Stuttgart.

Ortner, S. B. 1984. Theory in Anthropology since the Sixties. *Comparative Studies in Society and History* 26(1):126–66.

———. 1996. *Making Gender: The Politics and Erotics of Culture*. Beacon Press, Boston.

Parsons, E. C. 1925. *The Pueblo of Jemez*. Yale University Press, New Haven, Connecticut.

———. 1974. *The Social Organization of the Tewa of New Mexico*. Memoirs of the American Anthropological Association No. 36. Kraus Reprint Co., New York.

———. 1994. *Tewa Tales*. University of Arizona Press, Tucson. Originally published 1926.

———. 1996. *Pueblo Indian Religion*. University of Chicago Press, Chicago. Originally published 1939.

Peacock, D. P. S. 1970. The Scientific Analysis of Ancient Ceramics: A Review. *World Archaeology* 1(3):375–89.

Plog, F. 1979. Prehistory: Western Anasazi. In *Southwest*, edited by A. Ortiz, pp. 108–30. Handbook of North American Indians, Vol. 9, W. C. Sturtevant, general editor. Smithsonian Institution, Washington, DC.

Plog, S. 1978. Social Interaction and Stylistic Similarity: A Reanalysis. *Advances in Archaeological Method and Theory* 1:144–82.

———. 1983. Analysis of Style in Artifacts. *Annual Review of Anthropology* 12:125–42.

———. 2003. Exploring the Ubiquitous through the Unusual: Color Symbolism in Pueblo Black-on-White Pottery. *American Antiquity* 68(4):665–95.

———, and J. Solometo. 1996. Alternative Pathways in the Evolution of Western Pueblo Ritual. In *Debating Complexity: Proceedings of the 26th Annual Chacmool Conference*, edited by D. Meyer, P. Dawson, and D. Hanna, pp. 326–32. Archaeological Association of the University of Calgary, Calgary, Alberta.

———. 1997. Alternative Pathways in the Evolution of Western Pueblo Ritual. *Cambridge Archaeological Journal* 7(2):161–82.

Potter, J. M. 1997. Communal Ritual, Feasting, and Social Differentiation in Late Prehistoric Zuni Communities. Unpublished PhD dissertation, Department of Anthropology, Arizona State University, Tempe.

———. 2000 Pots, Parties, and Politics: Communal Feasting in the American Southwest. *American Antiquity* 65(3):471–92.

———, and E. M. Perry. 2000. Ritual as a Power Resource in the American Southwest. In *Alternative Leadership Strategies in the Prehispanic Southwest*, edited by B. J. Mills, pp. 60–78. University of Arizona Press, Tucson.

Rappaport, R. A. 1979. *Ecology, Meaning, and Religion*. North Atlantic Books, Richmond, California.

Rautman, A. E. 1997. Changes in Region Exchange Relationships during the Pithouse-to-Pueblo Transition in the American Southwest: Implications for Gender Roles. In *Women in Prehistory: North America and Mesoamerica (Regendering the Past)*, edited by C. Claassen and R. A. Joyce, pp. 100–19. University of Pennsylvania Press, Philadelphia.

Reckwitz, A. 2002. Toward a Theory of Social Practices: A Development in Culturalist Theorizing. *European Journal of Social Theory* 5(2):245–65.

Reed, E. K. 1949. Sources of Upper Rio Grande Pueblo Culture and Population. *El Palacio* 56:163–84.

Reid, J. J., and S. M. Whittlesey. 1982. Households at Grasshopper Pueblo. *American Behavioral Scientist* 25(6):687–703.

Rice, P. M. 1984. Change and Conservatism in Pottery Producing Systems. In *The Many Dimensions of Pottery*, edited by S. E. van der Leeuw and A. C. Pritchard, pp. 231–88. University of Amsterdam, Amsterdam.

———. 1987. *Pottery Analysis: A Sourcebook*. University of Chicago Press, Chicago.

Rinaldo, J. B., and E. A. Bluhm. 1956. *Late Mogollon Pottery Types of the Reserve Area*. Fieldiana: Anthropology Vol. 36, No. 7. Chicago Natural History Museum, Chicago.

Robbins, D. 1991. *The Work of Pierre Bourdieu*. Westview, Boulder, Colorado.

Roney, J. R. 1995. Mesa Verdean Manifestations South of the San Juan River. In *Special Issue: Migration and the Movement of Southwestern Peoples*, edited by C. M. Cameron. *Journal of Anthropological Archaeology* 14(2):104–24.

———. 1996. The Pueblo III Period in the Eastern San Juan Basin and Acoma-Laguna Areas. In *The Prehistoric Pueblo World, AD 1150–1350*, edited by M. Adler, pp. 145–69. University of Arizona Press, Tucson.

Rouse, I. 1939. *Prehistory in Haiti: A Study in Method*. Yale University Publications in Anthropology No. 21. Yale University Press, New Haven, Connecticut.

———. 1986. *Migrations in Prehistory*. Yale University Press, New Haven, Connecticut.

Rowlands, M., and K. Kristiansen. 1998. Introduction: Social Transformations in Archaeology. In *Social Transformations in Archaeology: Global and Local Perspectives*, edited by K. Kristiansen and M. Rowlands, pp. 1–26. Routledge, New York.

Ruscavage-Barz, S. M. 1999. Knowing Your Neighbor: Coalition Period Community Dynamics on the Pajarito Plateau, New Mexico. Unpublished PhD dissertation, Department of Anthropology, Washington State University, Pullman.

Sackett, J. R. 1986. Isochrestism and Style: A Clarification. *Journal of Anthropological Archaeology* 5(3):266–77.

———. 1990. Style and Ethnicity in Archaeology: The Case for Isochrestism. In *The Uses of Style in Archaeology*, edited by M. Conkey and C. Hastorf, pp. 32–43. Cambridge University Press, Cambridge.

Sahlins, M. 1981. *Historical Metaphors and Mythical Realities: Structure in the Early History of the Sandwich Islands Kingdom*. University of Michigan Press, Ann Arbor.

Sando, J. S. 1982. *Nee Hemish: A History of Jemez Pueblo*. University of New Mexico Press, Albuquerque.

Schaafsma, C. F., and C. L. Riley (editors). 1999. *The Casas Grandes World*. University of Utah Press, Salt Lake City.

Schaafsma, P. 1980. *Indian Rock Art of the Southwest*. School of American Research, Santa Fe, New Mexico, and University of New Mexico Press, Albuquerque.

———. 1981. Kachinas in Rock Art. *Journal of New World Archaeology* 4(2):24–31.

———. 1992. *Rock Art in New Mexico*. Museum of New Mexico Press, Santa Fe.

———. 1994. The Prehistoric Kachina Cult and Its Origins as Suggested by Southwestern Rock Art. In *Kachinas in the Pueblo World*, edited by P. Schaasfma, pp. 63–79. University of New Mexico Press, Albuquerque.

———. 2000. *Warrior Shield and Star: Imagery and Ideology of Pueblo Warfare*. Western Edge Press, Santa Fe, New Mexico.

———, and C. Schaafsma. 1974. Evidence for the Origins of the Pueblo Katsina Cult as Suggested by Southwestern Rock Art. *American Antiquity* 39(4):535–45.

Schaefer, J., and D. A. Huntley. 2000. *A Cultural Resources Inventory and Evaluation for the Laguna Pueblo Development Project, Pueblo of Laguna, New Mexico*. ASM Affiliates, Inc., Encinitas, California.

Schapiro, M. 1953. Style. In *Anthropology Today: An Encyclopedic Inventory*, edited by A. L. Kroeber, pp. 287–312. University of Chicago Press, Chicago.

Schroeder, A. H. 1979. Pueblos Abandoned in Historic Times. In *Southwest*, edited by A. Ortiz, pp. 236–54. Handbook of North American Indians, Vol. 9, W. C. Sturtevant, general editor. Smithsonian Institution, Washington, DC.

Seventh Southwestern Ceramic Seminar. 1965. Acoma-Zuni Pottery Types. Research Center, Museum of Northern Arizona, Flagstaff, September 24–25.

Shaffer, B. S., and K. M. Gardner. 1997. Reconstructing Animal Exploitation by Pueblo Peoples of the Southwestern United States Using Mimbres Pottery, AD 1000–1150. *Anthropozoologica* 25–26:263–68.

———, K. M. Gardner, and B. W. Baker. 1996. Prehistoric Small Game Snare Trap Technology, Deployment Strategy, and Trapper Gender Depicted in Mimbres Pottery. *Journal of Ethnobiology* 16(2):145–55.

Shennan, S. J. 1989. Introduction: Archaeological Approaches to Cultural Identity. In *Archaeological Approaches to Cultural Identity*, edited by S. J. Shennan, pp. 1–32. Routledge, London.

Shepard, A. O. 1936. *The Pottery of Pecos*, Vol. 2. Papers of the Southwestern Expedition No. 7. Published for Phillips Academy by Yale University Press, New Haven, Connecticut.

———. 1942. *Rio Grande Glaze Paint Ware: A Study Illustrating the Place of Ceramic Technological Analysis in Archaeological Research*. Contributions to American Anthropology and History No. 39, Carnegie Institution of Washington Publication 528, pp. 129–262. Carnegie Institution of Washington, Washington, DC.

———. 1956. *Ceramics for the Archaeologist*. Carnegie Institution of Washington, Washington, DC.

———. 1965. Rio Grande Glaze-Paint Pottery: A Test of Petrographic Analysis. In *Ceramics and Man*, edited by F. R. Matson, pp. 62–87. Viking Fund Publications in Anthropology No. 41. Wenner-Gren Foundation for Anthropological Research, New York.

Sheridan, A., and G. Bailey (editors). 1981. *Economic Archaeology: Towards an Integration of Ecological and Social Approaches*. BAR, Oxford.

Siegal, B. J., and A. R. Beals. 1960. Conflict and Factionalist Dispute. *Journal of the Royal Anthropological Institute* 90:107–17.

Snead, J. E., W. Creamer, and T. Van Zandt. 2004. "Ruins of Our Forefathers": Large Sites and Site Clusters in the Northern Rio Grande. In *The Protohistoric Pueblo World, AD 1275–1600*, edited by E. C. Adams and A. I. Duff, pp. 26–34. University of Arizona Press, Tucson.

Snow, D. H. 1989. A Very Brief Overview of Rio Grande Glaze and Matte-Paint Ceramics. Manuscript prepared for the New Mexico Archaeological Council, Rio Grande Ceramic Workshop, Santa Fe.

South, S. 1978. Research Strategies for Archaeological Pattern Recognition on Historic Sites. *World Archaeology* 10:36–50.

Spielmann, K. A. 1998a. The Pueblo IV Period: History of Research. In *Migration and Reorganization: The Pueblo IV Period in the American Southwest*, edited by K. A. Spielmann, pp. 1–30. Anthropological Research Papers No. 51. Arizona State University, Tempe.

———. 1998b. Ritual Influences on the Development of Rio Grande Glaze A Ceramics. In *Migration and Reorganization: The Pueblo IV Period in the American Southwest*, edited by K. A. Spielmann, pp. 253–61. Anthropological Research Papers No. 51. Arizona State University, Tempe.

Stanislawski, M. B. 1979. Hopi-Tewa. In *Southwest*, edited by A. Ortiz, pp. 587–602. Handbook of North American Indians, Vol. 9, W. C. Sturtevant, general editor. Smithsonian Institution, Washington, DC.

Stark, M. T. 1998. Technical Choices and Social Boundaries in Material Culture Patterning: An Introduction. In *The Archaeology of Social Boundaries*, edited by M. T. Stark, pp. 1–11. Smithsonian Institution Press, Washington, DC.

———. 2006 Glaze Ware Technology, the Social Lives of Pots, and Communities of Practice and in the Late Prehistoric Southwest. In *The Social Life of Pots: Glaze Wares and Cultural Transformation in the Late Precontact Southwest*, edited by J. A. Habicht-Mauche, S. L. Eckert and D. Huntley, pp. 17–33. University of Arizona Press, Tucson.

———, J. J. Clark, and M. D. Elson. 1995. Causes and Consequences of Migration in the 13th Century Tonto Basin. In *Special Issue: Migration and the Movement of Southwestern Peoples*, edited by C. M. Cameron. *Journal of Anthropological Archaeology* 14(2):212–46.

Stephen, A. 1936. *Hopi Journal*. Columbia University Contributions to Anthropology Vol. 23. Columbia University Press, New York.

Steward, J. 1937. Ecological Aspects of Southwestern Society. *Anthropos* 32:87–104.

Stewart, J. D., P. Matousek, and J. H. Kelley. 1980. Rock Art and Ceramic Art in the Jornada Mogollon Region. *Kiva* 55(4):301–20.

Stewart, O. C. 1984. Taos Factionalism. *American Indian Culture and Research* 8(1):37–57.

Strong, P. T. 1979. San Felipe Pueblo. In *Southwest*, edited by A. Ortiz, pp. 390–97. Handbook of North American Indians, Vol. 9, W. C. Sturtevant, general editor. Smithsonian Institution, Washington, DC.

Swift, M. K. 1988. *Archaeological Survey of the Access Road for a Proposed Landfill Site West of Los Lunas in Valencia County, New Mexico*. Office of Contract Archeology, University of New Mexico, Albuquerque.

Tainter, J. A., and B. B. Tainter. 1995. Riverine Settlement in the Evolution of Prehistoric Land-Use Systems in the Middle Rio Grande Valley, New Mexico. In *Desired Future Conditions for Southwestern Riparian Ecosystems: Bringing Interests and Concerns Together*. General Technical Report RM-GTR-272. USDA Forest Service, Rocky Mountain Forest and Range Experiment Station, Fort Collins, Colorado.

Throop, C. J., and K. M. Murphy. 2002. Bourdieu and Phenomenology: A Critical Assessment. *Anthropological Theory* 2(2):185–208.

Tierney, G. D. 1977. A Vegetative Survey of White Rock Canyon: The 5280–5400 Foot (1610–1646 Meter) Elevations. In *Archaeological Investigations in Cochiti Reservoir, New Mexico*. Vol. 1: *A Survey of Regional Variability*, edited by J. V. Biella and R. C. Chapman, pp. 39–67. Office of Contract Archeology, Department of Anthropology, University of New Mexico, Albuquerque.

Titiev, M. 1944. *Old Oraibi: A Study of the Hopi Indians of Third Mesa*. Papers of the Peabody Museum Vol. 22, No. 1. Peabody Museum of American Archaeology and Ethnology, Harvard University, Cambridge, Massachusetts.

Turner, J. 1992. Ritual, Habitus, and Hierarchy in Fiji. *Ethnology* 31(4):291–302.

Turner, V. 1968. *The Drums of Affliction: A Study of Religious Processes among the Ndembu of Zambia*. Clarendon Press, Oxford.

Vandiver, P. B. 1990. Ancient Glazes. *Scientific American* 262(4):106–13.

Van Keuren, S. 2006. Fourmile Polychrome and the Organization of Glaze-Decorated Pottery Production in East-Central Arizona. In *The Social Life of Pots: Glaze Wares and Cultural Transformation in the Late Precontact Southwest*, edited by J. A. Habicht-Mauche, S. L. Eckert, and D. Huntley, pp. 86–104. University of Arizona Press, Tucson.

VanPool, C. S. 2003. The Shaman-Priests of the Casas Grandes Region, Chihuahua, Mexico. *American Antiquity* 68(4):696–717.

VanPool, T. L., and C. S. VanPool. 2003. Agency and Evolution: The Intended and Unintended Consequences of Action. In *Essential Tensions in Archaeological Method and Theory*, edited by T. L. VanPool and C. S. VanPool, pp. 89–113. University of Utah Press, Salt Lake City.

Vivian, P. 1994. Anthropomorphic Figures in the Pottery Mound Murals. In *Kachinas in the Pueblo World*, edited by P. Schaasfma, pp. 81–92. University of New Mexico Press, Albuquerque.

Vivian, P. B. 1961. Kachina: The Study of Pueblo Animism and Anthropomorphism within the Ceremonial Wall Paintings of Pottery Mound, and the Jeddito. Unpublished MA thesis, Department of Art, State University of Iowa, Iowa City.

Voll, C. B. 1961. The Glaze Paint Ceramics of Pottery Mound, New Mexico. Unpublished MA thesis, University of New Mexico, Albuquerque.

Walt, H. 1981. Kiva Murals. Manuscript (acc. # 81.32.68) on file at Maxwell Museum of Anthropology, University of New Mexico, Albuquerque.

Ware, J. A., and E. Blinman. 2000. Cultural Collapse and Reorganization: Origin and Spread of Pueblo Ritual Sodalities. In *The Archaeology of Regional Interaction: Religion, Warfare, and Exchange across the American Southwest and Beyond*, edited by M. Hegmon, pp. 381–410. University Press of Colorado, Boulder.

Warren, A. H. 1976. The Ceramic and Mineral Resources of LA 70 and the Cochiti Area. In *Archaeological Excavations at Pueblo del Encierro, LA 70, Cochiti Dam Salvage Project, Cochiti, New Mexico: Final Report 1964–1965 Field Seasons*, edited by D. H. Snow, pp. B1–B184. Laboratory of Anthropology Notes No. 78. Museum of New Mexico, Santa Fe.

———. 1979. The Glaze Paint Wares of the Upper Middle Rio Grande. In *Archaeological Investigations in Cochiti Reservoir, New Mexico*. Vol. 4: *Adaptive Changes in the Northern Rio Grande Valley*, edited by J. V. Biella and R. C. Chapman, pp. 187–216. Office of Contract Archeology, Department of Anthropology, University of New Mexico, Albuquerque.

———. 1980. Prehistoric Pottery of Tijeras Canyon. In *Tijeras Canyon, Analyses of the Past*, edited by L. S. Cordell, pp. 149–68. Maxwell Museum of Anthropology and University of New Mexico Press, Albuquerque.

———. 1981a. Appendix 1: Description of Pottery Tempering Material of Gran Quivira. In *Excavations of Mound 7*, edited by A. C. Hayes, pp. 179–82. Publications in Archeology 16. USDI National Park Service, Washington, DC.

———. 1981b. A Petrographic Study of the Pottery of Gran Quivira. In *Contributions to Gran Quivira Archaeology*, edited by A. C. Hayes, pp. 67–73. Publications in Archeology 17. USDI National Park Service, Washington, DC.

———. 1981c. *The Micaceous Pottery of the Rio Grande*. Anthropological Papers No.6. Archaeological Society of New Mexico, Albuquerque.

———. 1982a. Pottery of the Lower Rio Puerco, 1980–1981. In *Inventory Survey of the Lower Hidden Mountain Floodpool, Lower Rio Puerco Drainage, Central New Mexico*, edited by P. L. Eidenbach, pp. 139–68. Human Systems Research, Inc., Tularosa, New Mexico.

———. 1982b. Prehistoric Mineral Resources of the Lower Rio Puerco. In *Inventory Survey of the Lower Hidden Mountain Floodpool, Lower Rio Puerco Drainage, Central New Mexico*, edited by P. L. Eidenbach, pp. 67–76. Human Systems Research, Inc., Tularosa, New Mexico.

Washburn, D. K. 1974. Nearest Neighbor Analysis of Pueblo I–III Settlement Patterns along the Rio Puerco of the East, New Mexico. *American Antiquity* 39(4):315–35.

———. 1980. *Hopi Kachina, Spirit of Life*. California Academy of Science, San Francisco.

———. 1983. Toward a Theory of Structural Style in Art. In *Structure and Cognition in Art*, edited by D. Washburn, pp. 138–64. Cambridge University Press, Cambridge.

———. 1992. Structure of Black-on-White Ceramic Design from the Mimbres Valley. In *Archaeology, Art, and Anthropology: Papers in Honor of J. J. Brody*, edited by M. S. Duran and D. T. Kirkpatrick, pp. 213–23. Papers of the Archaeological Society of Mexico Vol. 18. Archaeological Society of Mexico, Albuquerque.

———. 1999. Perceptual Anthropology: The Cultural Salience of Symmetry. *American Anthropologist* 101:547–62.

Weigand, P. C. 1977. Fingerprints as a Means of Artisan Identification from Southwestern Archaeological Ceramics. *Pottery Southwest* 4(3):4–6.

Whalen, M. E., and P. E. Minnis. 2001. *Casas Grandes and Its Hinterland: Prehistoric Regional Organization in Northwest Mexico*. University of Arizona Press, Tucson.

Whallon, R. 1968. Investigations of Late Prehistoric Social Organization in New York State. In *New Perspectives in Archaeology*, edited by S. R. Binford and L. R. Binford, pp. 223–44. Aldine Press, Chicago.

Whiteley, P. M. 1986. Unpacking Hopi "Clans," II: Further Questions about Hopi Descent Groups. *Journal of Anthropological Research* 42(1):69–79.

———. 1988. *Deliberate Acts: Changing Hopi Culture through the Oraibi Split*. University of Arizona Press, Tucson.

Whittlesey, S. M. 1978. Status and Death at Grasshopper Pueblo: Experiments toward an Archaeological Theory of Correlates. Unpublished PhD dissertation, Department of Anthropology, University of Arizona, Tucson.

Wiessner, P. 1983. Style and Social Information in Kalahari San Projectile Points. *American Antiquity* 48:253–76.

Wimberly, M., and P. Eidenbach. 1980. *Reconnaissance Study of the Archaeological and Related Resources of the Lower Puerco and Salado Drainages, Central New Mexico*. Human Systems Research, Inc., Tularosa, New Mexico.

Wobst, H. M. 1977. Stylistic Behavior and Information Exchange. In *Papers for the Director: Research Essays in Honor of James B. Griffin*, edited by C. E. Cleland, pp. 317–42. Anthropological Papers No. 67. Museum of Anthropology, University of Michigan, Ann Arbor.

Woodbury, R., and N. F. S. Woodbury. 1966. Decorated Pottery of the Zuni Area. In *The Excavation of Hawikuh by Frederick Webb Hodge: Report of the Hendricks-Hodge Expedition*, by Watson Smith, Richard Woodbury, and Nathalie Woodbury, Appendix II, pp. 302–36. Contributions from the Museum of American Indian, Heye Foundation Vol. 20. Museum of the American Indian, New York.

Young, J. 1994. The Interconnection between Western Puebloan and Mesoamerican Ideology/Cosmology. In *Kachinas in the Pueblo World*, edited by P. Schaafsma, pp. 107–20. University of New Mexico Press, Albuquerque.

Zedeño, M. N. 1995. The Role of Population Movement and Technology Transfer in the Manufacture of Southwestern Ceramics. In *Ceramic Production in the American Southwest*, edited by P. Crown and B. Mills, pp. 115–41. University of Arizona Press, Tucson.

Index

~

The letter *f* or *t* following a page number indicates a figure or table on that page.

Acoma Glaze Ware, 50, 110. *See also* Zuni/Early Acoma Glaze Wares

Acoma region/people, 50, 104. *See also* Zuni/Acoma region/people

Adams, Charles E., 82, 86–87

Adler, Michael, 21

African Americans, 11

agency theory, 10

Aluttiq people, 12–13

Archaic period, 18

ARMS site files, 18

Arnold, Dean, 59–60

Arroyo Hondo, 48

atypical style, 68. *See also under* design

Bandelier, Adolph, 20

Baringo, 60

binocular and petrographic analyses, 32, 44

Bourdieu, Pierre, 3, 10; critics of, 11; cultural transformations and, 11

Bradley, R. J., 47

Brody, J. J., 50

Capone, Patricia, 32

Casas Grandes: interaction sphere of, 47; Pottery Mound and, 53–54

ceramics by excavation levels, 117t–22t

ceramic sociology, 59–61

ceramic types, 72–75; defined, 72; human behavior aspects and, 77–78. *See also specific regions and types*

Cerros Mojinos, 20

Chacoan system, 19

Chada, B. R., 18

Cibola White Ware, 19

clans, 99

Classic Mimbres period, 53

communal feasting, 83

communities of identity, 3, 7; glaze ware technology and, 98–99

communities of practice, 40; migration and, 2, 7

Cordell, Linda, 18, 21, 23–24

Crotty, Helen, 25, 86

Crown, Patricia, 61, 62, 63–68, 82–83, 84, 85–86

DeBoer, Warren, 60

decoration and technology, 32, 35–36; attributes code sheet, 133–43

decorative style: archaeologists and, 61; art history, information exchange theory and, 60; defined, 59; habitus and, 62; interaction intensity and, 60; interpretation of, 59–62; social boundaries and, 58–62; technological style and, 75–78

Deetz, James, 11

design: attributes, study area, 69t; elements, definition, 108; habitus and, 64; layout, definition, 108; style, definition, 108

Dietler, Michael, 12, 60

Dittert, Alfred, 50

Duff, Andrew, 6, 38, 83

Eck, D. C., 18

Eidenbach, P. L., 18

Eleanor site, 19

Elizabeth Garrett Thin Section Collection, 23

› 197

Española Valley, 44
ethnic identity, 5
Evans, R. K., 12
excavation levels, 132; ceramics by, 117t–22t

factionalism, 6
filler, 108
firing technology: atmosphere, 35, 39–40, 98; slip color and, 35, 40–41
Fourmile Polychrome, 50, 82, 86
Friedrich, Margaret, 60

Garrett, Elizabeth, 23, 32–35
Gerow, P. A., 18
glaze-decorated pottery: burial ritual and, 84–85; as mortuary furniture, 84–85; religious imagery and, 85–91
glaze ware technology, 27, 56, 58; communities of identity and, 98–99; exterior designs and, 51f; immigration and, 37, 40–41; social change and, 37; timeline of, 49f
Gran Quivira, 92
Grasshopper region, 38–39
Graves, William, 83
Guadalupe Ruin, 19

Habicht-Mauche, Judith, 32
habitus, 3, 10, 12; African Americans and, 11; decorative style and, 62; migration and, 38; shared, immigration and, 47–52
Haury, Emil, 38, 39, 41, 47–48
Hegmon, Michelle, 5–6, 12, 61–62
Herbich, Ingrid, 12, 60
Herhahn, Cynthia, 32, 37
Hibben, Frank, 62–63, 104; Hummingbird Pueblo and, 21; Pottery Mound and, 20, 23, 77; Pottery Mound, Casas Grandes and, 53; Pottery Mound kivas and, 100
Hidden Mountain, 20, 32, 34f; abandonment of, 56; Western Pueblo immigrants and, 52. See also under Lower Rio Puerco Wares
Hill, James, 12
Hodder, Ian, 60
homelands: migration and, 43
Hopi region/people, 6, 47, 92, 101, 103, 104; migration and, 97–98; social domains and, 11; technological and decorative styles and, 77–78
Hopi Yellow Ware, 53, 75

Hummingbird Pueblo, 20–23; glaze ware technology and, 48; interregional contact, premigration and, 44–46; partial vessels recovered from, 63f; population of, 15; Zuni district immigrants and, 52
Huntley, D. A., 18

iconic motifs, 70–72
immigration. See migration
information exchange theory: style and, 60
interregional contact: postmigration, 46–47; premigration, Hummingbird Pueblo and, 44–46

Jornada Mogollon Rock Art Style, 82

kaolin paint, 108
Kashaya people, 12–13
katsina ritual/religion, 82, 91–92, 101; plazas and, 82; warfare and, 92. See also Southwestern Regional Cult
Kayenta region, 38, 48, 61–62
Keresan Bridge, 99
Keres people, 99–100
Kidder, Alfred, 123
kin: official versus practical, 10

kiva murals, 86, 92, 103; ritual developments and, 85–86

kivas, 21, 100; at Pottery Mound, 23–25; room ratios and, 87, 94t, 100

Kuaua, 92

Lightfoot, Kent, 12–13

Lino Gray pottery, 18

local production: method for determining, 32; results, 32–35

Lower Rio Puerco district, 3–5, 7, 16f; ceramic traditions of, 15; ceramic typology of, 29; communities of practice and, 29; continuity and, 29; cultural history of, 18–21; decorative style and, 62–75; diversity of pottery traditions in, 79; geology of, 17; glaze ware technology and, 29–30, 56; migration and, 4–5; nucleation of populations, 29–30; Paleo-Indian through Pueblo II periods, 18–19; population history of, 15; population reorganization of, 21; post-1300 ritual developments of, 84–91; settlement aggregation of, 19–20; social organization in Pueblo IV, 99–101; wild resources of, 17

Lower Rio Puerco Wares, 115–16; Hidden Mountain Polychrome, 52, 73–75, 77, 78, 116; Hummingbird Red-on-buff, 72, 74, 75–76, 115–16; Pottery Mound Polychrome, 66f, 73, 74, 77, 116

Luhrs, D. L., 18

Luo people, 12, 61

MacEachern, Scott, 60

Mandara Mountains, 60

Marxism, 9

mask iconography, 82, 83–86

material culture: seeming contradictions of, 8; social boundaries and, 3–5

Maxwell Museum, 21, 23, 25, 47, 63

McKusick, Charmion, 87

mean ceramic date calculation, 124

Medio period, 48

Mera, H. P., 123

Mesa Verde region, 16–17

micaceous pottery, 44

migration, 5, 7, 97–98; change of habitus and, 38–39; communities of practice and, 2, 7; consequences of, 5; daily practice and, 93, 95; diffusion and, 37; environmental and social uncertainty and, 55; ethnicity, ritual practice and, 5; evidence for, 55–56; glaze ware technology and, 37, 48, 98; Grasshopper region and, 38–39; habitus and, 38; history, pottery and, 78; homelands and, 43; iconic motifs and, 98; interregional contact and, 44–47; kin-based groups and, 3–4; Lower Rio Puerco district and, 4–5; practice of, 38; shared habitus and, 47–52; Tonto Basin and, 39; village aggregation and, 98

Minnis, Paul, 47

Mogollon region, 16–17, 44, 47

Moore, James, 60

mortuary furniture: glaze-decorated pottery and, 84–85

murals. *See* kiva murals

nonlocal production, 32

Nuvakwewtaqa, 93

Ortner, Sherry, 11

paints, 108; organic versus glaze, 35–36

Pajarito Plateau, 44

paste: definition of, 107

plazas: katsina ritual/religion and, 82; public ceremonies and, 87; room ratios and, 93, 94t

Point of Pines, 47–48

Potter, James, 83, 87
Pottery Mound, 20–21, 23–26; Casas Grandes and, 53–54; decorated bowls from, 67f; Hopi mesas immigrants and, 52–53; kivas at, 23–25; murals at, 25–26; population of, 15–16; roomblocks of, 23; Zuni region immigrants and, 52
Pottery Mound and Hummingbird Pueblo: chronological data, 26–29; contemporaneity and sample size, 28–29; excavation levels of, 28t; timeline of, 26–29. *See also specific subjects and pottery types*
practice theory, 3, 7, 9–10, 104; applications of, 11–13; social boundaries and, 12–13; style and, 61; style and social boundaries and, 62
production habitus, 39–41
Protohistoric period, 104–5, 149
Pueblo IV period, 7, 19–21, 23, 72, 104–5; ceramic production and decoration and, 56; decorated pottery and, 68, 72–73; Hummingbird Pueblo and, 27; kivas and, 93; nucleation of populations and, 29; pottery types of, 107–22; ritual system and, 102; social organization in study area, 99–101

Pueblo III period, 19–20, 72; pottery types of, 107–122; roomblocks of, 20
Pueblo II period, 19
Pueblo I period, 18

Ramos Polychrome, 53
Rappaport, Roy, 5–6
rim form, 21, 113f, 123; seriation and, 112, 124
Rio Grande Glaze Ware, 54, 112; Agua Fria Glaze-on-red (Gl/r), 73, 77, 112–14; Cieneguilla Glaze-on-yellow and Polychrome (Glaze A), 73, 114; Early Rio Grande Glaze Ware, 112; Early Rio Grande Gl/poly, 76–77; Glaze A, 64–65, 68; Glaze C, 115; Glaze D, 115; Glaze-on-polychrome (Gl/poly), 74, 76; Glaze-on-red (Gl/r), 73–74, 76, 78; Intermediate types, 74, 114–15; Largo Gl/y, Gl/r and Polychrome (Glaze B), 114; Rio Grande Glaze A, 112; San Clemente Glaze-on-polychrome style, 65f; San Clemente Polychrome, 73–74, 76, 112, 114
Rio Grande region/people, 4–5, 16–17, 44, 46–47, 92; and ceramic local variants, 107–22, 123; exchange networks of, 54; study area inhabitants and, 54–55

Rio Grande Rock Art Style, 82
ritual: access to knowledge and, 102–3; burial, glaze-decorated pottery and, 84–85; material culture and, 91; post-1300 developments, 82–84; practice, 5–6, 8; religious imagery and, 85–86; village-wide practice, glaze-decoration and, 101
ritual developments: architecture and, 86–87, 91; birds and, 87–91; faunal assemblage and, 87–91; independent evidence and, 86–91; kiva murals and, 85–86; rectangular kiva and, 87
rock art, 82
Roney, J. R., 18
roomblocks: demographic developments and, 20; at Hummingbird Pueblo, 21, 27, 132; at Pottery Mound, 23–24

Salado Polychrome, 61, 83, 85
sample size issues, 28–29, 47, 63, 68, 76
Sandia-Manzano ranges, 44
Santa Fe area, 44
Schaafsma, Polly, 25, 82
Schaefer, J., 18
seriation: ceramic types and, 125t; correspondence analysis and, 124, 126–27; definition of, 124; *k*-means cluster

analysis and, 124, 127–28; software and, 125; statistical methods of, 124–25

Shepard, Anna, 32, 123

Shipibo-Conibo, 60

Sikyatki style, 66, 68, 74, 77

site unit intrusion: migration practices and, 38; Point of Pines and, 38

slips, 68–70, 75–76; bichrome, 35; color of, 35–36; definition of, 108; group membership and, 68–70, 75; local pottery types and, 70t; self-, 40, 57

social boundaries: definition of, 2–3; ethnic groups and, 1; fourteenth-century Pueblo world and, 3–5; identification of, 1; material culture and, 3–5; other social dynamics and, 5–6; practice theory and, 12–13; technological style and, 31–32

social groups: definition of, 2; identity and, 3; integration of, 93, 95, 102; practice and, 2–3; ritual and, 79, 81–82, 83, 92; tension and, 102–4

Southwestern Regional Cult, 85–86; social group integration and, 92–93, 95, 102. *See also* katsina ritual/religion

Spielmann, Katherine, 83

Stark, Miriam, 11–12, 29, 39

Swift, M. K., 18

Taricá, 60

technological style: decisions and, 59; decorative style and, 75–78; social boundaries and, 31–32

temper(ing), 32, 76–77; definition of, 107–8; group membership and, 75; Pottery Mound and, 53; rock, 40; types, 44–46, 145–51

Tewa groups, 46, 99, 101

Ticul of Mexico, 59–60

Tijeras Pueblo, 48

Tonto Basin, 39

uncertainty: migration and, 55

Upper Little Colorado River area, 6, 83

utility ware: Indented Corrugated, 108–9; Indented or Smeared Corrugated, Smudged, 109; Plain Gray, 108; Smeared Indented Corrugated, 109; surface treatments of, 108

Vivian, Patricia, 25, 86

Voll, Charles, 77

volume organization, 6–8

Warren, A. Helene, 32

Washburn, D. K., 18

Western Pueblo glaze, 76

Western Pueblo region, 16–17, 47, 48, 93, 97–98; ceramic local variants of, 107–22, 123; glaze wares of, 77; glaze ware technology and, 27, 35, 50; ritual in, 103

White Mountain Red Ware, 48, 50, 110; St. Johns B/r and Polychrome, 72, 110

White Wares, 27, 32, 58, 78; glaze ware and, 58, 72; icons and, 58; Loma Fria B/w, 35, 109; Red Mesa black-on-white (B/w), 18, 109; Socorro B/w, 19, 20, 35, 109

Wimberly, M., 18

Zedeño, María, 38–39

Zuni/Acoma region/people, 6, 44, 48, 50, 78, 101; migration and, 43, 97–98; social domains and, 11; study area inhabitants and, 55. *See also* Acoma region/people

Zuni/Early Acoma Glaze Wares, 50, 110; Heshotauthla Gl/r and Polychrome, 64, 68, 110–11; Kechipawan Polychrome, 111; Kwakina Gl/poly, 111; Pinnawa Glaze-on-white (Gl/w), 111

E 99 .P9 E24 2008
Eckert, Suzanne L., 1970-
Pottery and practice

DEC 0 1 2008